AMERICAN BIBLE SOCIETY
SYMPOSIUM PAPERS
ON

THE
BIBLE
IN THE
TWENTY-FIRST
CENTURY

AMERICAN BIBLE SOCIETY
SYMPOSIUM PAPERS
ON

THE
BIBLE
IN THE
TWENTY-FIRST
CENTURY

Edited by
HOWARD CLARK KEE

Trinity Press International
Philadelphia

THE BIBLE IN THE TWENTY-FIRST CENTURY
Symposium Papers
Howard Clark Kee, Editor

Library of Congress Cataloguing-in-Publication Data

The Bible in the twenty-first century / edited by Howard Clark Kee.
    246 pp. 20.5 cm.
    Papers and comments collected from a 1991 symposium sponsored
    by the American Bible Society.
    Includes bibliographical references and indexes.
    ISBN 1-56338-047-1.
1. Bible—History—Congresses. 2. Bible—Translating—Congresses.
3. Bible—Study and teaching—Congresses. 4. American Bible Society.
I. Kee, Howard Clark.
BS445.B456 1992
220′.09′049—dc20   92–34043
                                                  CIP

Printed in the United States of America

THE BIBLE
IN THE TWENTY-FIRST CENTURY

Table of Contents

Foreword 1
    David G. Burke

Introduction 3
    Howard Clark Kee

New Documents: Qumran and Gnostic Writings 7
    Joseph A. Fitzmyer, Jr.
        Respondents
    James A. Sanders 26
    Sidnie A. White 30

New Bible Translations: An Assessment and Prospect 37
    Donald A. Carson
        Respondents
    Leonard Greenspoon 68
    Barclay M. Newman 76
    Pheme Perkins 84

New Finds that Illuminate the World and Text of the Bible:
The Greco-Roman Era 89
   Howard Clark Kee
      Respondents
      Eric M. Meyers 109
      Roger S. Boraas 118

New Approaches to Understanding and Study of the Bible . . . 125
   Katharine Doob Sakenfeld
      Respondents
      Melvin K. H. Peters 145
      J. Ramsey Michaels 154

New Media for Communicating the Bible: The Potential
and the Problems 161
   Richard M. Harley
      Respondents
      Thomas E. Boomershine 181
      Gregor Goethals 187

Appendix

Breakthroughs in Bible Translating 197
   Eugene A. Nida

Biblical Megatrends: Towards a Paradigm for the
Interpretation of the Bible in Electronic Media 211
   Thomas E. Boomershine

Index 233

Index of Biblical References 245

FOREWORD

Since its inception in 1816, the American Bible Society has held steadfastly to its paramount organizing purpose; namely, to provide easy access to the Scriptures to all people, everywhere, at costs they can readily afford. Thanks to the help of generous contributors, the Society has continued to carry out this purpose by translating, publishing and distributing Bibles, testaments, and a wide variety of needs-oriented Scripture portions and products throughout the USA. And, through the networking agency of the United Bible Societies, it has helped to enable this same work all over the world. Bringing the Scriptures to people everywhere in languages and forms that are appropriate and relevant to their life situations has been the Society's singular goal, but the underlying assumption of that mandate is the conviction that the highest quality scholarly work with the biblical texts must be involved in the preparation of those Scriptures for people's use.

At the heart of the American Bible Society's work, then, is translation of the Scriptures from the original language texts. Having produced the globally influential common language translation—*Today's English Version/Good News Bible*—between 1961 and 1979, the ABS is presently producing the *Contemporary English Version*, a fresh "functional equivalence" translation that is both innovative and pioneering as it applies new insights from the field of discourse structure and language use toward the development of a clear, natural and easily read English style. After a period of careful research, the Society is now also engaged in the preparation of experimental translations of Scripture portions in multimedia formats in an effort to bring the Bible to those for whom screen-centered technologies are fast becoming the communications medium of choice. In all its translation programs the Society's goal is always faithfulness and accuracy, ensuring that the modern receptor's understanding of, and response to, the translated text will be the equivalent of that experienced by the original hearers/readers.

2

Solid and careful scholarship in regard to the text and world of the Bible is thus a critical concern of the ABS and its partner Bible Societies. Such scholarship is the essential preparation for translating the Scriptures, and it is equally requisite for developing the kinds of supplementary readers' helps that Bible users are increasingly demanding as aids to understanding in an age of fading Bible literacy.

What better way, then, for a translating Bible Society to celebrate its first 175 years of service than a scholarly symposium that would provide a forum for discussion of the issues that are pertinent and vital to Bible scholarship and translation in today's world. As even a cursory sampling of the essays and responses presented in this volume will reveal, the symposium served as a very timely summing up of where things presently stand, and prospective of future developments in key areas of Bible scholarship and translation work. It is the hope of the Society that, as an integral part of its commitment to sound Bible scholarship, it will be able to sponsor similar symposia on a regular basis in the future.

As is usual in such a collection of essays as this book represents, the opinions and viewpoints advanced by the authors must be understood to be their own and not necessarily representing those of the ABS. In the editing process there has been no attempt to harmonize differences in either spellings or abbreviations (e.g., between B.C.-A.D. and B.C.E.-C.E.) used by the various authors.

David G. Burke, Director
Department of Translations
and Scripture Resources

INTRODUCTION

Howard Clark Kee

The year 1991 marked the one hundred seventy-fifth anniversary of the founding of the American Bible Society. It seemed appropriate on such an occasion to look back in gratitude to the founding of this widely-supported agency for publishing and distribution of the Bible, but also to look ahead to the ways in which translation, study and publication of the Bible will likely change as we approach the end of the twentieth century. With both these aims in mind—celebrating beginnings and contemplating the future—a symposium was convened at Independence National Historical Park in Philadelphia, with invited papers and responses from scholars representing a range of areas of expertise and theological orientation to consider new developments which bear on the future of access to and understanding of the Bible.

The location, in the First Bank of the United States, was chosen for the meetings in recognition of the fact that the first president of the American Bible Society, Elias Boudinot, was a native of Philadelphia and chaired the First Continental Congress, which met in nearby Independence Hall. Numerous other adjacent buildings in colonial architectural style served as reminders of the historic context in which the Bible Society had its beginnings. At the same time, the presence of eighteen churches in the vicinity—especially Old St. Joseph's Roman Catholic and St. Peter's and Christ Church (both Episcopal)—demonstrated the continuity of religious tradition over two centuries. A new colonial-style building overlooking the historic area, The Annenberg Institute for Judaic and Near Eastern Research, reminded us of the diversity and vitality of the Jewish tradition and of scholarly work in the fields relating to biblical studies.

HOWARD CLARK KEE is former Professor of New Testament and Director of Biblical-Historical Graduate Studies at Boston University.

The most appropriate and responsible way to celebrate this anniversary seemed to be to convene a group of those with expertise and insights who could shed light on various aspects of the Bible today and in the coming years. Four major questions emerged:

How should the Bible be translated in light of new information and insights which have come through discoveries of ancient manuscripts, and through the development of linguistic perceptions about the nature of language, both ancient and modern?

What new evidence from historical and especially from archaeological discoveries sheds new light on the Bible, the meaning of its texts, and the changing settings—in ancient Israel and in early Christianity—in which it was written?

What methods for analyzing and understanding the Bible have developed in recent decades, and what promise do they offer for the study and interpretation of the Bible?

Now that the contemporary world is shifting from the predominance of the printed word as medium for study and communication to audio-visual media, what methods and strategies should be developed and used by those who want to get the message of the Bible through to as wide an audience as possible?

Those who were asked to present papers were persons of demonstrated skill in their respective fields, but care was also taken to include representatives from a wide range of traditional backgrounds: Protestant and Catholic, reformed and evangelical, Christian and Jewish. In each case the presenter had demonstrated hands-on knowledge of certain aspects of the Bible and directly related material, as well as the ability to perceive and articulate how their areas of expertise have implications for use and understanding of the Bible in the future. Each participant was asked to describe and assess where matters stand in his or her respective field of expertise. From that base, each was to indicate what was seen to lie ahead on a range of issues, which include:

How can one determine as nearly as possible the original text of the Bible?

How are effective and responsible translations to be developed?

What new or freshly-assessed information can enrich and improve our understanding of the changing social and cultural circumstances under which the Bible was written, and thereby bring us closer to its original meaning?

Which modes of Bible study will enhance understanding of the text and lead to appropriation of its content?

What are the possibilities and the most promising ways for employing new media to make the Bible accessible and meaningful to a generation oriented much more toward audio-visual rather than literary modes of communication?

The structure of the symposium (which was attended by scores, including clergy, academics, professionals and interested laity) consisted of a series of five basic addresses, which were followed by responses from experts in each field. Two additional papers are also included this volume: (1) Dr. Eugene A. Nida, who for more than four decades has been a world-renowned leader in both linguistic theory and the bearing of that science on Bible translation, offered an address with the title, "Breakthroughs in Bible Translating." (2) Dr. Thomas E. Boomershine, who has taken leadership in exploring modes of communicating the Bible in forms other than print, was a respondent to the Dr. Richard Harley's paper on New Media, but had presented an essay on this subject to the Society of Biblical Literature at its national meeting, which is also included in this volume. The four main sessions of the symposium had the following titles:

I. New Translations of the Bible.
II. New Finds that Illuminate the World and Text of the Bible.
III. New Approaches to Understanding and Study of the Bible.
IV. New Media for Communicating the Bible

A brief biographical sketch of each presenter appears at the bottom of the opening page of each essay. The responses are printed following each of the presentations at the main sessions of the symposium, with the papers of Nida and Boomershine at the conclusion of the volume.

New Documents: Qumran and Gnostic Writings

Joseph A. Fitzmyer, S.J.

Documents stemming from two archaeological discoveries in the last fifty years have shed important light on the biblical world and text: documents from the Qumran Caves in what was then the Hashemite Kingdom of Jordan, and documents from Nag Hammadi in Upper Egypt. The latter were discovered in 1946, and the former in the decade 1947–1956. Together they have yielded a trove of ancient texts written in Aramaic, Coptic, Greek, and Hebrew that no one would have suspected possible. They have increased our knowledge in an incredible way about the ancient eastern Mediterranean world, the Palestinian Jewish background of the OT and the NT, and about developments within the early Christian church.

My remarks about these recently discovered ancient documents will be centered on the two corpora, the Qumran texts and the Nag Hammadi texts. In each case I shall review briefly the history of the discovery, the contents and publication of the texts, and then comment on the impact that they have made on the study of the OT and the NT and the worlds that developed from them.

I. *Qumran Documents*

A. *Discovery.* In the vicinity of Khirbet Qumran, an ancient site originally believed to have been a Roman fort near the northwest shore of the Dead Sea, Ta'amireh Bedouin and French, English, and American archaeologists discovered eleven caves that have yielded written materials dating from the end of the third century B.C. up to

JOSEPH A. FITZMYER is Professor Emeritus of Biblical Studies at Catholic University of America, Washington, DC.

shortly before the destruction of Jerusalem in A.D. 70. Cave 1 was discovered by a Bedouin boy, Muhammad edh-Dhîb, in 1947, caves 2-6 by other Bedouin and archaeologists in 1952, and caves 7-11 by archaeologists or Bedouin in 1956. Of these caves, 1, 4, and 11 have proved to be the most important.

B. *Contents.* In Cave 1 were discovered seven major scrolls and some 70 other fragmentary Hebrew and Aramaic texts of varying size and importance. The seven major scrolls included two copies of Isaiah, the Manual of Discipline (the Qumran community's rule book), the War Scroll, the Thanksgiving Psalms, a commentary on Habakkuk, and the Genesis Apocryphon, an embellishment of Genesis stories. Cave 2 yielded 18 fragmentary OT texts and 15 non-biblical fragments of narrative, prophetic, juridical, or liturgical character. From Cave 3 came three fragmentary OT texts, 11 non-biblical writings, and the Copper Plaque recording where treasures were buried. In Cave 5 were found eight fragmentary OT texts and 17 non-biblical writings. Cave 6 yielded seven fragmentary OT texts and 24 non-biblical fragments, again of narrative, prophetic, juridical, or liturgical character. Cave 7 produced the surprise: 19 Greek fragments, two of OT writings (Exodus and the Epistle of Jeremy), and 17 others of contested identification, some even alleged to be of NT writings! In Cave 8 were discovered four fragmentary OT texts and one non-biblical hymn. From Cave 9 came only a small papyrus fragment with Hebrew letters, and from Cave 10 an ostracon (writing on a sea shell) inscribed with part of a Hebrew name. In all, Caves 1-3,5-10 yielded 212 complete or fragmentary documents.

Cave 11, discovered in 1956 by Bedouin who rather thoroughly cleaned it out, yielded 25 fragmentary manuscripts, among which was the Targum of Job, an Aramaic translation of a sixth of the canonical Book of Job, the important Psalms Scroll A, and the equally important Temple Scroll as well as other texts of some significance.

Cave 4 was discovered by Bedouin in 1952; they began to clean it out but were eventually stopped by Jordanian authorities so that competent archaeologists could control the excavation of it. In some ways this cave has proved to be the most important, because it seems to have been the place where the Qumran community dumped its library of scrolls before the destruction of its community center by the Romans about A.D. 68. From Cave 4 has come not one complete scroll, but "at least 15,000 fragments," as reported by Roland de Vaux, the French Dominican who conducted the exploration of the caves and the excavation of Khirbet Qumran and 'Ain Feshkha.[1] These fragments were brought to the 'scrollery' of the Palestine Archaeological Museum in Jerusalem (now called the Rockefeller Museum); others were bought from the Bedouin. Then began the giant jigsaw puzzle. By the end of June 1960, 511 texts had been identified, distributed over 620 plates. In volume 7 of the Clarendon Press publication, *Discoveries in the Judaean Desert,* the French scholar M. Baillet definitively published the fragmentary texts 4Q482 to 4Q520.[2] This reveals that the number of Cave 4 texts identified by 1982 was 520, and another eight have since been identified. Hence 528 fragmentary texts from Cave 4. When these are added to the 212 from the minor caves, and 25 from Cave 11, the total number of texts from Qumran caves is something like 765, most of them fragmentary, but often of significant value.[3]

C. *Publication.* Of the 765 fragmentary texts about 40 per cent have already been published. All the 212 texts from Caves 1-3, 5-10 have been definitively published, either by Israeli or American scholars, or by some of the international and intercredal team set up

---

[1] See R. de Vaux and J. T. Milik, *Qumrân Grotte 4, II: I. Archéologie, II. Tefillin, mezuzot et targums (4Q128-4Q157)* (DJD 6; Oxford: Clarendon, 1977) 8.

[2] See *Qumrân Grotte 4, III (4Q482-4Q520)* (DJD 7; Oxford: Clarendon, 1982).

[3] See J. A. Fitzmyer, *The Dead Sea Scrolls: Major Publications and Tools for Study: Revised Edition* (SBLRBS 20; Atlanta, GA: Scholars Press, 1990) 31-67. This list includes many texts that are known to exist or have been described in survey articles, but have not yet been published, even in partial form.

in 1952 to work on the Cave 4 jigsaw puzzle.[4] Most of the 25 texts from Cave 11 have been published by American or Dutch scholars,[5] and the remaining few are to appear shortly. But Cave 4 has created the major problem. In addition to the 39 texts definitively published by Baillet in the DJD series,[6] J. T. Milik and J. M. Allegro have issued the definitive publication of texts 4Q128 to 4Q186, i.e. 59 texts in the Oxford DJD series.[7] Milik also published seven Aramaic fragmentary texts of Enoch (4QEn^{a-g}) and parts of five related texts, the Book of Giants (4QEnGiants^{a-e}).[8] He and other members of the

---

[4] Ibid. 11-19 (Cave 1), 20-22 (Cave 2), 23-24 (Cave 3), 25-25 (Cave 5), 27-28 (Cave 6), 29 (Cave 7), 30 (Caves 8-10).

[5] Ibid. 68-75.

[6] See n. 2 above.

[7] See n. 1 for 4Q128 to 4Q157 (phylacteries, mezuzot, and targums). Also J. M. Allegro, *Qumrân Cave 4, I (4Q158-4Q186)* (DJD 5; Oxford: Clarendon, 1968 [*pesharim*]). The miserable form in which Allegro published this material in DJD 5 was a scandal, noted by many; cf. J. Strugnell, "Notes en marge du volume V des 'Discoveries in the Judaean Desert of Jordan,'" *RevQ* 7 (1969-71) 163-276. One text that Allegro did not include in his DJD volume was subsequently published by him in an appendix to his book, *The Dead Sea Scrolls and the Christian Myth* (Buffalo, NY: Prometheus Books, 1984) 235-40. He labelled it 4QTherapeia and referred to it as a "medical writing." This is a highly questionable identification of the text, which Israeli scholars have rather identified as a "writing exercise." See J. Naveh, "A Medical Document or a Writing Exercise? The So-Called 4Q Therapeia," *IEJ* 36 (1986) 52-55; cf. J. C. Greenfield, ibid., 118-19.

One should also beware of the follow-up of Allegro's publication of this text by J. H. Charlesworth, *The Discovery of a Dead Sea Scroll (4Q Therapeia): Its Importance in the History of Medicine and Jesus Research* (International Center for Arid and Semi-Arid Land Studies Publ. 85-1; Lubbock, TX: Texas Tech University. 1985). Charlesworth now admits that he misunderstood the text; see "A Misunderstood Recently Published Dead Sea Scroll (4QM130)," *Explorations* (American Institute for the Study of Religious Cooperation, Philadelphia, PA) 1/2 (1987) 2.

[8] See *The Books of Enoch: Aramaic Fragments of Qumran Cave 4* (Oxford: Clarendon, 1976).

Cave 4 team have issued at times preliminary or partial publications of a number of other 4Q texts; and some of the graduate students of Frank Cross and John Strugnell (of Harvard University) have recently been given 4Q texts for their dissertations, of which about a dozen texts or groups of texts have now been published.[9] Yet one still awaits the definitive publication of roughly 70-75 per cent of the Cave 4 texts. Many of these unpublished texts are fragmentary OT texts, the contents of which have been revealed; others are important sectarian texts, about which we know only from preliminary reports or surveys.

D. *Significance of the Qumran Documents.* The Qumran texts have contributed in unexpected ways to four areas of biblical study: to our knowledge of ancient Hebrew and Aramaic, to the history of ancient Judaism, to the textual study of the OT, and to the Palestinian Jewish background of the NT.

1. *Ancient Hebrew and Aramaic.* When the Qumran documents are considered along with the texts discovered at Masada and the caves of Murabba'at, Khabra, etc., we see that a gap that long existed has been filled in. From all these texts we have acquired evidence of the use of Aramaic, Greek, and Hebrew in Palestine in the first centuries B.C. and A.D.—in a word, of a trilingualism used by the people of that time and place. These documents give evidence of Palestinian literary activity in Aramaic and Hebrew in the period between the final redaction of the Hebrew Scriptures and the beginning of rabbinic literature (end of the second century A.D.).

This is particularly noteworthy for Aramaic, because, though one often believed that this language had become dominant in Palestine after the return of Jews from the Babylonian Captivity, the evidence for it particularly between the final redaction of the Book of Daniel (about 165 B.C.) and the composition of the earliest Aramaic

---

[9] See *The Dead Sea Scrolls* (n. 3 above), 31-67.

rabbinical text, the מְגִלַּת תַּעֲנִית (ca. A.D. 100), was practically nil.[10] This question has a bearing on the study of the NT and on a famous debate some 50 years ago between two highly respected American biblical scholars. E. J. Goodspeed, of the University of Chicago, once espoused the thesis that in this period there was no 'creative Aramaic literary writing' and even questioned the possibility of 'an Aramaic Gospel' being written.[11] A. T. Olmstead, of the same university, disagreed with Goodspeed and sought to answer him in an article entitled, "Could an Aramaic Gospel Be Written?"[12] But Olmstead had none of the evidence available from the Scrolls, which now clearly reveal considerable literary creativity in Aramaic of this period. Among such works are the Genesis Apocryphon of Qumran Cave 1, the Enoch literature of Cave 4, and other Aramaic texts of lesser moment.

The evidence for the literary use of Hebrew is even more abundant in the Qumran writings. Sectarian manuals, hymns, prayers, and liturgical compositions bear witness to a form of postbiblical Hebrew which mediates between the postexilic Hebrew of late OT books and that of the Mishnah, the core of the Jewish Talmuds.

The evidence for Palestinian Greek comes mostly from the related discoveries in caves of Murabba'at and other wadis (seasonally dry mountain valleys) south of Qumran. In this case, the evidence is not as significant as that for Hebrew and Aramaic.[13]

---

[10] See the collection of Aramaic texts put together by D. J. Harrington and me, *A Manual of Palestinian Aramaic Texts (Second Century B.C.–Second Century A.D.* (Biblica et Orientalia 34; Rome: Biblical Institute, 1978). Since the publication of that manual, which includes Aramaic texts from places other than Qumran, Milik has published the Aramaic texts of Enoch (see n. 8 above), the targums of Job and Leviticus from Cave 4 (see n. 1 above).

[11] See *New Chapters in New Testament Study* (New York: Macmillan, 1937) 127-68, esp. 165-66.

[12] *Journal of Near Eastern Studies* 1 (1942) 41-75.

[13] See further my article, "The Languages of Palestine in the First

2. *History of Ancient Judaism.* Whether or not one accepts the identification of the Qumran sect as Essene (first proposed by A. Dupont-Sommer and until recently used by the majority of Qumran interpreters), the Qumran documents have revealed to us a form of life, a theology, and a mode of biblical interpretation that were in use among Palestinian Jews from roughly 150 B.C. to A.D. 68. Jewish to the hilt, this pre-Christian community led an ascetic communal life, with at least some parts of it celibate. Antecedents of later Christian monastic discipline, which had often been traced to the Fathers of the Desert in Egypt, have come to light in the sectarian literature of this Qumran community of *Palestinian* Jews.

What is now known about such Jews from the Qumran documents dispels the tendency one once had to refer to the Judaism of this period, especially in its pharisaic-rabbinic emphasis, as 'normative.' These texts give striking support to Josephus' account of the different 'sects' (αἱρέσεις) among the Jews of his time.[14] Initially, scholars thought that such Essenes emerged from the Hasidim, the 'pious ones,' who, though at first associated with the Maccabees (1 Macc 2.42), broke with their movement when it became more politically oriented and the high priesthood was usurped by one of its kings. But more recently, Jerome Murphy-O'Connor of the Ecole Biblique in Jerusalem, building on a suggestion of S. Iwry and others, has proposed that the Qumran sect emerged from Jews who had returned from Babylon to Palestine in the second century B.C. Having heard about the success of the Maccabean movement and the restoration of theocracy in the Land, they emigrated from Babylon. But on arrival in 'Israel' and not finding things as ideal or as traditional as expected, they broke with the Jerusalem priesthood and what they regarded as its tainted Temple-service to withdraw to a desert retreat to establish

---

Century A.D." *Catholic Biblical Quarterly* 32 (1970) 501-31; repr. in *A Wandering Aramean: Collected Aramaic Essays* (SBL Monograph Series 25; Missoula, MT: Scholars, 1979) 29-56.

[14] See Josephus, *J.W.* 2.8.2 §119. Here he refers to them as philosophies among the Jews. Cf. *Ant.* 13.5.9 § 171; 20.9.1 § 199.

there בֵּית נֶאֱמָן בְּיִשְׂרָאֵל "a trustworthy house in Israel" (CD 3.19). This explanation has seemed plausible to many because it helps to explain by a historical setting many details in the texts that were often interpreted earlier only in a symbolic or figurative sense. Noteworthy, above all, are the form of life and the theological tenets of such Jews that clearly set them off from other forms of Judaism then current in Palestine. The Temple Scroll of Cave 11[15] has been interpreted as their second Tôrāh.[16]

In recent articles, however, E. Qimron and J. Strugnell, reporting on a Cave 4 text not yet officially published, 4QMMT (מִקְצָת מַעֲשֵׂי הַתּוֹרָה), have stressed the halakhic difference that these Jews of Qumran insisted on.[17] The debate about the identification of the Qumran sect on the basis of this text has only begun.[18]

3. *The Textual Study of the OT.* When the texts of Cave 1 were first made known, W. F. Albright hailed them as "the greatest manu-

---

[15] See Y. Yadin, מגילת־המקדש: ההדיר וסירף מבוא וספירש (3 vols., with a supplement; Jerusalem: Israel Exploration Society, 1977; English version, *The Temple Scroll*, 1983).

[16] See Y. Yadin, *The Temple Scroll*, 1. 390-92. Cf. Y. Yadin, *The Temple Scroll: The Hidden Law of the Dead Sea Sect* (New York: Random House, 1985); B. Z. Wacholder, *The Dawn of Qumran: The Sectarian Torah and the Teacher of Righteousness* (Cincinnati, OH: Hebrew Union College, 1983).

[17] See "An Unpublished Halakhic Letter from Qumran," *Biblical Archaeology Today: Proceedings of the International Congress on Biblical Archaeology, Jerusalem, April 1984* (Jerusalem: Israel Exploration Society, 1985) 400-407; cf. *Israel Museum Journal* 4 (1985) 9-12. The text of this 4Q document has now been published; see Z. J. Kapera, "An Anonymously Received Pre-Publication of the 4QMMT," *Qumran Chronicle* (Cracow) 2 (1990) Appendix A (pp. 1-12).

[18] See L. H. Schiffman, "The New Halakhic Letter (4QMMT) and the Origins of the Dead Sea Sect," *BA* 53 (1990) 64-73; Y. Sussmann, "The History of *Halakha* and the Dead Sea Scrolls—Preliminary Observations on מקצת מעשי התורה (4QMMT)," *Tarbiz* 59 (1989-90) 11-76.

script discovery in modern times." In the Qumran documents we have OT texts that take us back a thousand years or more from the time of the oldest manuscripts of the Hebrew Scriptures known prior to 1947. All told, about 195 complete or fragmentary biblical texts have been recovered from Caves 1-11. On the one hand, they attest to the fidelity with which Jewish scribes copied the OT over the centuries. On the other, they have brought to light unsuspected forms or recensions of biblical books. From Cave 1 came the great Isaiah scroll A, which preserves all 66 chapters, save for a few words lost at the bottom of some columns. Dated palaeographically to 100 B.C., it contributed only 13 paltry textual variants to the translation of Isaiah in the RSV of 1952.[19] Among the 127 biblical texts of Cave 4 every book of the Hebrew canon is represented save Esther (and Nehemiah, which at that time was considered as one book with Ezra). Some Cave 4 texts, especially fragments of 1-2 Samuel and Jeremiah, brought to light forms of the books that differ from the medieval Masoretic text-tradition. One text turned out to be a shorter Hebrew form of Jeremiah, previously known in the Greek Septuagint. Another Cave 4 text, written in paleo-Hebrew script and dating from the early second century B.C., contains the repetitious, expanded form of Exodus known previously in the Samaritan Pentateuch. The result is that scholars tend to distinguish different local texts of OT books: a Babylonian form (= more or less the Masoretic tradition), an Egyptian form (= more or less the LXX tradition), and a Palestinian form (= more or less the Samaritan tradition).[20] But the contribution that the Qumran documents have to make to the study of OT textual

---

[19] See M. Burrows, *The Dead Sea Scrolls* (New York: Viking, 1955) 304-9.

[20] See F. M. Cross and S. Talmon (eds.), *Qumran and the History of the Biblical Text* (Cambridge, MA: Harvard University, 1975). For a different assessment of the value of the biblical manuscripts from Qumran to the study of OT textual criticism, see E. Tov, "Hebrew Biblical Manuscripts from the Judaean Desert: Their Contribution to Textual Criticism," *JJS* 39 (1988) 5-37.

criticism is still to be fully worked out; it awaits the definitive publication of the many fragmentary biblical texts of Cave 4.

4. *Palestinian Jewish Background of the NT.* So far nothing has been found in Qumran documents that refers to Christians, to Jesus, or even to John the Baptist. Part of the reason for this is that the majority of the texts were composed in pre-Christian times, or in the first half of the first Christian century.

In 1972 a Spaniard, José O'Callaghan, claimed to identify tiny Greek fragments of Cave 7 as NT texts, in particular 7Q5 as a copy of Mark 6.52-53.[21] Yet apart from a recent German writer, C. P. Thiede, who has supported O'Callaghan,[22] such an identification of these fragments has fallen on deaf scholarly ears. Again, an Australian scholar, Barbara Thiering, has tried to interpret the Qumran texts as speaking covertly of John the Baptist, Jesus, and Christians. For her John would be the Teacher of Righteousness mentioned in Qumran texts, Jesus the Wicked Priest.[23] But her thesis rides roughshod over archaeological evidence connected with the texts and their palaeographical dating, many of which were clearly composed and/or copied in the last centuries B.C.

The Qumran documents, however, have shed unexpected light on tenets of Pauline and Johannine teaching, on the Matthean Gospel,

---

[21] See his book, *Los papiros griegos de la cueva 7 de Qumrân* (Biblioteca de Auctores Cristianos 353; Madrid: Editorial Católica, 1974).

[22] See *Die älteste Evangelien-Handschrift? Das Markus-Fragment von Qumran und die Anfänge der schriftlichen Überlieferung des Neuen Testaments* (Wuppertal: Brockhaus, 1986). Cf. H.-U. Rosenbaum, "Cave 7Q5! Gegen die erneute Inanspruchnahme des Qumran-Fragments 7Q5 als Bruckstück der ältesten Evangelien-Handschrift," *BZ* 31 (1987) 189-205.

[23] See *Redating the Teacher of Righteousness* (Australian and New Zealand Studies in Theology and Religion 1; Sydney: Theological Explorations, 1979) 213-14; *The Gospels and Qumran: A New Hypothesis* (Australian and New Zealand Studies in Theology and Religion 2; Sydney: Theological Explorations, 1981).

and on the Epistle to the Hebrews. Of the Synoptic Gospels, least has been established for Mark, the Gospel usually regarded as the earliest, as containing more Semitisms than the others, and as more closely related to the Jesus-event itself. Apropos of the Pauline writings, one finds in Qumran literature interesting parallels and contacts for the Apostle's dualistic thinking (light/darkness, God/Belial), his doctrine of God's righteousness, his teaching on human justification rooted in God's mercy, some of his ideas on angels, and his use of μυστήριον, 'secret.' For the Johannine material, one can also appeal to Qumran dualism (but in a way different from its parallels to Pauline usage), the emphasis on God's foreknowledge, and the doctrine of the Spirit.

Qumran texts have helped the study of two christological titles, 'Lord' and 'Son of God.' R. Bultmann once maintained that the absolute, unmodified title κύριος, '(the) Lord,' did not stem from the early Palestinian church, but had been borrowed from Hellenistic usage as the kerygma was carried abroad by missionaries into the world where this absolute title was used for gods and human rulers: "At the very outset the unmodified expression 'the Lord' is unthinkable in Jewish usage. 'Lord' used of God is always given some modifier."[24] Yet we now have evidence from Qumran that Palestinian Jews did refer to God absolutely as '(the) Lord' both in Aramaic and Hebrew: in 11QtgJob 24.6-7 (= Hebrew Job 34.12) Aramaic מָרֵא, 'Lord,' not only translates Hebrew שַׁדַּי, 'the Almighty,' but stands in parallelism with אֱלָהָא, 'God.'[25] The Hebrew form אָדוֹן seems to be found in 11QPs[a] 28.7 (= Hebrew of Ps 151.4).[26] All of which raises

---

[24] *Theology of the New Testament* (2 vols.; London: SCM, 1952) 1.51.

[25] See J. P. M. van der Ploeg and A. S. van der Woude, *Le targum de Job de la grotte xi de Qumrân* (Koninklijke Nederlandse Akademie van Wetenschappen; Leiden: Brill, 1971) 58.

[26] See J. A. Sanders, *The Psalms Scroll of Qumrân Cave 11 (11QPs[a])* (DJD 4; Oxford: Clarendon, 1965) 49, 55. 1 have here followed the interpretation of Sanders, who takes מֵעֲשֵׂי אָדוֹן, "the deeds of the Lord," as a unit, but not everyone does. Some consider the unit to be הַכּוֹל אָדוֹן, "the Lord of All." If that were correct, then אָדוֹן would be a construct and not

the question why the absolute use of κύριος for Christ in the NT could not have been an extension on the part of Palestinian Jewish Christians, speaking either in Aramaic or Hebrew, of the custom of referring to Yahweh by such a title. It may well have been for such Christians either a confessional title or even part of their kerygmatic proclamation, "Jesus is Lord" (מָרֵא יֵשׁוּעַ); cf. 1 Cor 12.3; Ro 10.9.[27]

'Son of God' is also used of Jesus in the NT. It occurs in the OT for angels, the people of Israel collectively, the king on the Davidic throne, and even for an individual upright Jew. Given such an OT background, most NT interpreters have been reluctant to ascribe the use of it for Jesus to a Hellenistic background, but some have proposed as its source the Latin *divi filius* or its Greek counterpart θεοῦ υἱός used of the emperor. But, once again, 'Son of God,' a title previously unknown in Palestinian extrabiblical texts, has turned up in an unpublished Aramaic fragment on which J. T. Milik lectured at Harvard University in 1972, when he displayed the Aramaic text on a screen and passed to the audience an English translation of the whole text. It thus came into the public domain. The text is broken, however, and the name of the person of whom the title is used has been lost:

> [X] shall be great upon the earth, [O King! All (people) shall] make [peace], and all shall serve [him. He shall be called the

---

evidence for the usage mentioned. See J. Magne, "Orphisme, pythagorisme, essenisme dans le texte hébreu du Psaume 151?" *RevQ* 8 (1972-75) 507-47; J. Carmignac, "Nouvelles précisions sur le Psaume 151," ibid. 593-97; P. Auffret, "Structure littéraire et interprétation du Psaume 151 de la grotte 11 de Qumran," *RevQ* 9 (1977-78) 163-88; J. Magne, "'Serviteur de l'univers' ou David-Orphée? Défense de mon interprétation du Psaume 151," ibid. 189-96. — In any case, the Hebrew absolute is found in the canonical psalter itself (Ps 114.7)!

[27] See also Josephus, who in two instances uses the Greek equivalent κύριος (*Ant.* 20.4.2 §90; 13.3.1 §68 [quoting Isa 19.19]). Cf. my article, "New Testament *Kyrios* and *Maranatha* and Their Aramaic Background," *To Advance the Gospel: New Testament Studies* (New York: Crossroad, 1981) 218-35.

son of] the [G]reat [God], and by his name shall he be named. He shall be hailed (as) the Son of God, and they shall call him Son of the Most High.... (4Q246).

No one reading those lines can fail to see the pertinence of them to Luke 1.32-35, the words of Gabriel to Mary in the infancy narrative.[28]

These are, then, merely a few of the reasons why the Qumran scrolls have proved to be so important for our understanding of the Bible, of Jewish history, and of early Christianity. It is now time to turn to the Gnostic writings.

II. *Nag Hammadi Documents*

A. *Discovery.* In 1946 an Egyptian peasant found the remains of a library in tomb-caves in a cliff (Gebel et-Tarf), 6.2 mi. northeast of Nag Hammadi in Upper Egypt, near the ancient monastic center of Chenoboskion. Eventually recovered from the find were 12 papyrus codices and eight leaves of Cod. XIII, written in Coptic and dating from the fourth century A.D. Codex I (Jung Codex) was acquired by an Egyptian dealer (A. Eid), but it disappeared from Egypt in the winter of 1948-49. Offered for sale in New York, it was eventually purchased for the Jung Foundation (Zurich), but some folios of it remained in the Coptic Museum of Old Cairo, to which the Codex has been returned after publication. Codex III was bought in 1946 by the curator of the Coptic Museum (Togo Mina) and identified by J. Doresse in Cairo/Paris (1948). The remaining codices were sold to the Coptic Museum in 1948, and identification of them was made in 1949. P. Labib published photographs of Cod. I and of 110 pages of Cod. II in 1956; all parts of all the remaining codices were published

---

[28] See my article, "The Contribution of Qumran Aramaic to the Study of the New Testament," *New Testament Studies* 20 (1973-74) 382-420; repr. *A Wandering Aramean* (n. 13 above), 85-113, esp. 90-94.

between 1956 and 1973. The 13 codices have to be considered along with Berlin Cod. 8502, first discovered by C. Schmidt in 1896, but published by W. Till only in 1955; it is a 5th cent. codex related to the same material.

B. *Contents.* The 13 codices contain 52 tractates, some of which are duplicated so that the real number is 45 separate treatises. They represent various sorts of Gnostic writings and diverse literary genres. These genres are sometimes pure, sometimes mixed, but many of the tractates are not easily classified. There are (1) gospels: *Gospel of the Egyptians, Gospel of Mary* (Magdalene), *Gospel of Philip, Gospel of Thomas,* and the *Gospel of Truth.* None of these gospels, however, is similar in form to the NT canonical gospels. The *Gospel of Truth* is an unsystematic meditation on the person of Christ and on his saving work. The *Gospel of Mary* is a combination of a dialogue between the risen Christ and his followers and of a revelation-discourse. (2) Apocalypses: the *Apocalypse of Paul, 1 Apocalypse of James, 2 Apocalypse of James, Apocalypse of Adam, Apocalypse of Peter, Apocalypse of Asclepius, Nature of the Archons, Paraphrase of Shem.* Despite their name(s) none is like the NT Johannine Apocalypse. (3) Acts: *Acts of Peter and the Twelve Apostles, Acts of Peter.* The latter is not a gnostic text, but rather part of a larger body of apocryphal acts of Peter. But the *Letter of Peter to Philip* is modelled on the NT Acts of the Apostles, whereas the tractate's title is applicable only to the beginning of it. (4) Letters: These are epistles addressed to various persons: *Epistle to Rheginos* (On the Resurrection), *Epistle to Eugnostos* (the Blessed). (5) Dialogues: *Sophia of Jesus Christ* and *Dialogue of the Savior* are forms of a conversation between the risen Christ and his followers in which gnostic teaching is made known. (6) Secret Books: These are various tractates that bear the name *Apocryphon* and which are in part apocalypses and part revelation-discourses. So the *Apocryphon of John.* (7) Speculative Tracts: *On the Origin of the World* or *Eugnostos the Blessed.* (8) Sapiential Literature: The *Sentences of Sextus* is a collection of aphorisms, but of non-gnostic origin, whereas the *Teachings of*

Silvanus are not only modelled on OT wisdom literature, but clearly of gnostic background. (9) Exegesis: Despite its title, *Exegesis on the Soul,* the tractate is a mythical explanation of the soul entrapped in the world, which cites Homer, the OT, and the NT. (10) Revelation Discourses: Tractates in which a revealer-figure, such as Sophia, speaks in the first person singular; examples are the *Apocryphon of John, Trimorphic Protennoia,* and *Thunder: Perfect Mind* (an essay on the sound of thunder as the revealing voice from the divine sphere). (11) Prayers: The *Prayer of Apostle Paul,* the *Prayer of Thanksgiving.* (12) Sundry Tractates: *Melchizedek, Marsanes.*

When one reads most of these Nag Hammadi texts, one is impressed by their gibberish. One wonders whether they have been rightly understood by modern Coptologists or correctly translated.

C. *Publication.* In contrast to the Qumran documents, all the texts of Nag Hammadi and some others related to them have been fully published. Photographic reproductions are available in the series, *The Facsimile Edition of the Nag Hammadi Codices,* published between 1972 and 1984,[29] There is also a series of—to date—seventeen volumes of translations and studies, *Nag Hammadi Studies,*[30] as well as a subseries, *The Coptic Gnostic Library.*[31] Work on these documents has been greatly aided by the bibliographic survey of D. M. Scholer,

---

[29] 13 vols.; Leiden: Brill, 1972-84. They have been published under the auspices of the Department of Antiquities of the Arab Republic of Egypt in conjunction with the United Nations Education, Scientific, and Cultural Organization.

[30] Ed. by M. Krause et al.; Leiden: Brill, 1971–. A preliminary form of the translations to be used in this series has been gathered into one volume, under the direction of J. M. Robinson, *The Nag Hammadi Library in English: Translated by Members of the Coptic Gnostic Library Project of the Institute for Christianity* (ed. M. W. Meyer; San Francisco, CA: Harper & Row; Leiden: Brill, 1977). A third edition of the last title, completely revised with an afterword by R. Smith, the editor, appeared in 1988.

[31] Edited with English Translation, Introduction and Notes (Leiden: Brill, 1975–).

Nag Hammadi Bibliography 1945-1969, and its annual supplements published in *Novum Testamentum.*[32]

D. *Significance of the Nag Hammadi Documents.* It is not easy to assess the value or significance of this discovery of ancient writings. It is safe to say that they are in no way comparable in importance to the Qumran documents. The dating of their composition is not easy, since, by and large, they are fourth-century copies of texts. As a bulk they are important for what they reveal to us about various forms of Gnosticism from the late second century to that of the fourth century. They show that Gnostics of the second, third, and fourth centuries did indeed teach what the church Fathers, such as Irenaeus, said they did. In other words, the Nag Hammadi texts contribute to our knowledge of the battles that went on during the patristic period of the Christian church.

The relevance of this discovery for the study of the OT is almost nil. The same would have to be said for the Jewish literature that is now available in the Qumran documents. One can detect in the Qumran documents elements that fed into the development of gnosticism, however, just as one can find in the NT similar elements, in other words, protognostic ideas and tenets. But in neither the Qumran literature nor the NT does one find the full-blown gnosticism that is present in these texts. Some students of these Nag Hammadi texts have succeeded in showing from them how gnostics interpreted Paul's writings or the Johannine Gospel.[33] But what has *emerged* in these

---

[32] NHS 1; Leiden: Brill, 1971. The annual supplements began in *Novum Testamentum* 13 (1971) and the 18th appeared in *Novum Testamentum* 31 (1988) 344-78.

[33] E.g. E. H. Pagels, *The Gnostic Paul: Gnostic Exegesis of the Pauline Letters* (Philadelphia, PA: Fortress, 1975); *The Johannine Gospel in Gnostic Exegesis: Heracleon's Commentary on John* (SBLMS 17; Nashville, TN/New York: Abingdon, 1973). Cf. P. Perkins, *The Gnostic Dialogue: The Early Church and the Crisis of Gnosticism* (Theological Inquiries; New York/Ramsey, NJ/Toronto: Paulist, 1980).

letters scarcely gives any support to the work of W. Schmithals, *Paul and the Gnostics,*[34] which claims direct Gnostic influence on Paul.

The one exception to all of this is the very important Nag Hammadi text, the *Gos. of Thomas.* The Coptic form of this gospel was first published by P. Labib in 1956.[35] Eventually, it was reproduced as Cod. II/2 in FENHL II/2 (1974). The Coptic form is dated to the mid-fourth century A.D. and is written on ten papyrus leaves. It is a collection of 114 sayings of Jesus, most of which are introduced by "Jesus said."

Shortly after the first publication of the Coptic text, it was realized that this was a Coptic version of an earlier Greek writing, known from papyrus fragments found at Oxyrhynchus at the end of the last century and the beginning of this. These Greek fragments were (1) *Logia Iesou* (Oxy P 1), published by B. P. Grenfell and A. S. Hunt in 1897, dated ca. A.D. 200, and containing eight fragmentary Greek sayings of Jesus; (2) *New Sayings of Jesus* (Oxy P 654), published by Grenfell and Hunt in 1904, dated ca. A.D. 250, and containing the prologue plus six fragmentary Greek sayings of Jesus; (3) *Fragments of a Lost Gospel* (Oxy P 655), published by Grenfell and Hunt in 1904, dated ca. A.D. 250, and containing four fragmentary Greek sayings of Jesus.[36] With the aid of the Coptic version, I was able to restudy the Greek fragments and publish them anew.[37]

---

[34] Tr. J. E. Steely (Nashville, TN/New York: Abingdon, 1972).

[35] *Peuangelion pkata Thomas* (Cairo: Coptic Museum, 1956). A handy edition with an English translation appeared in A. Guillaumont et al., *The Gospel according to Thomas: Coptic Text Established and Translated* (Leiden: Brill; New York: Harper & Bros., 1959).

[36] They were conveniently gathered, along with other *agrapha,* into one volume by J. Jeremias, *Unknown Sayings of Jesus* (New York: Scribner, 1957).

[37] See "The Oxyrhynchus Logoi of Jesus and the Coptic Gospel According to Thomas," *TS* 20 (1959) 505-60; repr. in slightly revised form in *Essays on the Semitic Background of the New Testament* (London: Chapman, 1971; repr. Missoula, MT: Scholars, 1974) 355-433. See now the restudy of H. W.

It is clear that the Coptic version is not just a translation but a reworking of the Greek text of this Gospel.

It is not a gospel in the canonical sense, since it contains no narrative or personal information about the person of Jesus or his deeds or his death. The 114 sayings that it records are wisdom sayings (maxims and proverbs), parables, eschatological sayings (prophecies), answers to questions posed by a disciple, and community rules. They are all strung together with no logical order.

No saying among the 114 is word-for-word identical with a canonical saying. But (1) many are paraphrases or variants of canonical sayings, especially of the Johannine Jesus. (2) Some reproduce sayings not found in the canonical Gospels, but extant in patristic writings. (3) Many, in fact, almost half, of the sayings are previously unknown dicta, of syncretistic or gnostic background. Those in the first category may be derived from an independent oral or written Christian tradition, since some of the sayings are preserved in a more primitive form than the canonical form (e.g. Sayings 65, 8), whereas those in the third category stem from the same source as other gnostic Gospels (e.g. Saying 114). The *Gos. of Thomas* is ascribed to Didymus Jude Thomas, i.e. Thomas the Twin (of Jesus). The text seems to have stemmed from Syrian Church tradition.

Apart from this text, however, which is important for the study of the canonical Gospels, the rest of the corpus of Nag Hammadi has little of pertinence for the study of the NT.[38] The main reason is that

---

Attridge, "The Greek Fragments," in B. Layton (ed.), *Nag Hammadi Codex II, 2-7, together with XIII, 2*, Brit. Lib. Or. 4926(1) and P. Oxy. 1. 654, 655: Volume 1: Gospel According to Thomas, Gospel According to Philip, Hypostasis of the Archons, and Indexes* (Coptic Gnostic Library, NHS 20; Leiden: Brill, 1989) 95-128. Cf. J.-E. Ménard, *L'Evangile selon Thomas* (NHS 5; Leiden: Brill, 1975).

[38] Cf. C. M. Tuckett, *Nag Hammadi and the Gospel Tradition: Synoptic Tradition in the Nag Hammadi Library* (Edinburgh: Clark, 1986) 149: "One important, albeit negative, result of the analysis undertaken here is that there appears to be no evidence for the use of pre-synoptic sources by the authors of the texts studied. Insofar as they reflect synoptic tradition at all, the texts

the provenience of these texts dates from about 100-150 years after the formation of the NT itself.

These, then, are the new documentary finds, from Qumran in ancient Palestine and from Nag Hammadi in Upper Egypt, that have enabled us in a variety of ways to interpret anew different aspects of the Bible and the world in which it took shape.

---

examined here all seem to presuppose one or more of the finished gospels of Matthew, Mark or Luke. It would therefore appear that the texts of the Nag Hammadi Library (with the possible exception of the Gospel of Thomas) will not be of any assistance in dealing with the problem of development of synoptic tradition at a pre-redactional stage. Rather, these texts are witnesses of the post-redactional development of that tradition. There is thus no evidence here for the existence of texts earlier than probably the second century; there is also no evidence for the continuing survival and use of a Q source (or any other pre-redactional synoptic source) by Gnostic communities."

RESPONSE: James A. Sanders

It is always reassuring to read what Joseph Fitzmyer writes simply because one knows in reading Fitzmyer that the data have been scrupulously checked and verified. Furthermore, Fitzmyer is a strict constructionist; one knows that he is not going to build a new hypothesis on a greater measure of imagination than of data. His current paper is no exception. The first three sections of the paper, on the discovery, contents, and publication schedule of the Qumran discoveries are reference material of the first order.

The section of his paper on the significance of the Qumran literature and their impact on areas of common study is solid, as far as it goes. His thesis about the languages of Palestine in the first centuries B.C.E. and C.E. has already been commonly accepted in the field.

I would, however, have expanded considerably on the impact of the Scrolls on the history of Early Judaism. They significantly brought a close to the old George Foot Moore synthesis which distinguished normative from heterodox Judaism and ushered in a new one focusing on pluralism in Judaism prior to the fall of the Second Temple. The earlier work in this regard of scholars, especially that of Saul Liebermann, Elias Bickermann, Moses Hadas and Morton Smith (bibliography attached), has been broadly affirmed and advanced. Old facile distinctions between Palestinian and hellenistic Judaism, even in Judah, have been seen as misleading due to work spurred by discovery of the Scrolls.

Many scholars now question whether the group at Qumran should even be called Essene; and while no other known epithet seems appropriate, the emphasis has been on Jewish pluriformity in antiquity.

JAMES A. SANDERS is Professor of Intertestamental and Biblical Studies at the School of Theology, Claremont, CA; Professor of Religion, Claremont Graduate School; and President of the Ancient Biblical Manuscript Center for Preservation and Research.

Some have begun to speak of the Qumran group as a Jewish denomination to avoid the bias implicit in calling them a sect. I am pleased that Professor Fitzmyer has mentioned Jerome Murphy-O'Connor's thesis about the diaspora origin of the group in Babylon; often in the history of Judaism diaspora Jews have seemed more orthodox than those in the Land. The old appellative of 'Late Judaism' when speaking of Second Temple Judaism has now been abandoned, in large part due to work done as a result of the discovery of the Scrolls. Study of the Pseudepigrapha has likewise received considerable impetus because of the Qumran literature, some of which contains the Hebrew and Aramaic originals of the translations early churches had preserved.

Some of these observations are pertinent also to the impact of study of the Scrolls on study of the Second Testament. All that Fitzmyer says in this regard is true, but I would add that, in general, discovery of the Scrolls has caused greater awareness of how much Early Jewish literature was written Scripturally. The intertextual nature of Early Jewish literature is one of its salient characteristics. Most of the literature of Early Judaism from earliest times, as Michael Fishbane and others (including me) have shown, was written Scripturally. The observation extends on through the vast majority of Jewish literature and through the formation of early Second Testament literature. A book titled *Pseudepigrapha and the NT*[1], for which I was asked to write the foreword, edited by James Charlesworth and Craig Evans, will appear soon stressing the point.

A small but growing number of us are fascinated by how fruitful an intertextual reading of the Gospels and Paul's letters can be, in contrast to a primary focus on their early Christian sources. Minimally, I would say that of equal importance to Mark and Q for the formation of Matthew and Luke, as well as Mark, was Scripture—whether in fluid translations of pre-Massoretic texts of Scripture as in Paul, Mark and John, or adaptive uses of the Septuagint in Paul and Luke and to a limited extent in Matthew. Richard Hays' *Echoes of*

---

[1] Forthcoming from Sheffield (Charlesworth and Evans).

Scripture in the Letters of Paul,[2] and the forthcoming *Luke and Scripture*[3] by Craig Evans and me mark a new departure in study of the sources of New Testament formation.

One of my consuming passions has been the impact of study of the Scrolls on first Testament text criticism and on concepts of canons of Scripture as they were developing alongside stabilization of texts of Scripture. Here is where the American and United Bible Societies have been most helpful in their sponsorship of the Hebrew Old Testament Text Project (HOTTP), formed in 1969 by Eugene Nida and chaired by him the following eleven summer sessions. Emanuel Tov says in his edition of the *Greek Minor Prophets Scroll* from Nahal Hever (DJD 8), that Dominique Barthélemy in his *Devanciers d'Aquila* (1963) introduced a revolution in biblical study. I would be more cautious than Tov and speak rather of a revolution in First Testament text criticism insofar as that discipline is conceived broadly enough to include an understanding not only of the transmission of the text but also its earlier literary development. But revolution it has been. In this regard our work on the HOTTP for the past 22 years has been broadly consonant with the work of the Hebrew University Bible project over against the Albright/Cross hypothesis reflected in Fitzmyer's paper.

Leaving aside technical issues, let me simply conclude by saying that the question of canon can now no longer focus solely on the question of closure of canon but must deal as much with canon as *norma normans* (the process of selecting the normative text of scripture) as with that of *norma normata* (the conclusions about the definitive text). The issue in this regard at the present moment is what the real task of text criticism is and how it should be formulated, and that must now be seen in terms of fluidity and stability of both text and canon in the period we study. The introduction to the third volume of *Critique textuelle de l'Ancien Testament,* which is due out in

---

[2] 1989

[3] Forthcoming from Fortress (Evans and Sanders).

a few months, will probably be as important in development of the revolution to which Emanuel Tov referred as the publication of *Devanciers* was twenty-eight years ago. The introduction to *CTAT* 3 requires 238 pages; the volume covers problems we dealt with in Ezekiel, Daniel and the Twelve Minor Prophets—another 1,037 pages!

Realization of this revolution was the principal reason I left the faculty of Union Seminary fourteen years ago in New York to go to Claremont to help found the Ancient Biblical Manuscript Center: text criticism must now be done by study, primarily on film, of the extant biblical and cognate manuscripts themselves, and not based mainly on critical editions and apparatus which often reflect the biases of competence and interest of their editors in their time; and issues of the concept of canon must be studied as well on the basis of the apographs bequeathed us by ancient believing communities and not even primarily on extra-biblical lists of what was considered the content and order of Sacred Scripture, which may reflect not the reality of the situation but postures of the writers. Discovery of the Dead Sea Scrolls was a gift of the magnitude it may be difficult to assess fully for decades yet to come.

Bibliography:

Saul Liebermann, *Greek in Jewish Palestine* (1912)
_____, *Hellenism in Jewish Palestine* (1962).
Elias Bickermann, *Studies in Jewish and Christian History*, 3 vols. (1976).
_____, and Moses Morton, *The Ancient History of Western Civilization* (1976).
Michael Fishbane, *Biblical Interpretation in Ancient Israel* (1985).
Moses Hadas, *Hellenistic Culture: Fusion and Diffusion* (1963).
_____, and Morton Smith, *Heroes and Gods* (1965).

RESPONSE: Sidnie A. White

My thanks to the American Bible Society for inviting me to participate in this 175th anniversary celebration; and thanks to Professor Fitzmyer for his excellent paper. It is a pleasant duty to be a respondent for a paper with which I agree in all its substantive points!

In my response, I will discuss three points raised by Professor Fitzmyer: the identification of the Qumran sect as the Essenes, Jerome Murphy-O'Connor's hypothesis of the Babylonian origins of the Qumran sect, and the impact of the discovery of the Dead Sea Scrolls on Old Testament textual criticism.

The identification of the Qumran sect as the Essenes mentioned by Josephus, Philo and Pliny the Elder goes back to the first discovery of the scrolls, and is based on the fact that there is a substantial amount of agreement between the internal evidence provided by the scrolls and the classical sources. Recently, however, there have been challenges to that identification, most notably by Larry Schiffman, whose position I will discuss below. First, however, I will present the classical evidence.[1]

Pliny the Elder describes the lifestyle and beliefs of the Essenes, and there is a large correspondence between their descriptions and the evidence of the scrolls for the lifestyle and beliefs of the Qumran sectarians. According to Josephus and Philo (and I am lumping their evidence together indiscriminately), the Essenes share their property.

---

[1] An excellent discussion of the evidence of the classical sources is found in Devorah Dimant, "Qumran Sectarian Literature" in *Jewish Writings of the Second Temple Period* (Compendia Rerum Iudaicarum ad Novum Testamentum; Section 2; ed. Michael E. Stone; Philadelphia; Fortress Press, 1984), 483-550.

SIDNIE A. WHITE is Assistant Professor of Religion at Albright College, Reading, PA.

1QS, the Serekh ha Yahad, talks about the joining of the property of a new member to the community, evidence of shared property. Essenes, according to Philo and Josephus, engage in a lifestyle of work and study. 1QS states "and where the ten are, there shall never lack a man among them who shall study the Law continually, day and night, concerning the right conduct of a man with his companion. And the Congregation shall watch in community for a third of every night of the year, to read the Book and to study the Law and to pray together."[2] Josephus and Philo go on to tell us that the Essenes take their meals together, maintain a strict state of ritual purity, and organize themselves into a strict hierarchy. All these claims correspond to statements made in the Scrolls about the community and its rules. Finally, both authors inform us that the Essenes had a body of special teachings not shared by other groups of Jews in the Second Temple period, for example predestination. Again, in the Hodayot (1QH) we read, "For thou hast established their ways for ever and ever, and hast ordained from eternity their visitation for reward and chastisement; Thou has allotted it to all their seed for eternal generations and everlasting years...In wisdom of thy knowledge thou didst establish their destiny before ever they were."[3] So there is substantial agreement between the classical sources and the scrolls, leading to the identification of the Qumran sectarians with the Essenes.

But, as some scholars have pointed out, there are also some areas in which the scrolls and the classical sources disagree. Josephus and Philo both declare that the Essenes were celibate,[4] yet no mention of this is made in the published Qumran documents. In fact, there were a few skeletons of women and children in the cemeteries at Qumran and Ein Ghuweir, and the Damascus Document discusses rules for

---

[2]   G. Vermes, *The Dead Sea Scrolls in English* (3rd ed.; London: Penguin Books, 1987) 69.

[3]   Vermes, 167

[4]   Josephus (J.W. 2:160-161) does mention a 'second order' of Essenes, who married and lived in villages.

married sectarians. However, the settlement at Qumran does appear to be essentially male, and the scrolls, aside from the Damascus Document, make little or no mention of women. How can we reconcile these competing facts? It has been suggested, and this seems to me reasonable, that celibacy, or better the avoidance of sexual contact for reasons of ritual purity, may have been practiced by some, or perhaps the majority of Essenes, but that some of them, particularly in the villages, were married. Qumran, therefore, was not the only Essene settlement in Judea, but rather a large Essene center. In support of this, we know that there were Essenes active in Judea at large. For example John the Essene was a leader in the Jewish Revolt.

The weight of agreement between the classical sources and the scrolls makes the equation of 'Qumran settlers = Essenes' highly probable. Recently, however, Larry Schiffman has proposed that the Qumran sectarians were actually proto-Sadducees.[5] He bases this suggestion on the fact that some of the laws (namely four) found in 4QMMT, that is, Miqsat Ma'aseh Torah, a new document from Cave IV, agree with rabbinic reports of Saducean interpretation of these same laws. He states "The dominant Essene hypothesis, if it is to be maintained, would require a radical reorientation. It would be necessary to assume that the term Essene came to designate the originally Saducean sectarians who had gone through a process of radicalization and were now a distinct sect in the sense derived from the sectarian documents."[6] I find Schiffman's use of the term 'Sadducee' misleading, since he is doing precisely what the supporters of the Essene hypothesis have been accused of doing, retroactively applying a term from the Roman period to a group of Hellenistic Jews. I would suggest that Zadokite would be a better term. Also, we know from Pesher Nahum that, at least in a later period, the sectarians at Qumran differentiated themselves from the Sadducees, to whom they

---

[5] Lawrence H. Schiffman, "The Significance of the Scrolls." *Bible Review VI* (October, 1990), 19-27.

[6] Schiffman, "The New Halakhic Letter (4QMMT) and the Origins of the Dead Sea Sect," *BA* 53 (June, 1990) 64-73.

refer as 'Manasseh.'[7] It does not seem reasonable to scrap the identification of the Qumran sectarians as Essenes, when there is such substantial correlation between the scrolls and the classical sources, because we have new evidence that doesn't quite fit the old definition. Instead, what is needed is an expansion of the term 'Essene.' As Philip Davies so aptly illustrated, "A modern Josephus, writing for Muslims, might well divide Christianity into three sects, Orthodox, Catholics, and Protestants."[8] However, if you asked an Episcopalian and a Baptist what their doctrines and practices were, you would be hard-pressed to create a coherent picture of a Protestant! The same may be true of the word 'Essene.'

I would suggest that the group of Jews who inhabited Qumran may have evolved over time, from a group with deep roots in Palestinian Judaism, who split with other Jews over such disputed things as law and calendar, to a sect with highly developed doctrines of, for example, predestination and angelology, which set them apart from other Jews. This is the group that Josephus is describing. Therefore, I would argue for the continuing identification of the Qumran sectarians with the Essenes.

This brings me to Murphy-O'Connor's Babylonian hypothesis. As stated by Fitzmyer, Murphy-O'Connor has suggested that Qumran was settled by a group of Jews who returned from Babylon in the mid-second century, in response to the success of the Maccabaean revolt. Not finding things as they expected, they withdrew from the Jerusalem community and settled at Qumran. Murphy-O'Connor bases most of his theory on evidence from the Damascus Document.[9] This theory has not received much support because of two dubious suppositions: 1) the identification of Damascus in the Damascus

---

[7] Vermes, 282.

[8] Philip R. Davies, "The Birthplace of the Essenes: Where is 'Damascus'?" *Revue de Qumran* 14 (4, 1990), 503-519.

[9] J. Murphy-O'Connor, "The Essenes and their History," *RB* 81 (1974), 215-244.

document with Babylon, and 2) the supposition of a second century return. As far as is known, nowhere else in the literature of the Second Temple is Damascus used as a code for Babylon. Why not just say Babylon? But Murphy-O'Connor points out that Damascus is equated with a land of exile, and that the place of exile is always Babylon in later Jewish literature. Even if this equation is accepted, however, the second objection looms. Why posit a return in the second century? There is no evidence elsewhere in the scrolls for such a return, and the text of the Damascus Document is at best ambiguous. The term שבי ישראל which Murphy-O'Connor translates as "the returnees of Israel," may also be translated "those who repent in Israel," and, in the context of the entire scroll, makes better sense. Finally, the group at Qumran, which we have identified as the Essenes, appears to have deep roots in *Palestinian Judaism*, adopting ideas cherished earlier in Palestine, in particular the solar calendar. Evidence for this is found in the prevalence of books such as I Enoch 72-82 (the Astronomical Book) and Jubilees (14 copies) from the early phase of habitation at Qumran. Unless Murphy-O'Connor's group made a radical adaptation to Palestinian practices and beliefs almost immediately upon arrival, it is difficult to accept a second century Babylonian origin for the group. It is not yet clear what Damascus stands for in the Damascus Document, but a second century Babylonian origin for the group at Qumran seems untenable.

Finally, I would like to comment on the contribution the Dead Sea Scrolls has made to Old Testament textual criticism. As mentioned by Fitzmyer, complete or fragmentary copies of every book of the Old Testament were found at Qumran, with the exception of Esther. I have been informed by Emile Puech that J.T. Milik will publish, in the next volume of *Revue de Qumran*, fragments of an Aramaic text that he has labelled 'proto-Esther'! That is exciting news for Esther scholars, myself included! If Esther did exist in an Aramaic form at Qumran, that would give 100% representation of the Hebrew Bible at Qumran.

The field of Old Testament textual criticism has also undergone a revolution owing to the discovery of the Dead Sea Scrolls. Scholars who had discounted the reliability of the Septuagint were put to shame by the existence of Hebrew texts at Qumran which appeared to be prototypes of the Septuagint translations. The existence side-by-side at Qumran of different versions of the same biblical book led Frank Moore Cross to propose his theory of local texts as originating in Palestine, Egypt and Babylon. The geographical designations were never meant to be stringent (after all, they were all found in the Qumran caves!), but the idea of grouping witnesses together according to type lies at the heart of Cross's theory. This theory has been vigorously attacked by Emanuel Tov, among others, who argues that it is anachronistic to designate texts by their agreement with witnesses (the Masoretic text, the Septuagint, the Samaritan Pentateuch) which received their final form only after the destruction of the Qumran community. Tov sees a much more complicated evolution for the biblical text, and resists the idea of grouping texts together, although he admits to the existence of a proto-Samaritan group at Qumran. As study on these texts progresses, it seems fair to say that certain strands, or families of texts are clear in each separate biblical book (or group of books). For example, in the Pentateuch we have a clear proto-Samaritan strand, exemplified by 4QpaleoExod^m, 4QNum^b and 4QPentateuchal Paraphrases. Textual critics are now speaking about groups of texts which exhibit similar characteristics, the most complete examples of which often are the Masoretic text, the Septuagint, and the Samaritan Pentateuch. This is a modification of the original Cross theory.

As Fitzmyer has pointed out, the discovery of the Qumran texts has increased our knowledge about Second Temple Judaism exponentially. 1992 will mark the 40th anniversary of the discovery of Cave IV. Forty years is a biblical generation, so the second generation of Qumran studies has begun. I hope the work of this second generation will prove as fruitful and thought-provoking as that of its predecessor.

NEW BIBLE TRANSLATIONS:
AN ASSESSMENT AND PROSPECT

Donald A. Carson

I. *Introduction*

The number of new Bible translations around the world is steadily increasing, and one individual can be familiar with only a small number of them. By the end of 1990, parts of the Bible had been translated into 1946 languages and dialects, complete Bibles into 318 languages. These figures do not include the large number of languages in which multiple Bible translations are found. During 1990 alone, versions of the complete Bible appeared in four languages; versions of the New Testament were published in fifteen languages. Only three of these, however, were languages in which no version of the Bible previously existed.

If we focus on English versions, we cannot overlook the fact that the last half-century has seen more work than the previous century-and-a-half. Between 1808 and 1949, fifty new translations or systematic revisions of the New Testament were published in the United States. If we add the number of editions that involved slight revisions, that number rises to sixty.[1] By contrast, from the publication of the RSV Bible to the present, twenty-nine English versions *of the entire Bible* have appeared, plus an additional twenty-six English renderings of the New Testament. This does not include translations of the Hebrew Bible by Jewish scholars, which we shall consider later. It is

---

[1] These figures are supplied by John L. Cheek, "New Testament Translation in America," *JBL* 72 (1953) 103-114.

DONALD A. CARSON is Research Professor of New Testament at Trinity Evangelical Divinity School, Deerfield, IL.

not possible to make an accurate count of minor revisions during this period.

Although I have published reviews of five English Bibles during the past twenty years or so,[2] I cannot claim the breadth of knowledge of Paul Ellingworth of Aberdeen, who in a recent essay surveys translations in fifty-nine different languages.[3] My experience is limited to serving as a consultant for one project, and to leading occasional seminars for Bible translators. The discipline of Bible translation, like other areas of human knowledge, has exploded into a complex network of specializations.

My somewhat limited assessment of new Bible translations (by which I refer to those produced during the last few decades), must focus on trends in both method and result, so far as I am able to discern them.

II. *Assessment*

1. There is widespread recognition of the primacy of dynamic equivalence (increasingly referred to as 'functional equivalence')[4] as the best controlling model in Bible translation. This development owes an incalculable debt to Eugene Nida and his associates, whose influence through their writings is evident across the range of Bible translation projects. Although reviewers have voiced criticisms about them, a handful of seminal books has dominated both discussion of theory and the actual practice of translation.[5] Through seminars and

---

[2] The most recent being "A Review of the *New Revised Standard Version*," *RTR* 50 (1991) 1-11.

[3] "Bible translations (modern versions)," *The New Twentieth Century Encyclopedia of Religious Knowledge*, ed. J. D. Douglas (Grand Rapids: Baker, 1991) 80-100.

[4] This change in nomenclature has come about because of the influence of Jan de Waard and Eugene A. Nida, *From One Language to Another: Functional Equivalence in Bible Translating* (Nashville: Thomas Nelson, 1986). The authors are trying to avoid an undue emphasis on equivalence of audience response sometimes associated with the former term.

[5] In particular, see Eugene A. Nida, *Toward a Science of Translating*

training sessions, their principles are now being inculcated in the growing number of translators in the so-called Third World. In the English-speaking world, very few translations or revisions (notably the New King James Version [NKJV] and the New American Standard Bible [NASB]) have self-consciously set themselves *against* the controlling tenets of functional equivalence.

Our familiarity with this fact must not be allowed to obscure what a remarkable reversal this is. Until the end of WWII, English-speaking Bible readers who did not use the KJV would most likely appeal to the Revised Version (RV) or its American counterpart, the American Standard Version (ASV), or perhaps the Douay Version —and it is difficult to imagine competent English translations that are more 'literal' than these. When Today's English Version (TEV, also known as GNB = Good News Bible) first appeared, by and large it was roundly condemned by most people on the conservative end of the theological spectrum. A few years later, softened up perhaps by the huge popularity, at the personal if not the ecclesiastical level, of both J. B. Phillips and the Living Bible (LB)—which had of course been published earlier than TEV[6] but which for ecclesiastical and constituency reasons had not evoked the same degree of hostile criticism—the same segment of the theological spectrum expressed itself reasonably satisfied with the New International Version (NIV), whose underlying philosophy of translation is not easily differentiated from that of TEV. Today most competent translators recognize the following factors: that (1) 'literal translation' and 'free translation' exist on the same spectrum, distinguishable in the extremes but nevertheless

---

(Leiden: Brill, 1964); Eugene A. Nida and Charles R. Taber, *The Theory and Practice of Translation* (Leiden: Brill, 1974); and, to a lesser extent, Wolfram Wilss, *Übersetzungswissenschaft: Probleme und Methoden* (Stuttgart: Ernst Klett, 1977).

[6] Phillips's *Letters to Young Churches* was published in 1947; the entire New Testament appeared in 1958. *Living Letter* was published in 1962, the complete LB in 1971. The TEV New Testament appeared in 1966, the full GNB in 1971.

unavoidably connected;[7] that (2) meaning and form, though inter-
twined, are not only differentiable, but that very frequently meaning
in the donor language has to be packaged in a quite different form in
the receptor language; that (3) translation is never a mechanical
exercise, but entails countless decisions as to the text's meaning; that
(4) meaning is not only referential, but may embrace subtle overtones,
emotional loading, degrees of naturalness, pragmatic associations,
implicit moral obligation, and much more.[8] Indeed, some would go
further and insist that this spectrum-model is too simple, too one-
dimensional. To treat adequately the distinction between freedom of
form and freedom of meaning one is forced, ideally, to aim simultaneously for maximum naturalness (which usually requires some freedom of form) and maximum accuracy. What was a *line* from 'literal'
to 'free' becomes a *two-dimensional matrix* that covers the turf from
'literal' to 'free.'

This is not to say that adoption of functional equivalence as a
controlling priority entirely determines just where a Bible translation
will emerge on this matrix between 'literal' and 'free.' The theory has
become so sophisticated and so flexible that the application of its
principles by different parties can produce quite different results.
What is clear, I think, is that dynamic (or functional) equivalence has
exerted a profound influence even on Bible translators who have not
formally espoused the undergirding philosophy.

Consider the two most important recent English versions. The
Revised English Bible (REB), a revision of the New English Bible
(NEB), states that "the guiding principle has been to seek a fluent and
idiomatic way of expressing biblical writing in contemporary English.

---

[7] Cf. John Beekman and John Callow, *Translating the Word of God*
(Grand Rapids: Zondervan, 1974) 19-32. Today most translators prefer not
to use the term 'paraphrase' for the 'free' end of the spectrum, reserving that
term to refer to a re-expression of a message in another form of the *same*
language.

[8] For a useful summary, see Michael F. Kopesec, "A Translator's
Perspective on Meaning," *OPTAT* 2 (1988) 9-19.

Much emphasis has been laid on correctness and intelligibility." The New Revised Standard Version (NRSV), similarly, insists that the biblical message "must not be disguised in phrases that are no longer clear, or hidden under words that have changed or lost their meaning; it must be presented in language that is direct and plain and meaningful to people today." Even so, Robert Bratcher, in an important review of both these English versions,[9] insists that the two are based on "distinct philosophies of translation."[10] Only the former, he says, is a dynamic equivalence translation. Bratcher says that the guiding principle of dynamic equivalence adopts the memorable maxim of the British *savant*, Hilaire Belloc: "The question is not, 'How shall I make this foreigner talk English?' but, 'What would an Englishman have said to express this?'" Certainly the NRSV should be placed a little farther to the 'literal' end of the spectrum than the REB. Still, I suspect that Bratcher's sharp disjunction between two underlying philosophies is overstated. Perhaps, in part, he too quickly adopts at face value Bruce Metzger's remark in "To the Reader" in the NRSV: "this version," Metzger writes, "remains essentially a literal translation." After all, the NRSV committee adopted the maxim, "As literal as possible, as free as necessary." But everything depends on who is judging what is possible and what is necessary. For example, if the readership is university students in North America, and others who have been sensitized to the gender-bias of English, one must conclude that the NRSV is *less* literal and *more* sensitive to the priorities of functional equivalence than is the REB.

In short, dynamic (or functional) equivalence has triumphed, whether the expression itself be embraced or not; even among translators who think of their work as more 'literal,' its influence is pervasive. By and large, this has been a good thing. Nevertheless, a few cautions might not be entirely inappropriate.

First, it is salutary to remember that when dynamic equivalence

---

[9] "Translating for the Reader," *Theology Today* 47 (1990) 290-292.

[10] Ibid. 290.

theory was being developed and codified, its dominant foil was a more literal approach. Though that foil today has a few vociferous advocates, it has largely lost its power. But just as theological formulation can be seriously distorted if it focuses too narrowly on just one foil, so can the articulation of translation theory. One wonders what the shape of contemporary functional equivalence theory would be if it chose as a foil that approach to meaning associated with the less temperate forms of the new hermeneutic, in which all meaning is denied to the text itself and is reserved instead for the reader/hearer.

Second, the degree of explicitation advocated in some dynamic equivalence theory (and displayed in some translations) needs re-evaluation. Most scholars recognize that a certain amount of 'situational meaning'[11] lurks in any source text—*i.e.* meaning that is implicit in the text *for the original reader*, but not necessarily for the modern reader whose approach to the text must transcend differences in both language and time. Beekman and Callow offer Mk 2.4 as an example ("And when they could not get near him because of the crowd, they removed the roof above him...").[12] Where the people of the receptor language are familiar only with steeply sloping thatched roofs, language helpers have been known to assume the text is describing a miracle. At one level, of course, the problem turns on the meaning of one word, στέγη ('roof'); at another, the problem is more than one of *mere* definition, but is bound up with a complicated set of associations. The thatched-roof culture does not think of roofs as flat and made from packed, dried mud, places to which people frequently withdraw, accessible by an outside set of stairs, capable of holding the weight of many people, and something that could be easily dug through (Mk 2.4). But that is the problem: Ernst-August Gutt has argued that at some point one must distinguish between 'implicit information' that derives from language-specific principles, and

---

[11] To use the language of Mildred Larson, *Meaning-based Translation: A Guide to Cross Language Equivalences* (New York: University Press of America, 1984) 37.

[12] *Op. cit.* 47.

'encyclopaedic knowledge' that both the source-language readers and the receptor-language readers inevitably carry with them as they read the text.[13] The demands of the barrier erected by the differences in socially accepted knowledge can never be overcome by translation alone. Of course, this is not to say that there is some particular barrier that translation cannot bridge—all of contemporary linguistic theory stands against such a notion—but only that the *totality* of such barriers *cannot simultaneously* be bridged in the translation itself. Dynamic equivalence theory has doubtless helped us analyze the different kinds of meanings lurking in (or behind?) a text. By aiming to meet the exigencies of some of these attendant meanings (for example, by adding a number of explanatory words), it has sometimes opted to neglect other exigencies, as we shall see.

Third, single-eyed pursuit of what is 'natural' in the receptor language (remembering Belloc's distinction) can generate a host of insurmountable problems. I do not mean to despise natural renderings. One wonders, for instance, why the New Revised Standard Version (NRSV) utilizes 'saints' in Phil 1.1. Still, three contrary factors must be observed.

(a) Unremitting pursuit of what is natural in the receptor language may introduce problems elsewhere. Consider an oft-cited extreme case. Some tribal cultures may not be familiar with sheep and lambs, but be quite experienced at sacrificing pigs. In a single passage describing the sacrifice of a sheep, substituting a pig would make the result entirely 'natural' to the readers of the receptor language. But the cost is high, since pigs and sheep are tied to so many strands of the Bible. Are we quite prepared to have John the Baptist cry, "Look! The swine of God who takes away the sin of the world!"? What replaces pigs as unclean animals? Is Christ now sacrificed as a piglet without blemish?

Although this illustration is probably overdrawn, simply because

---

[13] "What is the Meaning we Translate?" *OPTAT* No. 1 (Jan. 1987), 31-58. Cf. also A. H. Nichols, "Explicitness and the Westernization of Scripture," *RTR* 47 (1988) 78-88.

it is so extreme that few translators would opt for the pigs, yet a host of borderline cases is not hard to find. Should the elements of the Lord's Table ever become yams and goat's milk (or the local fermented drink?), simply because yams and goat's milk function in the receptor culture much as bread and wine function in first-century Palestine? The desirability of cultural naturalness must be weighed against competing *desiderata*, not least, in this instance, the desirability of maintaining the many lines between 'bread,' say, and some related biblical themes and passages (e.g., Jesus as the bread of life, and the anti-typological connection with the manna in the wilderness [John 6]).

(b) The Bible is not a simple book. Doubtless translators should earnestly endeavor not to make it more difficult than it is, but is their work well done when they make it simpler than it is? For example, the ἱλαστήριον word-group is notoriously difficult. But NEB's "remedy for defilement" moves the semantic focus from the sacrificial realm to the realm of medicine; "sacrifice of atonement" (NIV and NRSV), in addition to not being idiomatic in contemporary English, is lamentably obscure; "the means by which people's sins are forgiven" (TEV) is far more natural (though the term 'sins' in North Atlantic English is more frequently accompanied by snickers than shame), but considerably simpler than the donor text. One remembers the biting irritation of the late Stephen Neill when the Tamil translation team of which he was a part managed to smooth out all the difficulties in Ga 3, including those the apostle had intended.

In addition, Margot rightly points out that unintended ambiguities in the source text, better thought of as obscurities in the source text, will largely be cleared up by the thoughtful translator, but intended ambiguities (such as a clever word-play, such as πνεῦμα in John 3) will be preserved if possible, or explained with a note if necessary.[14]

(c) A certain amount of 'foreignness' in versions of the Bible is surely a good thing. Modern novelists recognize the point when they

---

[14] Jean-Claude Margot, "Should a Translation of the Bible Be Ambiguous?" *BibTrans* 32 (1981) 406-413.

choose an ostensible setting for their works of fiction. Chaim Potok does not make Asher Lev sound like the *goyim*, though I know quite a few *goyim* who enjoy reading his work. Because his protagonist is a lawyer with a Yiddish background, Scott Turow's novels abound in legal jargon quite beyond me, and may throw in an unexplained *Gevalt*. The concern, of course, is for historical verisimilitude. But surely a book as deeply embedded in history as the Bible is bound to deploy some expressions and categories that will not sound 'natural' to twentieth-century American English ears (or for that matter to Swahili ears, or Kikuyu ears). At a certain point, to make an ancient text sound *too* natural ultimately makes it sound phony.[15] This is not to justify stilted, archaic language, or an arcane cherishing of the merely traditional. It is to say that no responsible translation can or should seek entirely to escape the 'scandal of historical particularity' inherent in a text like the Bible. Deployment of somewhat alien categories must not become so noxious as to destroy the basic intelligibility of the flow of the text. But in the translation of historical and ostensibly historical texts, intelligibility is perhaps a more laudable goal than naturalness.

Fourth, dynamic equivalence has often set its agenda in terms of 'equivalence of response.' "Dynamic equivalence," writes Nida, "is ... to be defined in terms of the degree to which the receptors of the message in the receptor language respond to it in substantially the same manner as the receptors in the source language."[16] Mundhenk insists, "In the final analysis, a translation is good or bad, right or wrong, in terms of how the reader understands and reacts."[17] Once

---

[15] For a competent if perhaps overstated defense of this view, cf. Edward L. Greenstein, "Theories of Modern Bible Translation," *Prooftexts* 3 (1983) 9-39.

[16] Nida, *Toward a Science of Translating* 166; cf. Nida/Taber, *Theory and Practice* 24.

[17] Norm Mundhenk, "The Subjectivity of Anachronism," *On Language, Culture and Religion*, ed. Matthew Black and William A. Smalley (The Hague: Mouton, 1974) 260.

again, there is great insight here. Formal equivalence while the message is lost can scarcely be construed as faithful translation. Many contemporary translations are remarkably effective in this area. Nevertheless, equivalence of response, no matter how carefully worked out, can never be given absolute status. Some of the first responses to, say, Jesus' parables, and doubtless to some of Paul's letters, were extremely negative. Responses are not only personal, but are deeply culturally conditioned. It is hard to imagine generating in a twentieth-century American Gentile the response to Leviticus that its first publication produced among the ancient Hebrews. Certainly it is true to say that increasing sensitivity to the limits of pursuing equivalence of response[18] has contributed (as we have seen) to the shift in nomenclature from 'dynamic' to 'functional' equivalence.[19]

To conclude the consideration of this translation feature, dynamic (or functional) equivalence has largely triumphed, and rightly so. Moreover, among its most competent practitioners, none of its principles or rules or insights is taken so absolutely as to prove embarrassing. They recognize that the 'rules' of functional equivalence translation are like the 'rules' of textual criticism: none can be given absolute status, because there are always countervailing factors that must be weighed. *Lectio difficilior potior* (the more difficult reading [of the original text] is to be preferred) is doubtless a powerful criterion, but it is useless if the production of a difficult variant was unintentional. So also with dynamic equivalence translation: explicitness is sometimes necessary, pursuing 'natural' renderings is a worthwhile goal, and equivalence of response an important consideration. But none is absolute. Neither textual criticism nor Bible translation is as mathematically secure as mechanical engineering. The same caution could be raised against other insights from functional

---

[18] Cf. especially Ernst-August Gutt, *Translation and Relevance* (Oxford: Blackwell, 1991), who has powerfully deployed Relevance Theory to highlight the limitations.

[19] Cf. p.3 n.4, *supra.*

equivalence theory (e.g., the elevation of meaning over form).[20] To ignore such cautions in the effort to raise translation to a 'hard' science can only discredit what is a powerful and useful approach to an extraordinarily difficult task.

2. During the past few decades, there has been an astonishing multiplication of disciplines connected with the task of Bible translation, most of them flourishing and producing voluminous specialist literature. The many branches of linguistics have spawned scores of doctoral programs. Many Bible translators have become passingly familiar with structuralism, discourse analysis, tagmemics, communication theory, sociolinguistics, the various branches of semantic theory, the new hermeneutic, computer tools, and much more. Even to begin to survey this material and assess its impact on new translations would be enormously complex. But perhaps I may venture four observations that have the greatest bearing on new translations.

First, the multiplication of these disciplines means that it is becoming increasingly difficult to control the literature relevant for Bible translators, let alone to become expert in these fields. In other words, while these disciplines have been a fecund stimulus to Bible translators around the world, they have to some extent so taken on a life of their own that the working translator is apt to be a bit daunted by it all. In fact, we are now moving into the era of edited books summarizing recent developments—such as the first book in the UBS Monograph Series, the one edited by Johannes Louw, *Sociolinguistics and Communication*.[21]

Second, at the risk of unwarranted generalization, my impression is that most Bible translators in the West, translating the Bible into

---

[20] For cautions in this area, cf. Keith Crim, "Philosophies, Theories, and Methods in Bible Translation," *Society of Biblical Literature 1985 Seminar Papers*, No.24, ed. Kent Harold Richards (Atlanta: Scholars Press, 1985) 161-167.

[21] Johannes Louw, ed., *Sociolinguistics and Communication*, UBSMS 1 (London: UBS, 1986).

English, French, German, and so forth, or revising earlier editions, remain fairly ignorant of such developments, though many are stellar scholars in the original languages, traditional exegesis, theology and related disciplines. By contrast, a very large number of translators working to produce vernacular Bibles in the so-called Third World, whether they be missionaries or indigenes, are informed—some of them very well informed—of developments in the linguistic and related arenas, but are woefully ill-equipped when it comes to more than a rudimentary knowledge of Hebrew, Aramaic, and Greek, not to mention exegesis, theology, or biblical history. I have met more translators than I care to think about, valiantly laboring in difficult conditions, who have never had a scrap of theological education, and are disturbingly proud of the fact. It is easy for each of these two groups to criticize the other, not least by quoting the worst examples from the other side. [22]

Some experts in translation theory argue that a thorough command of, say, *koine* Greek can get in the way of good translation. Far more important, they say, are a basic knowledge of linguistic theory and an appreciation of style. I doubt that the translators of, say, the NRSV, will be convinced by this assessment. The problem to which the translation experts point is a real one, I think, but not because students have learned too much Greek, but because they have learned it in a more or less traditional format. What they need is Greek *and* linguistics—or, better yet, much more Greek (not less), but taught in an atmosphere where linguistic principles and readings are passed on as well.

Third, like all young and flourishing disciplines, those surrounding Bible translation are churning out a fair bit of mediocre and repetitious theoretical material. At the same time, however, they are also producing some work of ground-breaking significance, and much of this work has not yet been culled by translators. One thinks, for

---

[22] Jean-Claude Margot has commented insightfully on the problem: see his "Exegesis and Translation," *EQ* 50 (1978) 156-165.

example, of the new lexicon of semantic fields,[23] the masterful proposal of Porter that aspect controls the verbal structure of New Testament Greek,[24] the forthcoming lexicon of *Key Biblical Terms* that Summer Institute of Linguistics/Wycliffe Bible Translators[25] is preparing for translators, the many *Handbooks* and *Helps* for translators published by UBS, and of the bearing that the GRAMCORD Project will have on understanding syntactic units.

Fourth, the rise of these disciplines has to some limited extent renewed an old debate about the place of theology in translation. At the time of the Protestant Reformation, the schoolmen wanted to preserve the Vulgate that had served them well for centuries, and were appalled by the effrontery of Erasmus. For his part, Erasmus, steeped in the rising humanist tradition of the Renaissance, felt that authority should rest in the text in the original languages, and argued that the Bible must be interpreted from the Hebrew and Greek, not from the Vulgate. In principle, that freed him to prepare his own Latin translation. Luther sided on many points with the humanists, including a closely-reasoned refusal to what would today be described as elevating formal equivalence above semantic equivalence (SW, IV, 184,185[26]). At the same time he elevated what he felt was his Spirit-given theological insight into 'justification by faith' to the point where it controlled not a little of his exegesis, and therefore of his

---

[23] Johannes P. Louw and Eugene A. Nida, ed., *Greek-English Lexicon of the New Testament Based on Semantic Domains*, 2 vols. (New York: UBS, 1988).

[24] Stanley E. Porter, *Verbal Aspect in the Greek of the New Testament, with Reference to Tense and Mood*, Studies in Biblical Greek 1 (Bern: Peter Lang, 1989).

[25] The work is being prepared by Katharine Barnwell, Anthony J. Pope, and Paul Dancy, and is scheduled to appear shortly. The name Summer Institute for Linguistics is used for academic/linguistic work; Wycliffe Bible Translators is used in reference to missionary and promotion efforts.

[26] Theodore G. Tappert, ed., *Selected Writings of Martin Luther: Volume 4: 1529-1546* (Philadelphia: Fortress, 1967).

translation. Small wonder he could write, "Ah, translating is not every man's skill as the mad saints imagine. It requires a right devout, honest, sincere, God-fearing, Christian, trained, informed, and experienced heart. Therefore I hold that no false Christian or factious spirit can be a decent translator" (SW, IV, 186).[27] Of course, similar disputes over translation and interpretation erupted in the early church between Augustine and St. Jerome, and continued in the writings of William Tyndale and Thomas More.[28]

Modernity has changed the shape of the debate a bit, but similar echoes are still heard. Translators have not been slow to dismiss the worst instances of theological control (not to say manipulation) of the translator's task. Versions cannot be assessed by how well they support, or fail to support special doctrines, such as pre-millennialism.[29] On the other hand, some English versions, though clearly well-informed at the linguistic level, seem to run into trouble because they lack exegetical and/or theological sophistication. The RSV of Gn 1.26 reads, "Then God said, 'Let us make man in our image, after our likeness ...'" The TEV, however, renders, "Then God said, 'And now we will make human beings; they will be like us and resemble us ...'" On first glance, 'like us' and 'resemble us' seems so much simpler and more straightforward than 'in our image' and 'after our likeness.' (I overlook for the moment that 'after' might be replaced by 'according to' or even 'in line with.') By the time the reader reaches Gn 3,

---

[27] See note 26. For fuller discussion, cf. W. Schwarz, *Principles and Problems of Biblical Translation: Some Reformation Controversies and Their Background* (Cambridge: University Press, 1955); *Martin Luther, Creative Translator* (St Louis: Concordia, 1965); more briefly, John L. Bechtel, "The Modern Application of Martin Luther's *Open Letter on Translating*," *AUSS* 11 (1973) 145-151.

[28] Cf. especially Heinz Holeczek, *Humanistische Bibelphilologie als Reformproblem bei Erasmus von Rotterdam, Thomas More und William Tyndale*, Studies in the History of Christian Thought (Leiden: Brill, 1975).

[29] Cf. Eugene Nida, "Quality in Translation," *BibTrans* 33 (1982) 329-332; Daniel C. Arichea, Jr., *BibTrans* 33 (1982) 309-316.

however, he or she runs into confusion, for there the serpent deceives Eve by telling her that she 'will be like God' (Gn 3.5, RSV and TEV). When the Lord purposes to banish Adam and Eve from the garden, he does so because (according to the TEV) "the man has become like one of us" (Gn 3.22). Did God change his mind about making humans 'like us', as TEV seems to imply? It appears as if the effort to keep the English of Gn 1.26 simple, natural, idiomatic and plain, laudable in itself, has not been matched by equal effort to preserve distinctions in the source text and therefore to avoid what must strike the thoughtful reader as nonsense.[30]

This is not the place to attempt to articulate the relationship between translation and theology. Though it is surely right to say that theology, to be properly based, must turn on the kind of understanding of the text that is the goal of responsible exegesis and the *sine qua non* for quality translation, we must also say that the theology the translator espouses, consciously or unconsciously, at the moment of translation, is bound to influence him. We may agree that certain priority must be given to the text; we must also agree that no one approaches the text *tabula rasa*. Elsewhere I have tried to work out ways of articulating these relationships; here I wish only to emphasize that the multiplication of disciplines connected with Bible translation leaves plenty of scope for scholars to learn from one another.

3. The previous two points have prepared us for this one. It is now widely recognized that translation cannot be undertaken apart from interpretation, that each translation is itself invariably an interpretation.[31] That in turn drives us to ponder the relationship between translation and hermeneutics. In line with seriously dated

---

[30] I draw this example from Jacob Van Bruggen, *The Future of the Bible* (Nashville: Thomas Nelson, 1978) 86-87, with whose approach to translation I am in very substantial disagreement, but some of whose exegetical and theological insights bear pondering.

[31] E.g., Charles R. Taber, "Translation as Interpretation," *Int* 32 (1978) 130-143.

textbooks and the eighteenth-century Enlightenment historiography of Leopold von Ranke, there are still a few conservatives who think of hermeneutics exclusively as the process by which I, the knower, come to understand the object, the text. At the other extreme, some, including Nida and Reyburn in a book published ten years ago, distinguish exegesis from hermeneutics by stating that the former reconstructs "the communication event by determining its meaning (or meanings) for the participants in the communication," while the latter "may be described as pointing out parallels between the biblical message and present-day events and determining the extent of relevance and the appropriate response for the believer."[32] Hermeneutics is thereby reduced to what used to be called application. More sophisticated treatments will accept neither simplification.[33] They envisage a hermeneutical 'circle,' or, to avoid solipsism, a hermeneutical spiral, or a principled fusing of 'horizons of understanding' to make the transfer of information from one horizon to another possible, even if not exhaustive.

But even if we agree, against deconstructionism, that not all meaning resides in the knower, and that the text does bear meaning that can in substantial measure be known, the impact of the new hermeneutic, filtered through the new history and some new forms of literary criticism, is deeply embedded in Western intellectual life. And this post-modern view of knowledge, both a cause and a symptom of the entrenched pluralism of Western culture, has come to affect our Bible translations. We have become comfortable with the view that different English translations have different constituencies, because those different constituencies have different theological commitments, different biases, different educational bases. The sheer diversity of translations is assumed to be not only inevitable, but a good thing.

---

[32] Eugene A. Nida and William D. Reyburn, *Meaning Across Cultures*, American Society of Missiology Series 1 (Maryknoll: Orbis, 1981) 30.

[33] One of the best studies is Anthony C. Thiselton, *The Two Horizons: New Testament Hermeneutics and Philosophical Description* (Grand Rapids: Eerdmans, 1980).

Indeed, there are some good things about it, as we shall note; but they are not all good, and, from the perspective of the history of Bible translation, the situation that has arisen in the West in this century is extraordinarily anomalous. But first we shall return to this question of the constituencies of various English versions from another perspective.

4. We must appraise some recent attempts of some English Bibles to avoid the gender-bias inherent in the language. TEV took some steps in that regard. REB goes considerably farther, but is remarkably inconsistent (or, from the British perspective, less doctrinaire). The NRSV is the first English Bible that systematically struggles with the question from first principles, and is remarkably consistent.[34] Published reviews are now readily available, so I need only sketch those principles here.[35] Readers wedded to more traditional language will doubtless take offense; readers who have already made the transition to principled gender-free use of the English language find it the only truly modern version. By another route we have returned to the question of constituencies for translations.

5. I must say something about the texts being translated. Others in this conference will consider the impact of the Qumran and Gnostic writings on biblical study, not least the bearing of the former on the textual criticism of the Hebrew Bible. Apart from the New King James Version (NKJV), defended by a small but vociferous rear guard,[36] all modern English New Testaments are based on an eclectic

---

[34] For a comparison of REB and NRSV in this regard, cf. Burton H. Throckmorton, Jr., "The *NRSV* and the *REB*: A New Testament Critique," *TT* 47 (1990) 281-289.

[35] "To The Reader," *New Revised Standard Version,* ABS, 1989.

[36] The most interesting recent production from this movement is the recently published edition of the Majority Text NT: Maurice A. Robinson and William G. Pierpont, *The New Testament in the Original Greek according to the Byzantine/Majority Textform* (Atlanta: Original Word, 1991).

text, the most recent ones being variations on the UBS Greek New Testament Third Edition and Nestle-Aland, 26th Edition. But that does not mean these editions are followed slavishly.

It is intriguing to compare the latest two major English Bibles with their immediate predecessors. The NEB is notorious for the freedom with which it emends texts and moves blocks of material around, especially in the Hebrew Bible. There are at least one hundred textual transpositions without a scrap of text-critical warrant. By contrast, the REB is far more conservative in this regard. When we compare the RSV and the NRSV, we discover far more textual information conveyed in the notes of the latter. Not less interesting is the fact that at many places the translators of the NRSV have opted for a different variant than their predecessors did, usually with very little new manuscript evidence. It would be helpful to have some guide to the basis for these decisions. Doubtless the arrival of UBS Greek New Testament Fourth Edition, with the same text as UBS Greek New Testament Third Edition/Nestle-Aland 26th Edition, but a substantially revised apparatus, will launch a further round of discussion.

I conclude this section with two observations. First, there is a small but growing theoretical literature on the relationship between the translator's task and the establishment of text, including not only traditional questions of textual criticism but the distinctive role of the final text form and the outer boundaries of the text in canonical constraints.[37] Second, although it is too much to expect Bible

---

[37] E.g., Daniel C. Arichea, "Theology and Translation: The Implications of Certain Theological Issues to the Translation Task," *Bible Translation and the Spread of the Church: The Last 200 Years*, ed. Philip C. Stine; Studies in Christian Mission 2 (Leiden: Brill, 1990) esp. 40-48; Hans Peter Rüger, "Was übersetzen wir? Fragen zur Textbasis, die sich aus Traditions und Kanonsgeschichte ergeben," *Die Übersetzung der Bibel–Aufgabe der Theologie: Stuttgarter Symposion 1984*, ed. Joachim Gnilka and Hans Peter Rüger (Bielefeld: Luther-Verlag, 1985) 57-64; Adrian Schenker, "Was übersetzen wir? Fragen zur Textbasis, die sich aus der Textkritik ergeben," ibid. 65-80; Harold P. Scanlin, "What is the Canonical Shape of the Old Testament Text we Translate?" *Issues in Translation*, ed. Philip C. Stine,

translators to use exactly the same textual base, it would be exceedingly helpful if translators and publishers could agree on some basic indicators in the footnotes. Expressions such as 'Some manuscripts read,' 'Alternatively,' 'Or,' and a host of similar ones, confuse rather than clarify the principles on which textual choices were made by the translators.

6. With a few notable exceptions, Bible translations in the Western world are now done by committee. Where Christianity has not yet penetrated new tribes, translation is done by a single translator or a pair of translators, backed up by consultants at regional centers. Between these two extremes are the many Bible translations currently being undertaken in some tribal language where many of the tribal people have already become Christians, perhaps through the medium of a regional trade language such as Swahili. Although missionaries still perform a great deal of this work, the increasing tendency is to train indigenes to some minimal standard, and use consultants more extensively in the revisions and editing.

What effect do these quite disparate approaches have on Bible translations? Specifically, what are the effects of committee translation process. At one level, of course, it is always important to remember that in many counsellors there is wisdom. On the whole, versions that are the result of committee work are less liable to eccentricity than are those produced by a single individual (even if that individual has solicited a fair bit of advice along the way). The flip side is not only that committee translations may sometimes be a trifle more staid, a trifle less colorful (compare, say, RSV and Moffatt),[38] but that now and then the committee may settle for compromises that offend no one on the committee.

UBSMS 3 (London: UBS, 1988) 207-219.

[38] Cf. Ernst R. Wendland, "Receptor Language Style and Bible Translation: A Search for 'Language which Grabs the Heart,'" *BibTrans* 32 (1981) 107-124; Ross McKerras, "Don't Put Out the Fire!" *NOT* 5/2 (1991) 1-20.

This example comes out of my personal experiences. When I offered a brief (and largely positive) review of the NRSV at last year's SBL, although I approved the translators' handling of 'son of man' in Ps 8 and its quotation in He 2, I suggested that in Dn 7 the text ("one like a human being") and the footnote ("like a son of man") should be reversed. In the rebuttal, I was told that 'son of man' really does mean 'human being,' and that it would have been wrong to ignore the sensibilities of the Jewish scholars on the committee. The irony is that I agree with both points: 'son of man' in Dn 7 does mean 'human being,' and translators need to beware of needlessly offending the sensibilities of their prospective readers, let alone their committee members, Jewish, Black, conservative Christian, or whatever. But in fact, my point was a technical one. Most scholars recognize that the roots of Jesus' persistent application to himself of 'son of man' lie in Dn 7. Although Jesus' usage, as reported in the Gospels, can occasionally be rendered by 'human being' or even by the first person personal pronoun, far too many of the occurrences carry enough technical force that most translations properly preserve 'son of man.' I am *not* saying that later, unambiguously messianic linguistic developments should be read back into earlier material. I am saying, rather, that to lose sight of the biblical roots of Jesus' most frequent expression of self-identity as God's agent is to lose something important.

Because these matters are delicate, and I have no wish that anyone take umbrage, I add a few clarifying reflections.

(a) I agree on the whole with Barclay Newman[39] when he criticizes the New American Standard Bible (NASB) for deploying capital letters for pronouns taken to refer to the Messiah in the Psalms (e.g., Ps 72.2). A note accompanying Ps 45.1b reads, "Probably refers to Solomon as a type of Christ." The Living Bible (LB) similarly utilizes notes to make these Christian connections.

(b) On the other hand, many New Testament themes are con-

---

[39] Barclay M. Newman, "Toward a Theology of Translation," *Bulletin of the UBS* 124/125 (1981) 10-21, esp. 14-15.

structed out of the trajectories of what is now called inner-biblical exegesis. Some of this is indistinguishable from the best of what used to be commonly called typology. Both inner-biblical exegesis and typology can easily run amok. But that does not mean that the phenomenon does not exist, or is not important. The subject is highly complex and is generating a substantial body of literature, and it interests me a great deal.[40] From the translator's point of view, the question to be considered in this case is the instrument by which the translation should preserve the linguistic *form* of an expression so that the appropriate inner-biblical link can be spotted by someone without access to the original languages.

(c) If it be argued that 'inner-biblical' exegesis inevitably has a broader set of links to consider when 'biblical' refers to the Christian canon than to the Jewish canon, I heartily agree. Bibles *are* attached to communities; committees that cross communities invariably make great gains in terms of fairness and rigor, but there may be some losses as well.

(d) In any case, it seems to me that Jewish scholars interested in, say, the 'son of man' in the "Similitudes" of 1 Enoch might also have an interest in preserving the linguistic form of the expression in Dn 7.

7. A great deal of Bible translation work has been tied to missionary movements.[41] This is less true, of course, where Bibles are being produced to meet the needs of established ecclesiastical bodies. Still, it is very largely true, and from a Christian perspective this is a good thing.

---

[40] For bibliography and discussion, cf. D. A. Carson and H. G. M. Williamson, ed., *It Is Written: Scripture Citing Scripture. Essays in Honour of Barnabas Lindars, SSF* (Cambridge: University Press, 1988).

[41] Cf. Philip C. Stine, ed., *Bible Translation and the Spread of the Church;* and esp. William A. Smalley, *Translation as Mission: Bible Translation in the Modern Missionary Movement* (Macon: Mercer University Press, 1991).

What is perhaps overlooked is that this reality in turn influences the way translators think of their task. Translators commissioned by the National Council of the Churches of Christ to produce the NRSV will not see their role in exactly the same way as will translators struggling to produce the first New Testament for a remote tribe in Papua New Guinea, precisely because the envisioned readers are so different. I do not mean that the respective cultures of the two reader groups are very different. I mean that one translation effort is overtly and immediately interested in evangelism, and cannot think of its task apart from that goal, while the other serves a more established constituency. Internationally, however, a far greater proportion of translators immediately serve the missionary and evangelistic task than otherwise, and so the preponderance of thought and research and publication in the area is inevitably shaped to serve this large group. When we delve into this literature on Bible translation theory, and try to understand the way it works out in new Bibles, we are being influenced to think of the priorities of translation in a certain way.

I am not criticizing these missionary goals. The sacrifices and achievements of Bible translators around the world are extraordinary, something for which to thank God. But I wonder if Bible translation theory has been shifted a little too far in the direction of simplification and clarity (even when the source text is obscure), precisely because the unstated assumption is that the *only* evangelistic 'agent' for the particular target group will be the Bible itself. Indeed, for all of its history the Wycliffe Bible Translators has adopted the policy of *not* sending out pastors or more traditional missionaries, of *not* setting up schools and hospitals and the like. Traditional missionary endeavor has been left to other organizations. This single-eyed commitment to Bible translation has been remarkably productive. However, it may slightly skew the vision of the translators themselves. One cannot help noting that when Paul established churches in highly diverse centers of the Roman Empire, he quickly appointed elders in every place. He did not simply distribute copies of the Septuagint.[42]

---

[42] I use the term loosely, without suggesting that the Septuagint as it has

The New Testament that translators are putting into the vernacular frequently describes and mandates the tasks of pastors and teachers and evangelists. Of course, this does not rule out a place for specialized ministry, in this case the work of translation. But unless such work is coordinated with other work, it may take on a disproportionate importance. And it may establish a certain expectation of what all translations *ought* to be.

No matter how excellent and comprehensible a translation is, there will always be a need for pastors and teachers. A few years ago, a friend of a friend was giving out modern English New Testaments (I believe it was the TEV) to students at a British university, on the condition that they agree to read them. A few weeks later this zealous Christian stumbled across one of the students to whom he had given a New Testament. This student had no background whatsoever in the Bible; he had never so much as held any part of the Bible in his hand before. When he was asked what he made of the New Testament he had been given, he cheerfully replied with words to this effect: "Oh, it was rather interesting. The first part was a bit repetitious: it more or less tells the same story several times. But I sure liked that bit of science fiction at the end!" Eugene Nida tells another story of how a Thai Buddhist first read the four Gospels and, asked how he liked the New Testament he had been given, responded, "Oh, that is a wonderful book, and such a remarkable man! Why, he was born and he died, he was born and he died, born and died, born and died. In four reincarnations he made it to Nirvana."[43] Considering that Buddha took 1,000, small wonder the Buddhist was impressed. The point, of course, is that more than translation is needed.

I am not making a surreptitious plea for obscurity in translations, nor am I justifying a secret guild of *cognoscenti* who will unpack esoteric mysteries for the unwashed. I am simply saying that the

---

come down to us is precisely the same as the Greek Bible the church used during the first decades of its life.

[43] Eugene A. Nida, "Bible Translation for the Eighties," *IRM* 70 (1981) 133.

Bibles that are translated with evangelistic purposes in view may in many cases survive for decades, even for a century or two, without substantial revision. In all likelihood, pastors will come along, standards of education will rise—and the same Bibles will still be used. Moreover, very frequently a certain inertia controls this indigenous church: the only Bible they have ever known is *their* Bible, it is *the* Bible, so that those who may want to revise it and upgrade the quality of translation face major hurdles.

These factors suggest two things. First, Bible translators in such areas may need to think about working in tandem with evangelists, pastors and teachers. I understand that there is an internal discussion within the Wycliffe groups on this issue, and that there have already been changes in practice in recent years. Second, although Bible translation is to be undertaken with a target group of readers in mind, that group should not be construed as so narrow in outlook, so ill-informed about Christianity, pre-Christian, and lacking in teachers and preachers that the resulting translation will be hopelessly dated by the time that same group has become an established church.

Clearly, we have swung round once again to the constituents of Bible translations, and so to this last topic I now turn.

8. Not least in the English-speaking world, Bibles have constituencies, some of them overlapping. This fact is in dramatic opposition to the sweeping dominance of the King James Version (KJV) for three hundred years.

The constituencies can be defined in different ways. The level of a reader's proficiency can establish the locus of a constituency.[44] The NEB was sometimes said to be "not in the language of our times but

---

[44] Cf. Eugene A. Nida, "Translating Means Communicating: A Sociolinguistic Theory of Translation II," *BibTrans* 30 (1979) 319: "But the content of a discourse is only one factor influencing the choice of vocabulary. Even more important are the capacities of the intended receptors. Precisely the same information may be communicated on a technical or nontechnical level, and the choice of a lexical register depends on the receptors for whom a translation is being made."

in the language of the *Times*"—a sort of Oxbridge vernacular. The REB has diluted this elitism somewhat. Contrast the TEV: its strategy of pitching a translation at a more popular level[45] was to produce a version for readers of English as a second language. Both ends of the market scale have advantages and disadvantages.

Constituencies can also be established to some extent by the sponsors of particular versions. British Catholic translators produced the Jerusalem Bible (JB), and now the New Jerusalem Bible (NJB). Their American counterparts gave us the New American Bible (NAB), plus a revision of the New Testament. The Jewish Publication Society published a fresh rendering of the Hebrew and Aramaic Scriptures (*The Tanakh, The Holy Scriptures*). During the last three decades, Protestants have sponsored, among other translations, the TEV, the NIV, the NASB, the NKJV, and now the NRSV. But Protestants are so divided that few who will purchase and read the NKJV will become familiar with the TEV or the NRSV, and vice versa. That means there are many sub-constituencies. Some of them are very small indeed: how many of us are intimately familiar with the New Testament portion of God's Word to the Nations (GWN)[46]?

But in an open society where individuals can make their own purchases, the marketplace competes with denominational leaders and publishing sponsors to define constituencies. Recently Arthur Van Eck wrote, "A 1988 survey of 10,000 households which owned one or more Bibles indicated that one-third owned a Revised Standard Version of the Bible. Only the venerable King James Version was owned by more households with all other versions coming below the RSV in this survey."[47] These figures are impressive, though I confess

---

[45] I use the expression in a non-technical sense. Some translation theorists distinguish sharply between common-language versions and popular versions, placing TEV and its related versions (e.g., *Die Gute Nachricht* and *Les Bonnes Nouvelles*) firmly into the former category.

[46] Biblion Publishing, Cleveland, 1988.

[47] Arthur O. Van Eck, "The NRSV—Why Now?" *RE* 85 (1990) 163.

I would be interested to know how the 10,000 households were selected. Were they tied, I wonder, to mainline denominations?

The reason I press the point is that, in preparation for this essay, I wrote to six major Bible publishers and asked them to give me their sales figures for the past five years. Since the bases for the figures sent to me were not always exactly the same, I have tried to be precise in the specifications. Here are the results.

(a) During the five year period 1986-90, Doubleday sold 250,000 copies of the JB or NJB.

(b) During the same period, the RSV sold 2,184,046 copies. The figure for NRSV, for 1990 alone, is 1,115,901.

(c) In the five-year period from April 1 1986 to March 31 1990, Oxford University Press sold, in the United States alone, 76,720 copies of the NEB. This does *not* include the number sold by Cambridge University Press, which did not respond to my inquiry. But let us be charitable and double or triple the figure released by OUP, and we arrive at a total of not more than 200,000. This does not include copies sold overseas, including the UK.

(d) The Lockman Foundation estimates it sold, from 1986 to 1990 inclusively, 1.2 million copies of the complete NASB.

(e) Thomas Nelson reports that 'to date' (which presumably means from publication to the present, i.e. the ten-year period 1982-1991) the NKJV sold approximately 14 million copies under the auspices of Nelson, and about 4 million more copies in the editions of Gideons International and the American Bible Society. If we halve these figures to reflect the five years from 1986 to 1990, the total is approximately 9 million.

(f) During that same five-year period, the NIV sold approximately 32 million copies, 11 million through Zondervan and 21,327,027 through the International Bible Society.[48]

---

[48] For various reasons I have not sought the figures on some other translations that might be mentioned. For example, the sales figures on the *Living Bible*, A.J. Holman Co., Philadelphia and New York, 1973, are doubtless very high. But the Living Bible has made relatively few inroads

Of course, the size of circulation does not say anything necessary about the quality of the work. However, if the *Annales* school of historiography is right, these figures do tell us something about who is reading and what is being read. The overwhelming sales of NKJV and NIV tell us something about constituencies!

Not all of this compartmentalization is bad. Various constituencies are being served. With the best will in the world I do not see how some of the barriers between the constituencies are likely soon to be bridged. The halcyon days when everyone was brought up on one version, memorizing it and absorbing it as part of the cultural heritage, are gone and will not return. Perhaps it is worth suggesting that when a family or a church does adopt a version, there is something to be said for not changing again too quickly: a certain amount of memorization takes place with much regular use, almost by osmosis. If we value hiding God's Word in our hearts (minds? memories?), rather than in our notebooks or computers, the advantages of some discipline in this area are plain.

III. *Prospects*

Since I am neither a prophet nor the son of a prophet, my perspective on the prospects of Bible translations can be brief. I have already indicated that gender-neutral English use is likely to increase, and that will affect future revisions. More linguistic research will churn from the presses. The first linguistically sensitive Greek grammars will appear shortly, and in the long haul they will help to change the shape of seminary education, and therefore perhaps of what the French call the 'formation' of translators. There are no signs that the flood of revisions and of revisions of revisions, not to mention fresh translations, is abating, but for all practical purposes only eight or ten versions are likely to be viable in the market-place. And if the sales figures are significant, ninety per cent of America's

---

into churches as pew Bibles (unlike the others mentioned in the list above), so I thought it best to leave it aside.

Bible readers (or, at least, Bible purchasers!) will primarily use one of three or four versions.

Perhaps I may put forward five or six further prospects:

1. During the past decade, computers have served as word processors to help many translators to produce successive drafts, enter corrections, change spellings, and prepare a new version for publication.[49] Although sophisticated computers have been used to produce first draft translations of scientific material, it is unlikely that they will be used to produce first draft translations of literary material as diverse and as complex as that of the Bible—at least in the foreseeable future, perhaps ever. But during the next decade or two a growing number of translators will use computers, linked to CDs or their successors, to access a large body of research. Perhaps more importantly, creative and complex database systems will become more 'user friendly,' with the result that more translators will use them for note-taking and research-organizing functions. At the same time, new advances in the textual criticism of the New Testament will probably occur as software is developed to utilize fully the remarkable system at Münster at the Institut für neutestamentliche Textforschung.

2. New advances in the textual criticism of the Old Testament will emerge as the rest of the Dead Sea Scrolls are published, provided they yield enough information to allow the currently competing models of Old Testament textual development to be substantially resolved.

3. There will probably be some major advances in the production of Bibles in languages where many of the people have already become Christians through the medium of a regional trade language. Almost a decade ago, Rachel Angogo Kanyoro laid out the challenges and prospects in Africa.[50] I would be interested to learn how her propos-

---

[49] See Harold W. Fehderau, "Using Computers in a Translation Project," *BibTrans* 36 (1985) 418-422.

[50] "A Proposal for Translation Research Strategy in Africa," *BibTrans*

als have prospered, and what the next steps are. But these matters cannot be rushed, not only because of the limitations of the resources available (both people and money), but also for a host of cultural reasons. For example, William Smalley has explicated the phenomenon of language hierarchies, in which multilingual people use different languages for different purposes.[51] I recall on one trip to Australia an Anglican bishop from eastern Zaire, who could speak three languages: his own tribal language, Swahili, and French (in which he had taken his theological education). He chose Swahili when he was describing the state of his diocese to Australian Anglicans—and several Australian missionaries were capable of providing fluent interpretation. But when the bishop was called upon to preach, he preferred to use French—whereupon I was called upon to translate, having been reared in French Canada.

4. There may well be a flurry of new Bible translations and revisions in what used to be called the Iron Curtain countries.

5. There will probably continue to be some concerted focus on the production of fresh translations for the various Muslim populations, replacing older works produced by missionaries who were not native speakers, and whose efforts, though ground-breaking in their day, were beset by numerous problems that cannot be probed here.[52]

6. In the West, there will be the continued production of expensive 'study editions' of the more 'successful' versions. In my view, most of these do little good except make money for the publishers.[53]

---

34 (1983) 101-106.

[51] "Thailand's hierarchy of multilingualism," *Language Sciences* 10/2 (1988).

[52] See the important article by K. J. Thomas, "The Challenge of Bible Translation," *The Reformed World* 39 (1987) 675-682.

[53] I would be less opposed to such editions if they restricted themselves to providing information of as neutral a sort as possible, to help the reader

IV. *Conclusion*

Perfect translations are impossible. As Andrew Walls puts it, "Politics is the art of the possible; translation is the art of the impossible."[54] That is overstated, of course, but it is a stark reminder that all translation is compromise. We might usefully compare one's educational choices, where there are few absolute 'rights' and 'wrongs.' Shall I send my children to the local school? To a private school? To a parochial school? To a junior college? To a state university? To a private university? Appropriate answers will vary from child to child, from city to city, according to the resources available. Whatever decision is taken, there are entailments one simply must live with. So it is with translation. It is impossible to achieve perfection in all the possible *desiderata* simultaneously. So responsible translators learn as much as they can, make and correct their choices, and live with the entailments—recognizing that other translators, in different situations and with different skills, targeting a quite different group of people, may make a different set of choices and be forced to live with a different set of entailments.

The 175th anniversary of the American Bible Society is an appropriate occasion to thank God for the advances that have been made, to confess our shortcomings and disappointments, and to

---

bridge the chasms carved out by distance in time and language and culture. For a variety of reasons too complex to be explored here, I would argue that the additional notes provided by most study Bibles would be better left to separate books.

[54] Andrew F. Walls, "The Translation Principle in Christian History," *Bible Translation and the Spread of the Church* 24-39. Cf. Werner Winter, "Impossibilities of Translation," *Problems in the Philosophy of Language*, ed. Thomas W. Olshewsky (New York: Hold, Rinehart, and Winston, 1969): "In a nutshell, we seem to have here all the challenge and all the frustration that goes with our endeavors to do the ultimately impossible. We know from the outset that we are doomed to fail; but we have the chance, the great opportunity to fail in a manner that has its own splendor and its own promise."

resolve to press on with the privilege and responsibility of the multifaceted task of translating the Word of God.[55]

[55] I am grateful to Dr. Katharine Barnwell for reading an earlier draft of this paper, and for offering a number of important insights and suggestions for its improvement.

RESPONSE: Leonard Greenspoon

Donald Carson has admirably covered the key issues and areas in the vast field he was asked to survey; his choices are judicious; and his evaluations, where presented, do not exhibit any ideological or theological bias of the sort that often colors and even overwhelms similar discussions.

The comments I offer take their starting point in each case from Carson's remarks.

1. I am not as convinced as he that the admittedly elastic principles of Functional or Dynamic Equivalence have indeed won the day, nor would I be as happy as he appears to be if that turns out to be the case. Part of my concern revolves around the question of the separability of meaning from form and the desirability of such a division even if it is possible. In this respect, I think more attention should be paid to the *Prooftexts* article by Professor Edward Greenstein[1] of the Jewish Theological Seminary and to the translations by himself and Everett Fox.[2] We need not accept everything they propose nor shy away from wincing at some of their 'translation' results, but their attempts to reproduce numerous formal aspects of biblical Hebrew (especially spoken Hebrew) should not thereby be devalued.

2. Much of one's feelings on this matter are connected with the distinction, which I find valuable to consider, between a translation

---

[1] Edward L. Greenstein, "Theories of Modern Bible Translation" (*Prooftexts* 3, 1983) 9-39, as noted by Carson.

[2] For Fox, see now *Genesis and Exodus* (Schocken, 1990); originally, *In the Beginning* (1983) and *Now These Are the Names* (1986).

LEONARD J. GREENSPOON is Professor of Religion at Clemson University, Clemson, SC.

that brings the text to the reader, and one that requires the reader to go to the (world of the) text. The net effect of functional equivalence is to bring the biblical text (which is to a greater or larger extent foreign to us all) to the reader; Greenstein and Fox and to a lesser degree more traditional English translations make greater demands on the reader. But I am not convinced that such efforts on the part of readers, or at least some readers, are without enormous value.

3. This is especially true in many academic settings, where, in my opinion, students benefit from gaining acquaintance with at least some of the stylistic and formal features of the Hebrew (and/or Greek) original. I recognize, of course, that one characteristic of the Bible market today, and one of the major causes for the proliferation of modern language versions, is that there are multiple constituencies among Bible purchasers. With that in mind, I would never deny the value of translations prepared utilizing the principles of functional equivalence. Nor, however, should we deny similar, positive worth to other types of translations.

4. A few years ago here in Philadelphia, at the Annenberg Research Institute, Edward Greenstein presented a preliminary version of his translation of the book of Esther. [3] As I recall, it was not well received by the scholars in attendance, with but one exception—a literary critic. This, I think, serves to remind us that somehow or other the older translations managed to achieve a higher level of literary merit than appears to be the case with many of the more recent renditions. There is very little memorable, very little oratorically exciting about most of the text of the newer versions. Now I am aware of the fact that in the past literary splendor was on occasion achieved at the price of accuracy, and I would not want to sacrifice

---

[3] Now published in Edward L. Greenstein, "What Might Make a Bible Translation Jewish?" *Translation of Scripture (Proceedings of a Conference at the Annenberg Research Institute May 15-16, 1989)* (Philadelphia, 1990) 77-101.

comprehensibility at the altar of stylistic niceties. Nonetheless, it is difficult for me to judge as totally successful a version that fails to engage, excite, or move me, as great literature should.[4] Nor, ultimately, do versions that are stylistically flat, if for no other reason than that they fail to do justice to the stylistic sophistication, elegance, and, yes, playfulness of the original. In this instance, I refer to the words of Max Leopold Margolis, who judged that the success of the King James Version (KJV) was in large measure the result of its ability to produce in the English language so many of the effects of the Hebrew original.[5]

5. Reference to Margolis brings to mind the question of Jewish translations of the Bible, to which Carson alludes in his paper. The question of what constitutes a Jewish translation and even the advisability of such an enterprise is as old as the Letter of Aristeas, if the interpretation of Harry M. Orlinsky and others is correct—and I think it is. As they interpret this 2nd century B.C.E. 'epistle,' it was a defense of the Old Greek translation of the Pentateuch as a work equal to the Hebrew original in value as well as in inspiration. Against those who apparently denied any authority to the Septuagint, Aristeas asserted that the work of the 72 translators was accepted by the Alexandrian Jewish community exactly as Moses' law had been received at Sinai.[6] Within Judaism it is now widely accepted that Bible translation is a practical, if not always desirable necessity, although there are still some who do not believe the Talmud should

---

[4] See also Gerald Hammond, *The Making of the English Bible* (New York: Philosophical Library, 1982).

[5] See my *Max Leopold Margolis A Scholar's Scholar* (Atlanta: Scholars, 1987), especially chapter 3, "Bible Translation."

[6] See the remarks by Greenstein in the articles cited above; see also my forthcoming article, "From the Septuagint to the New Revised Standard Version: A Brief Account of Jewish Involvement in Bible Translating and Translations," in The Solomon Goldman Lecture series published by Spertus College.

be consulted except in the original. Nonetheless, there is not equal unanimity as to exactly what constitutes a Jewish translation. I think it is fair to say that the New Jewish Version (NJV) has been received more positively within the general scholarly and ecclesiastical world than among Jews in general, although among the latter the reception has also been largely positive. Surely a Jewish translation should incorporate traditional Jewish exegesis, especially in key theological passages. However, given the dynamic and expansive quality of Jewish biblical interpretation, it is difficult not to find some support for almost any non-Christological exegetical point. Such considerations lead some Jewish scholars to look to style and 'feeling' rather than exegesis as the key to a Jewish translation.[7] On this point lively debate will, I hope, continue.

6. My earlier reference to Margolis recalls another remark Carson made in passing, about revisions. It seems to me that insufficient attention has been paid to the distinction between a fresh translation and a revision. In terms of the result, there may be little practical difference and the public may be largely unaware whether it is reading one or the other. But in terms of procedure or practice, there are significant differences: as distinct from a 'translation,' which entails the fresh rendering of a text from one language into another, a 'revision' is most dependent on an existing text in the same language. It is really a matter of degree: no translator, however original, is totally unaware of earlier renderings, nor is even the most slavish reviser without knowledge of the foreign language text that stands behind the earlier translation with which he works. Or, to put it another way, it is a matter of starting point: a translator begins with the text in a foreign language; the reviser, with a text in his own language. And it is an intriguing question why an individual or group of individuals fully capable of preparing a fresh translation should instead opt for the production of a revision. Because I had access to the official and unofficial papers of those involved in the 1917 Jewish

---

[7] See note 6.

Publication Society translation, I was able to demonstrate that this 'translation' was in fact a revision of the 1885 Revised Version (RV), itself part of the KJV tradition. Moreover, I could understand what motivated the principals to act as they did, to the point that they kept the public largely uninformed of this close linkage with the RV.[8] I have also tried to use insights achieved from a study of this modern translation/revision to gain some under-standing of an ancient revision, in this case the work of Theodotion, in the late 1st century B.C.E.[9] Whether or not my argument was persuasive, I have attempted to open the question up for further investigation. I shall return to this point at the end of my remarks.

7. Carson is to be congratulated, among other reasons, for his attempts to gain accurate sales or at least distribution figures for modern versions. Publishers tend to guard zealously such figures. Several years ago, a major Conservative religious publisher was willing to send me almost all of the results of an elaborate Bible-buying survey they had commissioned and conducted, on the condition that I keep it confidential. Given the fact that several publishers are involved in the sales and distribution of most translations, I am not sure that Carson's figures are anything more than an approximation. Allow me to add some data of my own: distribution figures for Today's English Version (TEV; formerly, the Good News Bible, GNB): between January 1, 1987 and December 31, 1987, over 110,000,000 partial or complete copies of this version were placed in circulation. (Only about 2% of that number were com-plete Bibles, but that 2% is, after all, a little over 2,000,000 copies. Individual testaments accounted for another one and a half million of this total, and I suspect these were mostly New Testaments. Approximately 3,000,000 portions [24 pp. or more] were listed as distributed; well

---

[8] See my article, "A Book 'Without Blemish': The Jewish Publication Society's Bible Translation of 1917," *Jewish Quarterly Review* 79 (1988) 1-21.

[9] See my "Biblical Translators in Antiquity and in the Modern World: A Comparative Study," *Hebrew Union College Annual* 60 (1989) 91-113.

over one hundred million of the figure are accounted for by "misc. and selections [of fewer than 24 pp.].") According to figures provided to me by Zondervan, the major publishers of the New International Version (NIV), more than 45,000,000 partial or complete copies of this version are in circulation. For the Living Bible (LB for short, among scholars; The Book, for publicity, among members of its sales staff): the year after the publication of this admitted 'paraphrase' of the entire Bible appeared (that was in 1971) the Living Bible was the best-selling book in the United States. Two years later it accounted for almost half of the Bibles purchased in America.

8. On a related matter, Carson refers to the fact that we can expect the packaging and re-packaging of several popular translations in the form of a variety of study Bibles and, I would add, 'specialty' editions. He appears somewhat dubious of the value of this phenomenon, and, for several reasons, I wholeheartedly agree. First of all, such editions, and in fact translations themselves, are often the recipients of what I would term an unseemly and totally unnecessary amount of hype: The Book, The publishing event of the Century, The Most Authentic, and so forth. As I have written elsewhere, it seems that the sales and publicity departments of many publishers are the most active, innovative, and creative parts of their operations. With respect to study Bibles or translations in general, as Carson notes, the educational value is frequently very disappointing. United Bible Society translator Harold Scanlin has looked at the notes of certain New Testament versions from this perspective, and I have investigated the introductions and notations of a number of Old Testament versions for the text critical, and especially Septuagintal, knowledge imparted therein.[10] Almost without exception the reader is given

---

[10] For Scanlin, see his "Bible Translation as a Means of Communicating New Testament Textual Criticism to the Public," *Technical Papers for The Bible Translator* 39 (1988) 101-113; see also my article, "It's All Greek to Me: the Septuagint in Modern English Versions of the Hebrew Bible," *VII Congress of the International Organization for Septuagint and Cognate*

partial, misleading, or confusing information on these subjects—and that is when any information at all can be found. In this regard, publishers and translators are missing a golden opportunity to perform a real service with respect to educating the large Bible-reading public on issues related to text and version. Gilt edges and leather covers certainly have their place. But so also does authoritative, clear, and useful information about the Septuagint, the Vulgate, and so forth.

9. Carson wisely eschews the role of prophet as foreseer. I would certainly not want to fill that breach. Instead, I close with remarks not so much about the future of Bible translating, but about some desiderata in the future of the *study* of Bible translations. Near the beginning of his paper, Carson pointed out that we cannot correctly understand the principles of dynamic equivalence without knowledge and appreciation of the conditions or circumstances in which Eugene Nida and others originally worked. This emphasis on what we might broadly term the social history of Bible translation is sorely needed. It is only slowly coming to be a factor in biblical studies at all; that is, up until a decade ago there was hardly anything even approaching a historiography of biblical studies. We have tended to emphasize the *what*, that is the finished product, the translation, to the virtual exclusion of the *who*, the *why*, even the *where*. Bible translations, in addition to whatever else they may be, are literary works that reflect the social, political, cultural, and religious environment in which they are produced. As 'works-by-committee,' most are also subject to the give-and-take of such enterprises. We do an injustice to the individuals involved in such projects when we fail to recognize the nitty-gritty of producing a translation, the forces at work in such a production, and the multiple allegiances and agendas each translator has, explicitly or implicitly, to deal with.

Studies (Leuven 1989) (Atlanta: Scholars, 1991), and "On the Textual Basis of Several Modern Translations of the Hebrew Bible" (a paper presented at the southeastern regional meeting of SBL in March 1990).

If politics is the art of the possible, translation the art of the impossible, we can all the more marvel that any translation of the Bible (with its political, religious and other accompaniments) ever gets produced. It is perfectly appropriate that we point to what we perceive as the shortcomings of any modern version. At the same time, we ought never to lose sight of the enormous odds against ending up with anything at all that is usable.

RESPONSE: Barclay M. Newman

Martin Luther, in his essay, *Defense of Translation of Psalms,* affirms:

Whoever would speak German must not use Hebrew style. Rather he must see to it—once he understands the Hebrew author—that he concentrates on the sense of the text, asking himself, "Pray tell, what do the Germans say in such a situation?" Once he has the German words to serve the purpose, let him drop the Hebrew words and express the meaning freely in the best German he knows.

To accomplish this goal—especially in poetry—certain sacrifices must be made. These sacrifices are best described by two translators of Arabic poems:

We have agreed to sacrifice form, rhyme, meter, and sound. The reason we have done so is because the Arabic language is categorically separate from the English language. It is not an Aryan tongue; it is Semitic. Moreover, the poetic tradition—the map of connotations, imagery, and verbal conventions—is different.[1]

In the translation of poetry, both formal equivalent and *functional equivalent* translations have, for the most part, sacrificed rhyme, meter, and sound. But they also have in common that have attempted to retain the *form* of the Hebrew, without considering the need for creating an effective and appropriate style in English. In particular,

---

[1] *Birds Through a Ceiling of Alabaster, Three Abbasid Poets,* translated with an introduction by G. B. H. Wightman and A. Y. al-Udhari (Penguin Books, 1975), pp. 28-29.

BARCLAY M. NEWMAN is Chief Translations Officer for the American Bible Society.

I refer to the matter of Hebrew parallelism, which does not carry over with equal effectiveness into English. This is especially true where publications of the Bible demand a double column format that results in a number of runover lines.

Observe what happens with Psalm 18 when squeezed into a two column format. When a poetic text is read aloud, there is generally a pause at the end of each line, especially where runovers are involved, because the reader's eyes must skip from the end of one line to the middle of the next line. Runovers are indented several spaces more than primary 'or secondary lines. Sometimes the result can be disastrous, as in verses 19, 25, and 28 of the NRSV:

> [19]He brought me out into a broad
>   place...
> [25]With the loyal you show yourself
>   loyal...
> [28]The Lord, my God, lights up
>   my darkness...

The unexpected shifts between second and third person references to the deity are also problematic, especially for the hearer of the text. This happens at least three times in the Psalm, and they can be quite disturbing to the discerning reader, as may be illustrated from verses 34-35 of the NRSV:[2]

> [34]*He* trains my hands for war,
>   so that my arms can bend a
>   bow of bronze.
> [35]*You* have given me the shield of
>   *your* salvation...

---

[2] Note verses 13-15, which constitute a single paragraph in the GNB: "The LORD thundered...*He* shot his arrows...*he sent them running...when* you rebuked *your* enemies, LORD." See also "the power... *You* have kept... *You* gave... *You* make...they call out to *the LORD*, but *he* does not save them."

Verse 29 compounds the problem by retaining the second to third person shift and simultaneously having the psalmist sound as if he is swearing:

> [29]By *you* I can crush a troop,
>   and *by my God* I can leap over
>   a wall.

I completely agree with Donald Carson: No translation is perfect; all translation is compromise, but the Contemporary English Version (CEV) has attempted to deal creatively with poetic passages in the Bible.

1. *Measured Lines.*

The choice of line breaks in poetry is no less integral to the translation than is the choice of words, and to alter the lines may result in a *mis*-translation, especially for the *hearer*. One should keep in mind that more people *hear* the Bible read than read it for themselves. For this reason, the translators of the CEV determine the line breaks, rather than leaving that decision to either the typesetter or the computer. The CEV line breaks are not always ideal, because we still have a problem of double columns, but we can at least control where the breaks are made.[3]

2. *Use of Second Person References to God.*

In liturgical, confessional, and poetic passages, Hebrew frequently shifts between second and third person references to God, whereas for English speakers it is generally more natural to employ only a second person pronoun (that is a 'you' form).

---

[3] Our Translation Team considers the choice of line breaks so important, that the American Bible Society has made a contract with Thomas Nelson Publishers that breaks can be made in no other places, without consultation with the ABS Translations Officer.

Where shifts are made in longer sections, and where the biblical writer is obviously shifting from addressing God to making an open declaration about God, the shifts are honored in the CEV. But in a psalm such as Psalm 18, the shifts seem rather arbitrary and obtrusive to English speakers. And so, in this particular psalm the CEV uses a second person reference throughout.

This style also has the supplementary advantage of making the language more inclusive, by having fewer masculine pronouns for God.

3. *Economy of Words and a New Poetic Form.*

In the CEV, Psalm 18 consists of 173 lines, making it 25 lines shorter than the NRSV and 33 lines shorter than the GNB. This is significant, since functional equivalent translations tend to be longer than formal equivalent translations. We will employ the traditional A/B style, consisting of alternating primary and secondary lines. But we have also introduced a different form—that of an AA/B style, in which two primary lines are followed by one secondary line. The result is a wider variety of format, no runover lines, and, quite often, fewer lines overall in a poetic section. Moreover, these factors contribute significantly toward achieving an ease of oral reading without stumbling, of hearing without misunderstanding, and of memorization.

4. *The Paragraph as the Basic Discourse Unit.*

In Hebrew Psalms, God is often addressed more frequently within a paragraph than might be desirable in English. For this reason, in the CEV one noun of addressing is sometimes pushed forward to the beginning of a paragraph, while others within the paragraph may be dropped. Occasionally, two nouns of address (for example, 'Lord' and 'God') that occur on separate lines (or in separate verses) of the Hebrew text are brought together near the beginning of the paragraph, as in verses 1-2 of Psalm 18:

[1]I love you, *LORD God*,
    and you make me strong.
[2]You are my mighty rock,
    and my fortress, my protector,
  the rock where I am safe...

Compare this with the NRSV, which retains the form of the Hebrew text:

[1]I love you, *O LORD*, my strength.
[2]*The LORD* is my rock, my
    fortress and my deliverer,
my God, my rock in whom I
    take refuge...

5. *Abbreviated and Embedded Nouns of Address.*

Unfortunately, the forms 'O Lord' and 'O God,' as well as 'my Lord' and 'my God,' especially when occurring at the beginning of a sentence, may sound like swear words, and so these expressions have usually been avoided in the CEV. In fact, we have often embedded the nouns of address for the deity, as in verses 1, 3, 20, 28, 30, and 49.[4]

6. *Parallelism.*

Parallelism is a primary feature of Hebrew poetry, but it is not so prominent in English poetry, and for persons unfamiliar with the biblical tradition, it may sound cumbersome and awkward. Parallelism does exist in CEV Psalms, but to a lesser degree and in a different format than in traditional translations, whether they be formal or functional.

---

[4] A notable exception is found in Psalm 22, where we have maintained the traditional form, "My God, my God, why have you deserted me."

7. *Textual Visualization.*

For the most part, the style of the CEV poetry is significantly different from that of other translations, because the translators are concerned with matters of *textual visualization* and *aesthetics.* It is expected of poetry, not only that is *sound* good, but that it *look* good!

Here I wish to incorporate one brief example (consisting of only six words in Hebrew) that illustrates numerous important aspect of translating Hebrew poetry into English. The passage is Lamentations 5.11, which reads as follows in Hebrew:

> "Women in Zion were raped,
>   virgins in the towns of Judah."

When translating this into English, at least five questions must be asked:

(1) Who is the speaker? Perhaps this is best dealt with as several translations have done in the Song of Songs, that is, by indicating in italics either *Jerusalem Speaks* or *The Prophet Speaks.*

(2) What is the function of this verse? I would answer by saying that it underscores the worst possible scenario in the downfall of Jerusalem—the city walls and temple have been destroyed, the young men have been slain in battle, and now the most senseless and degrading crime of all, the rape of helpless women and children.

(3) What is the primary focus—the women and girls, the geographical designations, or the event? The placement of the verb in the Hebrew text (linking the two subjects, as opposed to the more natural order of coming first in the sentence), though not altogether unusual, is significant enough to at least suggest that it is the horror of the event (the verb) that is central in the mind of the writer.

(4) Were women raped only on Zion and virgins only in the towns of Judah? Were women safe in the towns of Judah and virgins protected in the city of Zion? The obvious answer to both questions is 'No!'

(5) What about the ellipsis? Is it more effective to retain one verb with dual subjects? Would it be better to use the same verb twice or to have two different verbs with essentially the same meaning? Is there yet another option?

Note that has been done in the NRSV:

> "Women were raped in Zion,
>   virgins in the towns of Judah."

Contrast this with the restructuring of the GNB:

> "Our wives have been raped on
>   Mount Zion itself;
> in every Judean village our
>   daughters have been
>   forced to submit."

The differences between the 'formal' rendering of the NRSV and the 'functional' restructuring of the GNB are significant:

(1) The formal equivalent has retained as much of the Hebrew form as is allowable in an English sentence. This is in keeping with the stated purpose of the NRSV: "as literal as possible, as free as necessary."

(2) The functional equivalent has (a) created a chiasm [wives/Zion...every Judean village/daughters], (b) used two essentially synonymous verbs [raped/forced to submit], (c) seen Zion as the item in focus [Zion itself],[5] and (d) produced a text that consumes five lines in a double column format.

Are there other options? I would suggest two possible methods of restructuring, both of which involve combining the subjects ('women'

---

[5] There is no support in the Hebrew text for introducing the reflexive pronoun 'itself' as an intensifier.

and 'virgins') and the geographical designations ('Zion' and 'towns of Judah').

If *prose* arrangement is intended, the text may be restructured in the order subject + verb + place:

> Our women and young girls
> were raped in Zion
> and everywhere in Judah.

On the other hand, a *poetic* effect is better achieved by rearranging the elements as follows:

> In Zion and everywhere in Judah
> our women and young girls
> were raped.

This proposed poetic restructuring in English is significantly different from that of the Hebrew text. But it is much more effective for readers of English, and it would convey the intended impact of the Hebrew text far better than either the formal equivalent of the NRSV or the functional equivalent of the GNB.

RESPONSE: Pheme Perkins

Dr. Carson has provided an admirable overview not only of new Bible translations but of the task of translating itself. There is no substantive point of disagreement between us, so my remarks will be confined to highlighting important issues raised by his paper. Dr. Carson speaks of the segmented audiences for the major Bible translations. I am besieged as I am sure many biblical scholars are with people who ask "What translation is the best?" My standard response is always to ask what the individual intends to "use it for." If it is one of the people from my Tuesday morning Parish Bible study group, I usually narrow it down to a couple of choices and then let them 'test drive' one of my copies to see which version they are most comfortable reading. In our 'great books' course for Freshmen, we have adopted the *New Oxford Annotated.* Many of our other courses use either the annotated *New Jerusalem Bible* (especially in Hebrew Bible courses) or the annotated version of the *New American Bible* put out by Oxford as the *Catholic Study Bible* (especially in courses for which Bible is a section of a theology course and the lengthy essays on each book are desirable). Foreign students are urged to go down to the Bible Society and obtain a copy in their own language, which has always been possible, or failing that to use the *Good News Bible.* The latter is also commonly used in high school programs but is not appropriate for college or graduate students.

Contrary to Dr. Carson's disparaging remark about 'study editions,' the cultural gap between the modern world and the Biblical one is so great that some annotated version is essential. People can learn to use the explanatory notes and introductions to provide a context for 'what's going on' or to explain a difficult passage. When they get over the initial hurdle of doing so, they actually enjoy such features.

PHEME PERKINS is Professor of Theology (New Testament) at Boston College, Boston, MA.

1. *The Bible as Cultural Artifact.*

The 'cultural gap' poses one of the biggest challenges to Bible translation. Dr. Carson's essay referred to the problem of 'situational meaning' (p. 42) or 'encyclopaedic knowledge' (p. 43) that existed for the original reader but not for the modern readers. We bring an entirely different cultural framework to reading the Bible. The principle of *dynamic equivalence* which has taken over as the fundamental strategy for translation requires some form of paraphrase. One might note that the ancient versions had a strategy to confront that problem. The rendering of the Hebrew scriptures into the Aramaic of Jesus' day was an explanatory translation. We refer to them as Targums. Our pastor reading the Martha and Mary story from the pulpit the other day substituted for the 'much serving' of Luke 10.40 (NAB), the following two expressions, "Martha was burdened with *the details of hospitality*" and "do you not care that my sister has left me to *do the household chores.*"

That's a Targumic rendering—painful to my ears, but not to those of the people around me. For them, the story was more lively and immediately effective than the version printed in the lectionary. Of course, this highlights another difficulty which Dr. Carson has mentioned, can we really translate for 'effect'? I have been trying for two weeks to persuade my senior citizens Bible study group that when Jesus told his disciples that they would have to 'become like little children' to enter the kingdom, he was offending them. No self-respecting adult male would want to be compared to a child, much less asked to return to the status of one! But they all have pictures of their adorable grandchildren...and they'll never believe it!

At the academic level, the problem is just as tough. The more we know about literary forms and genres, the more difficult it is to translate the Bible. Whether it is the ironic transformation of the ancient 'war oracle' genre in the oracles against foreign nations in Amos[1] or

---

[1] Amos 1.3-2.16; cf. Shalom M. Paul, *Amos* (Hermeneia; Minneapolis: Fortress, 1991) 7-11.

the ironic conversion of the polluting yeast into a symbol of the Kingdom's presence in Jesus' parable[2], not even a Targumic translation could get the point across. It requires a full-fledged explanation. The 'best' translations in such situations are those which have not become so simple or inculturated that the reader no longer recognizes that the world of the Biblical text is different from our world.

But in the more detailed instances of rhetorical forms and literary conventions, no translation can hope to reproduce the original. It would be ludicrous to attempt to find modern equivalents. Richard Longenecker's new commentary on *Galatians* in the Word Commentary series lists thirty-one passages in which Paul is using conventional non-literary letter formulas.[3] Since these involve expressions of astonishment, distress and rejoicing, which have no equivalents in English letter-writing, we cannot convey the tone of the Pauline text without radically changing the expressions used. We should perhaps admit that in the end the older generation of British scholars who translated the classics were right. The only access to a text is in the original. Everything else is paraphrase, so 'free translation' was the norm.

2. *The Translations and the Academy.*

This observation brings me to my last comments. Those in charge of the public use of the Bible—that is clergy and many theologians—no longer have access to the text. They are dependent upon translations just as the field has splintered. In practical ecumenical projects like common lectionaries, pulpit exchange and shared Vacation Bible schools, we run the risk of going separate ways again. Training students in seminaries is also increasingly problematic, since they come from different Bible-reading constituencies. Dr. Carson

---

[2] Mt 13.33//Lk 13.20-21; cf. Bernard B. Scott, *Jesus, Symbol-maker for the Kingdom* (Philadelphia: Fortress, 1981) 73-77.

[3] R. Longenecker, *Galatians* (Waco, TX: Word, 1990), cv-cix.

referred to another translation problem: *translating for canon criticism*—though he did not use those words. This means translating so that the reader of one part of the Bible can recognize its reuse of an earlier tradition. That is notoriously difficult and none of the new translations is able to carry it out with any consistency.

Another academic challenge is to translate so that the best exegesis is reflected in one's choices. That is also problematic. Two examples from the NRSV. In the first case, What to do with an obscure word?:

Amos 7.7 has the Lord standing by a wall of *'anak* with *'anak* in his hand. Though this unknown word has been rendered 'plumb line' as in the NRSV, this rendering is a bad guess. Akkadian *annaku* 'tin' requires some rendering of a 'tin wall', that is an ironic reversal of the usual imagery of a nation or its army as an iron or bronze wall (Jer 1.18; Ezek 4.3).[4]

But the NRSV ignores this data and continues with the old 'plumb line' which is easier to understand even though it hardly portends disaster.

The second example raises the problem of theological convictions and translations, which Carson has also noted. Most studies of Paul, sensitive to anti-semitism in earlier scholarship, now recognize that Paul was far more committed to the Jewish law than previously thought. He even uses Jewish *halakah*, formal legal interpretations, to guide the life of his communities.[5] Translations of Paul's letters have yet to catch up:

Take for example, Ga 5.4. The Greek present tense δικαιοῦσθε makes good sense as present, 'you are righteous,' and is no

---

[4] Paul, *Amos*, 233-35.

[5] Cf. Peter J. Tomson, *Paul and the Jewish Law* (CRINT; Minneapolis: Fortress, 1990).

different from Paul's own statement about his past life in Phil 3.6, "being blameless according to righteousness in the law." But because it is assumed that no Christians (especially Gentiles) might 'be righteous' according to the Law, the NRSV follows its predecessor and translates it as a connotative present, "you who want to be justified..."

The choice makes a major difference in understanding. It would appear that there are already Christians practicing righteousness according to the Law (also Ga 4.10).[6] Their expectation of intensified participation in God's Spirit is being rejected by the apostle. The NRSV translation skews the history of early Christianity away from the on-going involvement with Jewish life that continues to be evident on the part of Christians, even in the fourth century. Not only is the translation issue a theological challenge, it is also a challenge to the story that Christians have told themselves about their history.

Thus the most difficult problem facing Bible translators is that of cultural, theological and ethnic hegemony. Does our translation practice make the Bible more the property of one group than another? If so, we must constantly ask ourselves who is the God, who stands behind the text:

Or is God the God of Jews only? Is he not the God of Gentiles also? Yes, of Gentiles also, since God is one; and will justify the circumcised on the ground of their faith and the uncircumcised through their faith. (Ro 3.29-30).

---

[6] Cf. Charles H. Cosgrove, *The Cross and the Spirit: A Study in the Argument and Theology of Galatians* (Macon, GA: Mercer, 1988) 150-51.

New Finds that Illuminate the World and Text of the Bible: The Greco-Roman Era

Howard Clark Kee

When Elias Boudinot and his associates were launching the American Bible Society in the second decade of the nineteenth century, a German philosopher at the height of his powers was promoting a method of intellectual and historical analysis that would profoundly influence scholarly assessment of the Bible, especially in relation to the post-exilic period and to Christian Origins. I refer, of course, to Georg Wilhelm Friedrich Hegel (1770-1831), whose basic principle of human thought and institutions asserted that they develop by a pattern in which an emergent thesis is countered by an antithesis, which then produces a new synthesis. This analytical strategy was adopted by F. C. Baur and the so-called Tübingen School which pictured a *thesis*—what he regarded as a narrow-minded Jewish Christianity—set over against an antithesis—the law-free gospel of Paul. The gospels and Acts represent efforts to develop a synthesis. Even though the specifics of Baur's proposal have been largely abandoned, the Hegelian principle of historical interpretation of Judaism and early Christianity as reflected in the Bible by setting features over against each other has continued to dominate biblical studies down through the present century. The pairs of opposites in recent decades have included Jewish wisdom vs. apocalyptic, Palestinian Judaism vs. hellenistic Judaism, and the Jesus tradition vs. the Pauline tradition.

What I shall present seeks to show how artificial are these distinctions, and to do so by calling attention to archaeological

---

HOWARD CLARK KEE is former Professor of New Testament and Director of Biblical-Historical Graduate Studies at Boston University.

discoveries of the past 50 to 60 years which require us to perceive the biblical material in a very different light from the false distinctions that have too long dominated biblical understanding. We shall concentrate our attention on four types of information which require a reappraisal of evidence about the biblical world, since is each case we may now discern cultural and conceptual features of diverse origins. Our focus will be (1) on excavations in Jerusalem, (2) on some problematical sites in Judea and Galilee, (3) on fresh analyses of synagogues in the wider Mediterranean world, (4) and on synagogue sites in Galilee.

Before turning to these themes, we should note that one of the most important sources of new information and insights about the biblical text and the biblical world is the recovery of manuscripts from the centuries just before and after the turn of the eras. Professor Fitzmyer analyzed these in detail: those from the Dead Sea and from the Gnostic Library from Nag Hammadi in Egypt. Both sets of documents were found more than forty years ago. These discoveries were followed in the early fifties by the discovery of caches of correspondence between Bar Kochba, the leader of the Second Jewish Revolt, in 132-135 C.E., written in Aramaic, Hebrew and Greek. How completely unexpected was the discovery of such manuscripts in that land is illustrated by the remark of one of my professors at Yale in 1949, uttered when Professor Millar Burrows, who was on leave in Jerusalem then, was getting the first scholarly glimpse of the Scrolls. In a course in archeology of the Greco-Roman world my professor declared that "the changing pattern of the climate in Palestine—hot and cold, wet and dry—precludes the survival of any ancient manuscripts there such as one finds in Egypt." Among the manuscripts found in the caves between Qumran and the Jewish revolutionary stronghold at Masada were several written in simple Greek, suggesting that this was a common language even among those Jews who were fomenting a revolution against the Romans. We shall see other evidence of the wide use of Greek among Palestinian Jews in the period of our investigation.

Other manuscripts found at Qumran that shed light on the world of Judaism in the Second Temple Period (but have no significance for our knowledge of the biblical text) are two fragments of a Hebrew astrological document (4Q186, 1 and 2) and another Aramaic document which may be a horoscope of the Messiah (4QMessAr).[1] We shall have occasion to comment on astrological features of Judaism in the rabbinic period when we examine the evidence from synagogues in Galilee. The important feature of this astrological material is that the determinative force of the position of the signs of the zodiac was perceived by pious Jews as evidence of the divine, determinative power that is shaping the history of the world, and especially of God's people.

I. *Excavations in Jerusalem*

The changing size of Jerusalem and the changing manner in which the hills and valleys of the area were occupied during the period from Israel's return from exile through the hellenistic, Hasmonean and Roman periods is far clearer as a result of excavations in various parts of the city during the past twenty-five years. In the time of Persian control, the city was on the eastern hill, extending from the temple area on the hill to the older city below and south of the temple mount. The wall built there to the south seems to date from the time of Nehemiah. Under the Ptolemies (301-198 B.C.E.) and the Seleucids (198-165 B.C.E.), the hellenistic rulers developed the western hill, installing a fortress there, as well as one that overlooked the north end of the temple precinct. On the western hill a formidable military structure was built, which came to be referred to as the Citadel.

The Hasmoneans (165-63 B.C.E.) strengthened the fortifications, and enclosed the two sections of the city on the eastern and western hills, with a bridge joining the two, of which the so-called Wilson's Arch was a major feature in the Tyropoean Valley between the two

---

[1] G. Vermes, who includes translations of these texts in his *The Dead Sea Scrolls in English*, thinks that the Aramaic text may refer to the miraculous birth of Noah.

hills. Tombs and other burials in the Kidron Valley to the east and south of the Temple Mount were multiplied in this period. In the Herodian and subsequent Roman period, the Antonia Fortress (named by Herod in honor of Mark Antony, who lost his claim to imperial Roman power in the Battle of Actium in 31 B.C.E.) provided a base of control adjacent to the temple on the north. The Citadel area on the western hill was the location of the great Herodian palace, remains of which have been excavated in the courtyard of the still-standing parts of the Citadel and in the adjacent garden of the Armenian Convent. Other houses in the vicinity of Herod's palace have been excavated, which are luxurious and include representational art, some of it in a style recalling the palaces of Pompeii.

Some of the features traditionally identified as early Christian holy sites, such as the Ecce Homo Arch, are now seen to be part of structures from the second century C.E. The Antonia Fortress, which has often been assumed to have been the scene of Jesus' interrogation by Pilate and the *lithostratos* mentioned in Jn 19.13, now appears to have been far smaller than the usual reconstruction of a building, often identified as the seat of the governor in Pilate's time, but which probably dates from the second century C.E. What is commonly identified as the remains of the fortress of Antonia is more likely of Byzantine or even medieval origin. The *praetorium* where the hearing is now thought to have taken place was in the complex of Herod's palace on the western hill of the city, which is where both Josephus and Philo report that the Roman governors stayed and carried out their official functions while in Jerusalem.

The line of the city wall in the Second Temple period is difficult to trace with certainty. M. Avi-Yonah, who has analyzed carefully the archaeological evidence, says locating the wall is "one of the greatest mysteries in topography." The line of the wall east of the temple and in the northeastern section of the city are easily determined, and the fact that some of the structures near the Church of the Holy Sepulchre have been shown to have been outside the city wall in the period of the Second Temple suggest that the wall turned south just west of the present Damascus Gate before turning west again toward

Herod's palace area. Complicating this picture is some evidence that portions of this wall come at the earliest from the time of Herod Agrippa I (who ruled 41-44).

The results of excavation in the vicinity of the temple give a much clearer picture. Remains of the long-known southern wall of the temple enclosure which have recently been excavated and analyzed, as well as those of adjacent structures, have made possible the recovery of the outline and vast extent of the grand entrance to the temple that this section offered worshippers and visitors. The circumference of the temple wall was nearly a mile. The entire enclosure, it has been estimated, could "comfortably hold a capacity crowd of 75,000."[2] The southern side of the temple area consisted of a grand Royal Portico, resembling the stoas of the Athenian Agora. Remains indicate the grandeur of the columns. Ornamental fragments abound, all of which are geometric or floral in design, presumably intentionally avoiding animal or human features. The double gates which gave access to the temple area from the lower city opened into ramps which led to the vast platform on which the courtyards and the temple proper stood. Access to the Tyropoean Valley to the west was by a grand stairway built on what has long been known as Robinson's Arch, and farther north the bridge (of which Wilson's Arch is a surviving feature) led across the valley to the western hill. The magnificence of this structure erected by Herod can be sensed even more vividly now, as can both pride of Jews in this place where they believed God dwelt among them, and the dismay that greeted the prediction of Jesus that it was soon to be destroyed (Mk 13.1-2 and parallels).

Also found in the rubble adjoining the southern wall of the temple area was a fragment of a column honoring Vespasian and Titus, as well as the 10th Legion of the Roman army which defeated the Jewish revolutionaries and captured the city in 70 C.E. Both bricks and rooftiles found there bear the imprint of the 10th Legion. Pottery frag-

---

[2] From Eric M. Meyers and J. F. Strange, *Archaeology, the Rabbis and Early Christianity* (Nashville: Abingdon, 1981), 52.

ments and decorated lamps have been found which are stamped with
C.Ael.C.—the new name given to the city by the Romans under
Hadrian: Colonia Aelia Capitolina. Thus the picture of changes in the
temple and the city of Jerusalem from the time of Herod until the
new situation following the Second Revolt led by Bar Kochba is
confirmed by the archaeological finds there. Only traces have been
found of the Third Wall, built by the Zealots in a vain effort to
withstand the attack of the Romans in 66-70, when the city was
"surrounded by armies" as Luke puts it in retrospect (Lk 21.20).

II. *Problematical Synagogue Sites in Judea and Galilee*

There is no certain archaeological evidence of a synagogue
building in Jerusalem prior to the fourteenth century C.E., when a
public hall was converted into a synagogue in the Jewish quarter of
Jerusalem. The sole archaeological basis for the claim that there were
synagogues in Jerusalem during the period of the Second Temple is
the standard interpretation of the well-known Theodotus Inscription,
discovered early in the present century and published by Adolf
Deissmann in his landmark work, *Light From the Ancient East*.[3] The
inscription, as Deissmann noted, had been found in a heap of rubble

---

[3] The fourth edition of the German original was published in 1922. The
English translation was published in New York: Harper, n.d., Appendix V,
431-441. The announcement in the public media in August 1991 that a
synagogue dating from the hellenistic period had been excavated in the
Shuafat section of Jerusalem has not been confirmed by publication of
supporting archaeological evidence. A recent survey of leading archaeologists in the USA and Israel concerning this alleged find produced two kinds
of response: (1) most of those whose major interests includes ancient
synagogues had never heard the report, since it did not appear in a scholarly
publication; (2) those who heard the claim dismissed it as an unwarranted
publicity-seeking act by an inexperienced archaeologist. A leading scholar,
Lee Levine of the Seminary of Judaic Studies in Jerusalem said that the
claim lacks any 'substantive evidence,' and that his survey of the site led him
to see that an 'interesting room' had been found, but with no evidence of
any kind that it had ever functioned as a synagogue.

at the bottom of an abandoned cistern. There was no basis for dating it from its context by what would be regarded today as archaeologically reliable criteria. When it was shown to archaeologists and epigraphers shortly after its discovery, they assigned it a date no earlier than the mid-second century. On what is now known to be an erroneous assumption that Jews were not permitted to live in Jerusalem, much less to develop synagogues there after the Second Revolt, Deissmann arbitrarily assigned a pre-70 C.E. date to the inscription. This date has been taken by many scholars as a given, even though S. Safrai[4] has shown that as early as the time of Nerva and Trajan, the Jewish system of limited self-government was operative, not only in relation to religious issues (such as setting the date of the new moon) but also in legal matters such as fines and modes of punishment in accord with Jewish law.[5] The inscription states that Theodotus, who is being honored by the tablet was a ruler of the synagogue, and the son and grandson of synagogue rulers; that he had built the synagogue for the reading of the law and the teaching of the commandments; that it served as a lodging for strangers and pilgrims from abroad; and that the foundation for the building had been laid by fathers and elders, including one Simonides. From this single inscription scholars have inferred that in the first century synagogues were buildings (rather than meetings), and that these structures functioned as places of instruction for local Jewish families and for rabbis-in-training, and also as hostelries for pious pilgrims. The question is, Does the archaeological evidence support this hypothesis?

On the basis of a random sample of opinions which I solicited from some leading current classical epigraphers, it seems clear that the

---

[4] In *Compendia Rerum Judaicarum*, Vol. 1, *The Jewish People in the First Century*, "Jewish Self-Government," Philadelphia: Fortress, 1974, 406-409.

[5] See my article on "The Transformation of the Synagogue after 70 C.E." in *New Testament Studies* 36 (1990), 7-8; and the forthcoming essay in a volume on Galilee in the two centuries before and after the turn of the eras, edited by Lee I. Levine and to be published in Israel.

epigraphic style of the inscription could be as late as the third century C.E., and that it by no means demands a first century date. Excavations of synagogues in Galilee, and of structures alleged to be synagogues, tend to confirm the negative judgment about the date of the Theodotus inscription. The evidence which has been found does, however, clarify the image of both synagogues—and by extension, of the earliest churches—in both Jewish and early Christian sources. Let us survey that evidence.

In Galilee, as we shall note below, the earliest gathering places unambiguously identified as synagogues are from the third and fourth centuries C.E. These remains include inscriptions in Greek, and with the twelve signs of the zodiac in the mosaic pavements and Yahweh represented as Helios in the center, driving the chariot of the sun. It is only in the fifth and sixth century synagogues that the iconography disappears, and the inscriptions are in Hebrew or Aramaic. What is the situation about synagogues in Judea? Excavations at Herodium, Herod's fortress-refuge southeast of Bethlehem, uncovered a meeting room which was first identified as a synagogue used by pious Jews during the First Revolt. Architectural features of what is demonstrably a synagogue, however, are completely lacking. A similar room at Masada, a center for the leaders of the Second Revolt [132-135 C.E.] located near the lower end of the Dead Sea, has been found. Joseph Gutman, however, declares that the evidence is lacking for identifying as synagogues either of these assembly halls excavated at Herodium and Masada.

Two possible candidates for first century C.E. synagogue buildings are those at Gamala and Magdala in Galilee. Similar meeting rooms, with stones benches have been excavated at Magdala and Gamala in Galilee. At neither site is there evidence of Jewish symbolism or any anticipations of the later distinctive features of synagogues. Yet the room at Magdala has been called 'a putative synagogue'[6] and a cautious, provisional identification of the room as Gamala as a

---

[6] J. F. Strange, in *Interpreters' Dictionary of the Bible, Supplement* (Nashville: Abingdon, 1976), article on Magdala.

synagogue[7] has been offered by Gutman, who writes, "Thus, assuming our interpretation is correct (and despite the lack of any conclusive evidence), Gamala would be the earliest known synagogue uncovered so far in Roman Palestine."[8] Z. Ma'oz's observation that at Masada and Herodium, rooms originally built as reception or ceremonial halls seem to have been improvised into houses of worship during the First Revolt[9] seems plausible for these structures at Gamala and Magdala as well.

III. *Synagogues in the Jewish Diaspora*

Further complicating the analysis of the beginnings of the synagogue is the documentary and inscriptional evidence from the Jewish Diaspora across the Mediterranean world, which has been assembled and assessed by Martin Hengel.[10] The oldest inscriptional references to structures for Jewish worship in the diaspora are from Egypt in the 3rd cent. B.C.E. There and in the papyri the standard term is προσευχὴ τῶν Ἰουδαίων and the language is Greek rather than Hebrew or Aramaic. This term was not in common use in Greek, but appears in the LXX in relation to prose prayers and sung hymns. Similarly, Philo depicts these institutions as providing instruction for Jews and thereby confirmation of ethnic identity. One poorly preserved papyrus seems to refer to the group that meets in the προσευχή as a συναγωγή. The oldest preserved papyrus that uses συναγωγή for

---

[7] J. Gutman, in *Ancient Synagogues Revealed*, ed. L. I. Levine (Jerusalem: Israel Exploration Society, and Detroit: Wayne State University Press, 1982).

[8] Gutman, "The Synagogue at Gamla," in *Ancient Synagogues Revealed*, p. 34 (see note 7).

[9] Z. Ma'oz, in *Ancient Synagogues Revealed*, p.35.

[10] In "Proseuche und Synagoge: Jüdische Gemeinde, Gotteshaus und Gottesdienst in der Diaspora und Palästina," originally in a Festschrift for K. G. Kuhn, pp.157-183; now in *The Synagogue: Studies in Origins, Archaeology and Architecture*, ed. J. Gutman (New York: KTAV, 1975).

the place, rather than for the group gathered there dates from 291
C.E. Hengel makes the generalization that this distinction stands in
the Roman inscriptions from the first century C.E. to the time of
Diocletian, and in inscriptions from the Bosphorus and Black Sea
area as well. The merging of the terminology is evident in the writings
of Josephus, who writes about συναγωγαί in Antioch, Dora and
especially in Caesarea, where he is referring to the building, but who
uses προσευχή for the gathering place of Jews in the strongly
hellenized city of Tiberias. In reference to Tarichaeae, he describes a
huge structure (οἴκημα) which he calls a προσευχή, where all the
Jews συνάγονται. Hengel thinks that in general προσευχή was
avoided by Jews in Palestine in order to preserve the distinction
between these indigenous gatherings and the temple in Jerusalem,
which in Isa 56.7 is described as the House of Prayer (בֵּית תְּפִלָּה).
Epiphanius uses προσευχή of the gathering places of Jews near
Nablus and in cities of Asia Minor. Only after the temple had been
destroyed were the terms treated as interchangeable.

More recent analyses of the archaeological evidence from the
synagogues in the cities of the Diaspora add some important dimensions to the evidence. This is conveniently summarized in L. Michael
White's recent book, *Building God's House*.[11] He concentrates on
the six sites where Diaspora synagogues have been responsibly excavated and published: Priene and Sardis in Asia Minor; Stobi in Macedonia; Delos in the Aegean; Ostia at the port of Rome, and Dura
Europos in Syria. Of these six structures, all but one were originally
homes which were transformed from domestic architecture into structures more appropriate for public use. The single exception is the
monumental public building at Sardis, but the fact that Josephus
refers to the gathering place of Jews there as merely a τόπος (that
is, 'place') probably means that there too the group originally met in
a house and then shifted to the more spacious facility as the commu-

---

[11] *Building God's House in the Roman World: Architectural Adaptation
among Pagans, Jews, and Christians.* Baltimore: Johns Hopkins University
Press, 1990.

nity flourished in numbers and resources. From this evidence it seems likely that the setting for a synagogue in the Diaspora was determined by local needs and inclinations rather than by any set pattern of expectations or performance.

At Delos was found what seems to have been the oldest of this surveyed group of synagogue structures. Originally a house of the late second century B.C.E., it was adapted for additional space and ease of public access in the mid-first century B.C.E. There is no evidence of a Torah shrine or of distinctive Jewish symbols. Nearby was found an inscription set up by some people calling themselves 'Israelites' who gathered to 'pay homage to Hallowed Argarizein.' Although no building has been identified as the original meeting place—probably because it was also only a slightly adapted house—it appears that Samaritans likewise gathered in Delos to confirm their identity and link their worship with the God they believed dwelt on Mt Gerizim, which is the meaning of the reference to Argarizein. At Ostia in the second century C.E. a presumably larger and more affluent group of Jews than those in Delos expanded their meeting place from a house to include parts of adjoining structures. Multiple stages of the renovation of originally domestic property is evident there, where what was originally a house had been developed by the fourth century C.E. into a complex that included a dining hall, corridors and a large assembly hall. Similar successive phases of development at Stobi (in what is now Yugoslavia) began in the second or third century C.E. and became a large synagogue hall by the fourth century. In the fifth century this was transformed into a Christian basilica.

More radical transformation is evident at Sardis, where what probably began as a house-based meeting grew to such an extent that it took over the municipal bath-gymnasium complex, and in the second century converted it into a great assembly hall for the Jewish community there. Subsequent renovation and decoration made it into what White has described as "an opulent showpiece for the Jews of Sardis" which continued to function well into the sixth century.[12] At

---

[12] White, op. cit., 74.

Dura Europos in Syria in a block of ten irregularly-shaped dwellings Jews gradually transformed a house into a synagogue building in the mid-second century C.E., including a small assembly hall with a small Torah shrine. In the middle of the third century the exterior was completely changed, and the interior was expanded into a larger assembly hall and an entry forecourt. A neighboring house was linked with the new complex to provide additional meeting space for community functions. In the latest stage, representational art was added, not only depicting events from biblical history but reproducing the signs of the zodiac as well.

In spite of differences in detail, the basic pattern is similar in the evolution of these other diaspora synagogues: they began as house-based informal gatherings of expatriate Jews who met to reinforce shared social and religious traditions. With the destruction of the temple as the symbol and substance of Jewish corporate worship, the gatherings and the structures where they met assumed increasingly formal appearance and practices. In the process of this development, certain features of the contemporary Gentile culture were adopted or adapted by the Jewish communities, as is evident in Galilee as well.

IV. *The Synagogues in Galilee*

Before analyzing the results of excavation of what are unambiguously synagogue buildings in Galilee, it is important to sketch the social and cultural atmosphere of this region in the early centuries of the Common Era. The impact of hellenization from the time of Alexander onward into Roman times in Syria-Palestine and Egypt is obvious, especially in the cities of the Decapolis which were established and developed as hellenistic models, but also in Jerusalem and especially in the new capital built by Herod and his successors at Caesarea Maritima. This city served as the administrative center of Roman power throughout the region. But was not Galilee in the time of Jesus a kind of cultural back-water, bucolic and a preserve for pristine Jewish life and culture? Was not Jesus a product of this rural environment? And did not the pure traditional modes of Jewish piety nurture his faith and ethics? Did this socially and culturally pure area not provide a refuge for the rabbis after the temple was destroyed and Jerusalem was converted by the Romans into a pagan metropolis named Aelia Capitolina?

These romantic images simply do not fit the evidence, historical or cultural. Crossing Galilee were some of the major trade routes of the ancient Near East, linking the major ports of Tyre and Ptolemais/ Acco on the Mediterranean coast with the fruitful district of Galilee, with the hellenistic cities of Damascus and others of the Decapolis east of the Jordan, and with the regions of Arabia and Mesopotamia that produced prize luxury items for the wider Roman world. Sepphoris and later Tiberias were significant centers of Greco-Roman culture, with populations numbering in the tens of thousands. Sepphoris in the time of Herod Antipas (4 B.C.E.-39 C.E.) was made administrative center for Galilee. Later it became the location of the rabbinic council until that was moved to Tiberias. Recent excavations at Sepphoris show that it was a typical Greco-Roman city, with impressive open market areas, public baths, and a theater seating 5000 (which may date from the later first or early second century). The major regional routes converged at Sepphoris and Tiberias.

Sean Freyne, in his study *Galilee from Alexander The Great to Hadrian*[13] details the impact of the cities of Tyre and Ptolemais/Acco on the region of Galilee, as evidenced by the wide use of their coins in the hinterland and the literary evidence for the dependence of these cities on the food produced in Galilee, but he then goes on to downplay the cultural influence of hellenization on Galilee, apart from the major cities, especially Sepphoris and Tiberias—neither of which is mentioned in the New Testament. He notes, for example that Tyre's role as an important agricultural market for Israel in the time of the prophet Ezekiel (Ezek 27.17) was still operative under Herod Agrippa (40-44 C.E.) according to Acts 12.20. He infers that the numismatic evidence from Khirbet Shema in Upper Galilee and from Tell Anafa near Lake Huleh shows commercial links with Tyre. But

---

[13] Wilmington, Del., and Notre Dame, Ind.: Michael Glazier, 1980.

engaging in social psychology at a remove of about two millennia, he simply asserts that aristocratic Jewish cities of Galilee were despised by pious Jews living in the surrounding villages, even though economic necessity required the villagers to maintain daily links with the cities. At the same time he notes the widespread use of Greek among Jews in the area, and goes so far as to assert that "From being a *lingua franca* [Greek] could become a first language for many, but without thereby necessarily indicating a radical break with older [Jewish] tradition."[14]

Although the excavations at Sepphoris are still in progress, what has been excavated confirms what was known from literary sources: that the city was a strategic military site with an arsenal and protective walls, law courts and a royal bank. The excavated remains show that it had the typical colonnaded streets and markets of a hellenistic city, baths and an acropolis. Whether its 5000-seat theater was erected in the early or late first century, or even in the second century, is still in dispute. The main routes that the city overlooked led from Tiberias to Ptolemais/Acco, from Tiberias to Caesarea in the southwest, and from Scythopolis to Ptolemais. The Roman proconsul of Syria (57-55 B.C.E.) located one of the five συνέδρια for the province there. Josephus describes Sepphoris as *autokratis*, since it was the largest and best-fortified city in Galilee.[15]

As M. Broshi has noted, Lower Galilee covered an area of approximately 15 by 25 miles. With its many villages and cities, he concludes that it was one of the most densely populated districts in the entire Roman Empire. The Letter of Aristeas comments on the overpopulation of this area (Aristeas 113) as does Josephus in several of his writings.[16]

Located only five kilometers distance from Sepphoris, the village of Nazareth could not have avoided commercial and cultural

---

[14] Freyne, *Galilee*, 141.

[15] Josephus, *J.W.* 3.511.

[16] Josephus, *J.W.* 3.3.2; *Ant.* 17.11.4; *Life* 45.230.

influences from the major urban center of the region.[17] It is even plausible that construction workers from that village—like Joseph and Jesus—would have found employment most readily in the developing city so close at hand and in the process of development as capital of the district precisely in the early decades of the first century C.E. At the same time, the farmers in the villages would be painfully aware of their bondage to the absentee owners of their lands, as Jesus' parables note. But their links with the larger towns and cities of the region would be constant and would shape their own cultural outlook. The interchange between village and city is dramatically apparent in the ceramic evidence that the pottery produced in one village on the border between Upper and Lower Galilee, now known as Kefer Hananiah, was distributed throughout both sections of Galilee, and pottery produced there and elsewhere in Galilee was shipped across the region and as far north as the Golan.[18] As for Nazareth, in addition to its proximity to Sepphoris, it was even closer (one and a half miles) from Japha, which was on the main road that led from Judah to Sepphoris. Contact with the currents of life and culture in the Roman world could scarcely have been avoided in a village located as Nazareth was.

According to the gospels, when Jesus launched his public activity he moved from his family home in Nazareth to a new base of operations in Capernaum. The romantic image of Capernaum offered by an early generation of biblical scholars as a tiny, isolated fishing village has been shattered by evidence that the town covered approxi-

---

[17] Useful surveys of the evidence for the impact of hellenized urban life on the villages of Galilee in J. Andrew Overman, "Who were the First Urban Christians? Urbanization in Galilee in the First Century" (SBL Papers 1988, 160-168) and Douglas R. Edwards, "First Century Urban/Rural Relations in Lower Galilee: Exploring the Archaeological and Literary Evidence," 169-182.

[18] David Adan-Bayewitz, "Manufacture and Local Trade in the Galilee of Roman-Byzantine Palestine" (Doctoral dissertation at Hebrew University, 1985).

mately 300,000 square meters, which would likely have been occupied by 12,000 to 15,000 inhabitants.[19] Some of the remains lie under the present water level of the lake. A block of dwellings excavated there show the pattern of rooms constructed around a central court, with a staircase leading to the roof, which was constructed of beams, branches, rushes and mud—which fits the Markan account of those who "dug through the roof" of the house where Jesus lived in order to the lower the paralytic before him (Mk 2.1-4).

Two sacred sites there—a synagogue and the House of Saint Peter—both date from the fourth-fifth century, and are both built on top of earlier houses. In spite of what pious Christian pilgrims were told, the synagogue was built 400 years too late for Jesus to have preached there. Josephus refers to Capernaum as a polis, but none of the features of a city—hippodrome, walls, theater—are to be found there. Yet the location of the town on a major trade route along the Sea of Galilee, the presence of a tax collection office, and the recently-found evidence of the harbor and an abundance of fish-hooks show that the town was more than an agricultural village. Residence there would have exposed one to the diverse cultural and ethnic factors operative in this increasingly hellenized part of the Roman world. Contrary to the pronouncements of form-critics earlier in this century who dismissed the stories of Jesus having had contacts with Gentiles as later developments of Pauline Christianity read back into the time of Jesus, we may now see that such incidents as Jesus conversing with a Roman centurion, or visiting in the region of Tyre and Sidon or the cities of the Decapolis are fully credible from the cultural setting of Lower Galilee.

Archaeologically, the late date and architectural simplicity of the synagogue in Capernaum contrast with the evidence from the synagogue at what was apparently a suburb of the much more thoroughly hellenized Galilean city of Tiberias. At Hammat Tiberias the older level of the synagogue dated from the first half of the second century, with a central court and rooms along at least three

---

[19] Estimate in Meyers and Strange, *Archaeology*, 58.

sides—a plan which suggests a public building, although it may have been used as a synagogue. In the third/fourth century structure, however, there is a mosaic pavement with Yahweh as Helios and the twelve signs of the zodiac. More than 50 dedicatory inscriptions in Greek were also found. By the fourth century the transition from synagogue as a group meeting in available space for study and worship to synagogue as distinctive structure and institution was well advanced. In the latter years of the first century C.E., Josephus in his *Life* (277) refers to what was later to be designated a synagogue as a προσευχή, which he describes as an assembly hall for a community.

V. *Συναγωγή in The New Testament*

In the New Testament there is only one text which uses συναγωγή unambiguously as a reference to a building. This is Lk 7.5, where a Roman centurion is reported by some Jews to have 'built us our synagogue.' In all other texts the force of the passage may well be understood if the connotation of the term 'synagogue' is taken to be the gathering, wherever it may have met, and not the meeting place itself. In all four of the gospels this usage is represented (Mk 1.21; 6.2; Mt 6.2; Lk 12.11; Jn 6.59), where a meeting is implied. Possible hints of formalization are offered in what I regard as a late tradition in Mt 23.6, where there is condemnation of those who "love the first seats in the synagogue." Even mention of the rulers of the synagogues may also be merely a designation of one who heads an organized community (Mk 5.22; Lk 8.41; Mt 9.18?), rather than one in charge of a formal ceremony in an institutionalized structure. Also significant, and yet little noted by scholars, is the frequent contrast implied between the Jewish and the Christian meetings by the distinction between 'their' or 'your' synagogues, and those which are implicitly 'ours,' (that is, the Christians'). This feature is especially common in Matthew 4.23; 9.35; 10.17; 12.9; 13.54; 23.24, but also appears in Mark 1.23. Thus there are two kinds of informal meetings of the pious: those of the Jews and those of the Christians.

Similarly, in Acts most of the references to synagogue make sense if understood as referring primarily to the gathering rather than to a distinctive structure. This is the case with Paul's initial activity in Damascus (Acts 9.2), and his preaching in Cyprus (13.5), Iconium (14.1), Thessalonica (17.1) and Beroea (17.10).

A shift in location of the Christian meeting at Corinth is mentioned in Acts 18 and at Ephesus in Acts 19. In both cases, the details are revealing. When Paul was expelled from the synagogue in Corinth, he shifted his base of operations to the house next door (Acts 18.6-8). The inscription found early in this century in Corinth reading in Greek, Συναγωγὴ Ἑβραίων, is epigraphically from a considerably later date than the time of Paul. The first century synagogue in Corinth depicted in Acts would have met in a house from which Paul moved to an adjacent house, where the Christians began to meet. Another possible type of location for a synagogue is indicated in the report in Acts 19.8-10 that with Paul's departure from the synagogue in Ephesus he shifted location to presumably rented quarters in the σχολή of Tyrannus. This also fits the pattern of locating gatherings wherever appropriate and suitable space for study and worship was available. Further, one can discern parallel developments between the house or public hall bases for συναγωγαί on one hand and for Christians on the other, who chose to designate themselves by an analogous Greek term for gatherings, ἐκκλησίαι. The familiar house-church phenomenon had its antecedent model in what we might call the house-synagogue. Only later are special adaptations of existing structures made in order to provide facilities for the meetings. It is in such a late strand of the New Testament tradition as Luke-Acts, which I should want to date no earlier than the first decade of the second century, that there is a reference to *building* a synagogue.

The shift in meaning of συναγωγή from a meeting to a meeting-place has a rough analogue in the change in significance of συνέδριον to Sanhedrin. The term συνέδριον was used throughout the hellenistic and Roman periods for local councils and courts to which the central royal or imperial power assigned a considerable degree of authority for decision-making in a given region. We have noted above that one was established by the Romans in Sepphoris. It is such an institution in Jerusalem that is mentioned in the gospels as conducting the initial inquiry about the legality of Jesus' activities. Their decision was to turn his case over to the procurator, Pontius Pilate. In the process of development of Mishnah and Talmud, a religious council was set up by the Jewish leaders to make decisions on their own internal disputes about interpretation and applicability of their law. To this body was assigned the borrowed title of Sanhedrin, even though the function as indicated in the tractate that bears that name indicates, was very different from the role and authority of the συνέδριον in the gospel accounts.

This historical conclusion from archaeological evidence concerning the evolution of the synagogue in the first and early second centuries C.E. is matched by the historical and literary investigations carried out by Jacob Neusner over the past two decades.[20] In his studies of the origins of rabbinic Judaism and of its basic documents, the Mishnah and Talmud, he showed that the Pharisees were originally a lay reform movement among Jews who sought to strengthen identity and commitment of Jews to their tradition and hopes of renewal by home-based study of scripture and informal worship. They worked to appropriate the standards of the Mosaic law in such a way as to establish and maintain a distinctive identity of their group as the people of God, as would be implicit in their self-designation as *Perushim*, 'the separate ones.' After the failure of the nationalist revolt of 66-70, they took courage—perhaps with encouragement from the Roman authorities in view of the group's non-political stance—in defining the scriptural basis on which they operated and by fostering worship, discussion and study in ways which developed into rabbinic Judaism and which in the period from the second to the sixth

---

[20] Jacob Neusner, hundreds of publications build on the foundational work he did in *The Rabbinic Traditions about the Pharisees Before 70*, 3 vols. (Leiden: E.J. Brill, 1971); also *Meaning and Method in Ancient Judaism* (Chico, CA: Scholars Press, 1981), and *Formative Judaism: Religious, Historical and Literary Studies* (Scholars Press, 1985).

centuries produced the literary materials for documentation and direction that we know as the Mishnah and Talmud.

The changing nature of the archaeological evidence concerning the synagogue from the first to the fifth centuries fits well with this historical reading of the literary evidence. The period of synthesis with Greco-Roman literary, conceptual and artistic features which is evident in the writings and archaeological remains down to the fourth century is then balanced by a repudiation of these conceptual and artistic features in the fifth and sixth centuries. Conversely, the establishment of Christianity under Constantine and the dominant influence on it by his successors, beginning in the fourth century, were to lead the church in a very different direction of synthesizing Greco-Roman thought and culture with the Christian tradition. But analysis of the material from the centuries before and after the change of eras during this period of cultural synthesis from both the Jewish and the Christian side enables the interpreter of the biblical material to perceive more clearly how the leaders of both these movements were able to engage their contemporaries across the traditional cultural and ethnic boundaries of that time, and how they were able to speak to needs, hopes and anxieties that transcended those cultural limits.

RESPONSE: Eric M. Meyers

The following observations are made with the full realization that they may be contradicted or modified by the chance discovery of a shepherd, as was the case with the discovery of the Dead Sea Scrolls in 1947, or by the results of a scientific excavation. The report in August 1991 from Israel that a late hellenistic synagogue was uncovered in a rescue excavation in the northern area of Jerusalem known as Shuafat certainly raises many serious question about the Second Temple period synagogue and Jewish religiosity at the time of Jesus. This discovery also reminds us of the delicate balance in historical reconstruction between texts and monuments.[1] In archaeology at least, the answers always lie below.

The topics I have chosen to discuss, albeit very briefly, hopefully will reflect upon the dynamic and changing character of the field that is the topic for our discussions. If I were to select a single American scholar who more than any other contributed to launching the general field that might be called 'the archaeology of early Judaism' I would name the late Erwin R. Goodenough, author of the programmatic work, *Jewish Symbols in the Greco-Roman World.* Though this series (13 volumes) has been rightly criticized for its overarching theory of hellenistic Judaism and the origins of early Christianity, as well as for its uncritical approach to dating artifacts, more than any other biblical scholar Goodenough placed non-written sources on the agenda of New Testament studies and scholars of early Judaism. In Jewish studies and in Israel I would name the late Michael

---

[1] E. M. Meyers, "Judaic Studies and Archaeology: The Legacy of Avi-Yonah," *Eretz-Israel* 19 (1987), pp. 21-27.

ERIC M. MEYERS is Professor of Religion at Duke University, Durham, NC; Director of the Annenberg Institute for Judaic and Near Eastern Research, Philadelphia, PA.; and editor of *Biblical Archaeologist.*

Avi-Yonah, whose achievements I have applauded in a Festschrift.[2]
His synthetic works in Jewish history and archaeology, historical geography, and Jewish art set him apart from many other Israeli
contemporaries, whose work may be in many ways just as distinguished, could not and did not impact so many sub-fields of Judaica
as did the work of Avi-Yonah. In this connection I would mention
the following other luminaries: the late Eliezer L. Sukenik and his son
Yigael Yadin, and Benjamin Mazar, and Nahman Avigad.

I. *Literacy and Belles Lettres*

While other presentations in this symposium are devoted to the
general area of the study of language and literature I wanted to begin
my presentation with a few comments on the questions of literacy and
belles lettres in the period under consideration.

Although the amount of written materials uncovered in Palestine
from the early hellenistic period is fairly limited, numerous scholarly
conclusions regarding this era are pertinent. First and foremost is the
consensus that at least two segments of the Hebrew Bible, Torah and
Prophets, were completed and redacted no later than the end of the
Persian period (ca. 4th century B.C.E.) and that most of the third
segment, the Hagiographa, was also available in a more or less fixed
form at this time. This means that an extraordinary effort on the part
of the Jewish community was expended from ca. 550-350 in editing,
redacting, and promulgating the major portions of the Hebrew Bible
in their proto-Massoretic form, i.e. in the form that was to become
normative in Judaism at least after 70 C.E.

---

[2] *Editors note:* Archaeological authorities in Israel assert that the claim
that a room excavated from the hellenistic period was a synagogue lacks any
substantive evidence. The young and inexperienced archaeologist who made
this claim was given wide publicity by the popular media, but no credence
from responsible archaeologists. No formal report and no evidence to
support the claim have been produced. The room is said to be architecturally interesting but to be wholly lacking in features which would indicate its
use as a synagogue when compared with the oldest examples which have
been responsibly excavated and reported.

By the third century B.C.E. there was a similar effort expended to make the Hebrew Scriptures more accessible by translating them into Greek. We know the results of that to have been the early Greek translation of the Bible, ultimately to be known as the Septuagint. The lively, inquisitive and increasingly cosmopolitan world that was the third century B.C.E. is also reflected in the famous Greek archives of ancient records, the Zenon papyri.

But equally as important in this connection are the Dead Sea Scrolls themselves, which represent a level of literary creativity that extends far beyond the canonical boundaries of Scripture. We know also that the date of composition and place of origin of many of these extra-canonical compositions extend far beyond the chronological and geographical confines of the Qumran community to the heart of Judea itself, where the majority of the Jewish community resided. The languages were mainly Hebrew, Greek, and Aramaic, and their scope and breadth embrace the highest compositional standard of the time; some of those documents are also dated to the pre-Qumran era, i.e. the third century. The publication of the remaining documents in the coming years will doubtless shed additional light on the all-important matters of place of origin, genre, and date of many of these compositions.

II. *Hellenism and Regionalism*

The aftermath of Alexander the Great's introduction of Hellenism into the Levant was nothing less than earthshaking and epochal. If the first century after his conquests represents an age in which the local Semitic population gingerly flirted with the new culture, the second century after Alexander revealed the true parameters of a struggle between two initially colliding worldviews that ultimately were to be supportive of one another. The second century B.C.E., however, in which the Maccabees fought to oppose the incursion of a new world order was also the century in which the Hasmonean leadership installed a series of administrations that actively sponsored a program of accommodation to hellenism in a style of leadership that was inspired by hellenistic tyrants.

Contrary to the commonly-held view that Palestine was thoroughly hellenized at an early stage in the Second Temple period, I am
inclined to view the process as a much more complex series of developments, with the heyday of accommodation coming in the middle
Roman period, i.e. around the third century C.E. Herod the Great's
active sponsorship of hellenistic and Roman architecture and the
decorative arts, while it literally succeeded in brightening the material
world of Jesus and the sages with frescoes and mosaics, resulted mainly in the hardening of intellectual positions that were uniquely
Semitic.

To put it another way, by the first Christian century despite
enormous inroads of hellenism in language, literature, and in material
culture, Palestine had retained its unique character. The Jewish
population still eschewed immortality of the soul and clung to its
traditional view of resurrection; they adopted a more or less fixed
corpus of biblical books as normative in their community, albeit with
competing and fluid views of what many of those books would be;
and developed a system of biblical interpretation or hermeneutic that
they could claim as their own, despite the fact that some Roman
rhetorical rules were employed in doing so.

Some geographical areas remained relatively immune to or isolated from the major characteristics of hellenism, namely, language,
literature, and material culture, such as the Upper Galilee or Tetracomia, and the Golan, also known as Gaulanitis. Other areas closer
to the oriental cities were touched more deeply by hellenistic culture:
along the main roads, e.g., the Via Maris, in the Rift Valley, alongside the coastal port cities, and in some corners of the Lower Galilee.
Sepphoris, for example, was presumably beautified by Herod Antipas
early in the first century but it is fairly clear to me that the character
of the place remained very Jewish in the first century and that the
great theater there was built only after Roman legionnaires moved
into the area after the two great wars with Rome in 70 and 135 C.E.

In short, the character of hellenism in Palestine was greatly
affected by the changing demographics of the Jewish and oriental
non-Jewish population between 66 and 135 C.E. The chief result of

the two wars with Rome was that Jewish attitudes towards Rome shifted once again toward accommodation and compromise. Indeed, so great was the impact of the second, Bar Kochba War, that the Jewish community more or less disavowed political power and sovereignty for nearly two millennia, save perhaps for the so-called Gallus Revolt of 351-2 C.E.

III. *The Ancient Synagogue*

The emergence of the ancient synagogue in the second to fourth centuries C.E. as the main vehicle for Jewish self-expression as a community and the study of it as institution and unique sacred structure provide extremely fertile ground for understanding the extent of change that had impacted Jewish society in the Roman era. Whether or not there were one or four Second Temple synagogues or hundreds, as Josephus would have us believe, is secondary to the mere fact that the synagogue more than any other institution enabled Judaism to be portable and to survive the traumatic challenges brought about by the Roman wars.

From an archaeological standpoint the earliest Galilean synagogue is the broadhouse synagogue of the mid second century at Nabratein. A genuine upsurge in the construction of synagogue buildings seems to occur in the third century, which from my point of view coincides with the floruit of Palestinian Judaism on the eve of the rapid spread of Christianity after Emperor Constantine's conversion. Surprisingly perhaps, the momentum of that activity extended well into the fourth century, despite a high inflation rate and years of severe drought. In third century Sepphoris, for example, there are reported to have been eighteen synagogues in a city of 20,000-25,000 inhabitants. The cultural ambiance is best epitomized by the now famed Dionysos mosaic with its Greek labels and endearing portrait of the 'Mona Lisa of Galilee.' All of these developments occur concurrently during the Patriarchate of Rabbi Judah the Prince, editor and redactor of the Mishnah promulgated at Sepphoris.

There is also speculation that prior to the fourth century the Judaeo-Christians of Palestine also prayed in synagogues, which we cannot properly identify. In any event the synagogue as architectural entity adopts both the Roman basilica and the old Syro-Palestinian temple in its form and calls upon both native Jewish, Greco-Roman, and pagan symbols to adorn its walls and floors. By using a raised platform or βῆμα in its liturgy the Jewish community demonstrated their abiding recognition of the central authority of the Bible in their lives. The Torah Shrine (or sacred ark and sacred niche) reinforces that idea also. The idea of a wall of orientation, pointing to Jerusalem, moreover, illustrated their loyalty to the holy city and its Temple and past traditions.

The synagogue in Jewish tradition is sacred because of what transpires there—it does not draw its sanctity from the place itself. Moreover, the sanctity of the place moves with the living community; and so in Jewish law you cannot sell or destroy a synagogue without building a new one. Nor does Jewish law permit one to lower its status even should it be destroyed and lie in ruins. Therefore the sanctity of a community can only truly be reflected in the norms of that community as expressed in worship, law, and in the acts of loving kindness to other human beings. The colorful mosaic floors which adorn the synagogues at Hammat Tiberias or Naaran near Jericho or at Ein Gedi illustrate how at home were the Jews of Palestine in Greco-Roman culture in late antique Palestinian society.

The legacy of the synagogue in western civilization is such that the church and mosque bear many of its salient features: sacred orientation, the raised platform, and sacred niche to name but a few. But in their very nature all three give eloquent testimony to the sacred writings, the Bible and the Koran. Archaeology has illuminated this three-fold heritage as no other discipline.

IV. *Jewish Burial Practice*

The unusual and varied manner in which Jews interred and re-buried their dead in Roman Palestine demonstrates the tenacity with which they clung to traditional, Semitic patterns of thinking about afterlife. The decorated coffins or sarcophagi in which they buried some of their dead—like much of the data already mentioned—also suggest a gradual accommodation to hellenistic customs and decorative techniques by the third century C.E. Furthermore, the tombs and catacombs in which these containers were deposited and in which a variety of burial customs were carried out reveal as much about Judaism in the rabbinic period as any other corpus of data from the period. On the other hand the inability of scholars to identify definitively any Christian burials prior to the fourth century in Syro-Palestine suggests strongly that Christian self-definition and beliefs were more closely aligned with Judaism than is normally believed.

The excavations in Beth She'arim fifty years ago, for example, demonstrated the remarkable extent to which the rabbis had adopted both Greco-Roman decorative elements in their art and how at home in Greek language they were. Approximately 80% of all the inscriptions found there are in Greek, a number of them exhibiting intimate familiarity with the highest standards of contemporary Attic poetry. In addition, the vast majority of burials there, approximately two out of three, are reburials from elsewhere, many from outside the land of Israel. The chronological span of this data is the second to the middle of the fourth century C.E. The custom of reburial or ossilegium testifies vividly to the growing centrality of the land in rabbinic eschatology and to the emerging notion of expiatory suffering as a category of posthumous existence linked to either a strict view of resurrection or immortality.

The necropolis at Beth She'arim would appear to have been destroyed around 352 in the so-called Revolt of Gallus, possibly the last gasp of Jewish nationalism. In any case either this event or the great 363 earthquake, the same year as Emperor Julian embarked on an abortive attempt to rebuild the Temple in Jerusalem, or both, marked the end of an era in Roman Palestine. The Jerusalem Talmud was never completed and the focus of attention in Jewish history shifted to Babylonia. In my view the catacombs in Italy, Malta, Sardinia, Sicily, and North Africa attest to the flight and condition of the Jew in the Diaspora sometime toward the end of the Roman period. The adoption of that style of communal burial by the early

Christians also testifies to the healthy state of relations between the two communities.

V. *Conclusions*

The changing patterns of Jewish thought as reflected in the archaeology of Roman Palestine may be partially explained as arising out of the disappointments with history after the two Roman wars. But equally, it seems to me, can it be explained as a result of Judaism's now open embrace of hellenistic culture without the fear of defilement or ideological challenge. It was a period of cultural symbiosis rather than syncretism. The emerging confrontation with Christianity, however, did not always produce constructive results, and whereas Judaism in Palestine seemed on the upsurge prior to Constantine, by the mid-fourth century construction of new synagogues and other buildings is down and there appears to be a demographic shift if not departure of Jews from Palestine proper.

From the vantage point of archaeology the emergence of Judaism in Roman Palestine may be viewed as a steady accommodation to hellenism in the most constructive sense. While ultimately Jewish and Semitic ways of understanding the world and afterlife were modified to some extent, the clash of cultures created a dynamic synergism that is reflected in the Dionysos villa at Sepphoris in the time when Rabbi Judah produced the Mishnah there, in the catacombs of Beth She'arim during the heyday of the sages when they often decorated their coffins with Greek mythological scenes, and in the synagogues which often remind one of Roman basilicas. But despite these outward signs of hellenism, Palestinian Judaism charted a course in religious history that was true to its biblical moorings and Semitic heritage.

There is no doubt also that Judaism remained a religion and culture that paid unique and extraordinary homage to the sacred book. The influence of the Bible was such that it spawned an unending series of commentaries on it. So important was its message that in synagogues it was read only upon a raised platform, could be read in many languages, and frequently depended on translators to spread its word. Whoever cannot discern and hear the "still small voice" of Scripture in the mute stones of the archaeological record has failed truly to touch the past of ancient Israel.

For further reading:

Levine, L. I., ed., *The Synagogue in Late Antiquity*. ANSOR and The Jewish Theological Seminary of America: Durham, 1987.

Meyers, E. M., "Synagogue." The *Anchor Bible Dictionary*, Doubleday: 1992.

_____, Netzer, E., and C. L. Meyers, *Sepphoris*. Eisenbrauns: Winona Lake, 1992.

_____, and J. F. Strange. *Archaeology, The Rabbis, and Early Christianity*. Abingdon: Nashville, 1981.

RESPONSE: Roger S. Boraas

Let's make a couple of things clear from the beginning. First, I'm no New Testament scholar. I recognize the superior grasp of the materials which Professor Kee has made the subject of his illustrious career, and I express gratitude for the benefits that I have received from his work as my teacher.

Second, I'm no expert on synagogue excavation, such as you have in my friend, your prior respondent, Professor Eric Meyers. His work on synagogues in the Upper Galilee and other regions has been unmatched in our generation, and is here cheerfully celebrated.

If by now you are wondering how I am here at all, let me say that my approach is that of a person primarily interested in field archaeological methods of recording practices, and that will be reflected in this response. With that clarification, I would make three comments on the presentation and the archaeological situation behind it.

I. *Focus Points in the Field Have Changed*

First, with Jack Finegan's publication of *The Archaeology of the New Testament*[1] twenty-two years ago, the biblical student was given a range of evidence purporting to reflect archaeology's contribution to that segment of biblical studies. While it opened with a review of sites associated with John the Baptist and with Jesus, the range of special evidence sections encompassed Tombs, Catacombs, Sarcophagi, Ossuaries and a special study of the Cross mark. Focus in the site reviews was on architecture, including floor plans, mosaic designs,

---

[1] Jack Finegan, *The Archaeology of the New Testament* (Princeton: Princeton University Press, 1969).

ROGER BORAAS is Professor of Religion at Upsala College, East Orange, New Jersey.

sundry building inscriptions and some art motifs, but there was not a single plate of pottery profiles or any artifact material analysis. There were no studies of wood involved. Neither were there any examinations of lithics, either construction or decorative material. The sole presentations of ceramics were in photos and drawings of inscribed material. No numismatic analyses were included despite extensive materials available illustrating the coinage of the times. No correlations of either numismatic or ceramic evidence with the relevant stratigraphy were presented. And of course, it was simply too early to have available such details as the particular evidence of crucifixion technique which has since been made available from analysis of the ossuary at Giv'at Ha-Mivtar.[2] Nor were the more recent rolling stone tombs on the east bank of the Jordan available for report and comparison.[3]

That things have changed drastically is most sharply put by Professor Kee's attention to social and economic pattern studies now affecting our views of Nazareth, and the observation that pottery from Kefer Hananiah was distributed throughout both Upper and Lower Galilee and shipped as far as the Golan. The latter is now likely to be concluded on stylistic and ware observations alone, but is subject to proof by analysis of the clay used in the manufacture. The same techniques allow for identification for the source clay beds from which the raw materials were drawn. The precision of materials

---

[2] For reassessment of the evidence see Joseph Zias and Eliezer Sekeles, "The Crucified Man from Giv'at Ha-Mivtar—A Re-appraisal" in *Biblical Archaeologist* 48:3 (September 1985): 190-191.

[3] See preliminary report on the excavation of Tomb F.1 at Tell Hesban in Roger S. Boraas and Siegfried H. Horn, eds., *Heshbon 1971: The Second Campaign at Tell Hesban: A Preliminary Report* in Andrews University Monographs VI (Berrien Springs, Mich.: Andrews University Press, 1973): 115-117. See also the preliminary report on the excavation of Tomb G.10 at Tell Hesban in Roger S. Boraas and Lawrence T. Geraty, eds., Heshbon 1974: *The Fourth Campaign at Tell Hesban: A Preliminary Report* in Andrews University Monographs IX (Berrien Springs, Mich: Andrews University Press, 1976) 103-106.

analysis is what is allowing very precise tracing of trade patterns and the lines of economic interdependence that exchanges of trade goods provided for ancient communities.

II. *When is a House a Synagogue?*

Second, taking a referent from Kee's argument that before the mid-second century the synagogue (as also the earliest church) was a community likely meeting in an ordinary home rather than a specialized building, one can ask what, archaeologically, would be helpful in identifying such 'home' sites as functioning locations of synagogue communities. What to look for may be suggested by Meyers' studies of the synagogues excavated at Nabratein, located in the Upper Galilee but with social and economic connections more to the south. Field work done in 1980-1981 indicated a series of three synagogues, the middle of which went through two phases of construction and rebuild. Times involved the years 135-250 for Synagogue 1, 250-350/363 for Synagogue 2, and 564-700 for Synagogue 3.[4] The physical evidence of Synagogue 1 (our chief interest for providing clues) was excavated primarily in the 1980 season, and comprised a building 11.2 m. x 9.36 m. (exterior) with some benching on the eastern wall, and partial evidence of some βῆμα (step, seat, platform?) construction along the south wall.[5] Evidences of roof support were problematic. A depression in the center of the internal floor was conjectured to have been the location of a wooden lectern

---

[4]   Eric M. Meyers, James F. Strange, Carol L. Meyers, "Second Preliminary Report on the 1981 Excavations at en-Nabratein, Israel" in *Bulletin of the American Schools of Oriental Research* (hereafter *BASOR*) 246 (Spring 1982), 35.

[5]   Eric M. Meyers, James F. Strange, Carol L. Meyers, Joyce Raynor, "Preliminary Report on the 1980 Excavations at en-Nabratein, Israel" in *Bulletin of the American Schools of Oriental Research* 244 (Fall 1981), 7-10, and *BASOR* 246, 40.

or other item of liturgical furniture.[6] Ceramic and numismatic evidences fit the Roman style and motif profiles for the Early and Middle Roman periods [Early dated to 1-135 C.E., Middle to 135-250].[7] They contributed significantly to the dating by their deposit location in a sealed fill under the earliest synagogue floor. "The ceramic material beneath the plastered floor of this building and from the foundation deposits at all four walls was uniformly Early Roman to Middle Roman, with no later material."[8]

So what might show archaeologically that a 'house' was functionally a synagogue? Architecturally, the house may have been of the broad house or other design, with a central room and adjacent rooms on the sides. It may have been fitted with benches, some form of βῆμα, and possibly a lectern. In addition, one might expect some form of Torah Ark (firmly attested in the later Nabratein structures by both stone carved pediment and incised pottery).[9] The ark may have been portable and might have been made of wood (perishability our biggest problem here). Were any ceremonial lamps used? And should there have been some standard symbols of the community's life? From the obvious evidences of later structures and furnishings, one would expect regular symbols such as a menorah (incised on a lintel of Synagogues 2 and 3 at Nabratein),[10] possibly stamped or incised pottery, or representations common in later mosaics and catacomb decorations such as shophar, lulab (springs), or ethrog (citrus).[11] Then there's always the hope for additional inscriptions.

When one considers 1) that archaeology is dependent on a

---

[6] *BASOR* 246, 40.

[7] *BASOR* 246, 35.

[8] *BASOR* 246, 36.

[9] *BASOR* 246, 42 and *BASOR* 244, 21-24.

[10] *BASOR* 244, 4, Fig. 2.

[11] J. Gutman, "Art, Early Jewish" in *The Interpreter's Dictionary of the Bible* (Nashville: Abingdon, 1976) Supplementary Volume: 69.

society's material production evidences as clues, 2) that only a small percentage of what ancient peoples produced as material artifacts survives the ravages of decay or deliberate destruction, and 3) that only a small proportion of what survives is likely to be found by the limited efforts of excavation, one may grow skeptical about the chances of solving our question archaeologically at all. For a vast majority of the evidences likely to be recovered from any house, their significance for our question is neutral at best. I refer to such items as the location and orientation of the building, and the occurrence of coins, pottery, tools, weapons, toys, or ordinary furnishings. Was a house-synagogue fitted with benches at all, or were the activities served by wooden stools, long decayed and gone? Were the rituals served by ordinary household types of pottery, now indistinguishable from everyday family wares? Were the essentials, such as a Torah Ark also made of perishable materials, thus gone and beyond recovery? And what of the symbolism? Were the symbols carried primarily on cloth, leather, or wooden equipment and hangings, thus rendering their survival and recovery next to impossible? Given present techniques of data recovery, the task is complex at best.

III. *Wither the Process?*

Third, a final comment comes from growing complexities within the archaeological discipline itself. Increased technological applications in chemistry, physics, biology, and geology have drastically improved our capacity to learn from small bits of data. However, the shift of focus to increasingly broader anthropological interests on the part of large numbers of field archaeologists in the younger generation of scholars, leaves the specter of a diminishing supply of folk interested in relating the results of field research to biblical problems of this sort. The large investment now required of any expedition to do justice to environmental studies, from pollen to bone pathology, from butchering techniques to neutron activation analyses of clays and pottery manufacture and distribution, yields a growing shortage of money. The range of expertise needed at the field site continues to expand. Sampling to allow accurate data recovery is sometimes highly specialized. Needs are there for palynologists (the study of spores and pollens), paleobotanists, paleozoologists, metallurgists, ornithologists, hydrologists, entomologists, and physical anthropologists just to deal with material analyses which reflect the environment of the settlement. Attention for the illumination of biblical history, everyday life in biblical times, and details of possible correlation with biblical texts has to profit from the wide ranging new computerized statistical studies of social and physical contexts. One can only urge that encouragement and support be given to scholars interested to keep that quest alive and healthy. It may be that both theological training institutions and the best programs in Ancient Near East studies in major research universities will need to mount closer cooperation to make that happen.

New Approaches to Understanding and Study of the Bible

Katharine Doob Sakenfeld

I. *Introduction*

In 1971, just twenty years ago, retiring Harvard University president Nathan Pusey spoke of an upcoming era of "radically altered conditions, sharp change, and formidable obstacles..."[1] Pusey was speaking of the future of education in the United States, but his words are applicable to changes in biblical scholarship as well. The year of Pusey's address was the very year I completed my Ph.D. work, and after two decades I still respond at a personal as well as a professional level.

A chief theme and source of excitement during my graduate years had been the possibility that scholars from different religious traditions, Protestant, Catholic, and Jewish, could at last study the Hebrew Bible in common and in conversation, able to use a common critical methodology, a critical methodology that could be shared and appreciated even by scholars who did not see themselves as adhering to any religious group that regarded the Bible as foundational to its faith. I remember rejoicing in that commonality, being delighted to share a method with people of very different religious background from myself. Yet there have been "sharp changes" in the past twenty years, and we already work in "radically altered conditions." That is not at all to say that the old barriers among religious groups such as

---

[1] *Harvard Magazine,* July-August 1991, p. 89.

KATHERINE DOOB SAKENFELD is Professor of Old Testament Literature and Director of Ph.D. Studies, Princeton Seminary, Princeton, N.J.

Catholic, Protestant, Jew have re-arisen, but rather that a whole new series of divisions have emerged. The consensus concerning method in biblical studies, which was probably already showing signs of crumbling as early as 1971, has all but disappeared, and a host of new questions have arisen both about how to study the biblical text and about what in the biblical text deserves our special attention.

When those who organized this Symposium discussed with me their ideas for the focus of this lecture, two themes emerged. The first goal was to sketch some of the newer approaches to biblical studies in the scholarly community; the second was to suggest something of how the Bible is appropriated by communities of faith and what the role of the academic study of the Bible might be or become in the lives of those faith communities. In the preceding statement of the task of this lecture, the words 'sketch' and 'suggest' are very important; even at that level the task seems most challenging.

Because the task is so vast, I have elected to approach each of the two goals by way of concrete illustration. I will look at the question of new scholarly approaches concretely by reviewing recent scholarly discussion of Numbers 12, a story about Moses, Miriam, Aaron, and a Cushite woman. A spate of recent publications on this text illustrates many of the new directions of scholarly inquiry and its methodological uncertainty. The second part of the presentation then moves into the question of appropriation in faith communities by describing three methods of Bible study that are typically used in small groups in Christian churches, with comments about what each method presupposes about how the Bible functions authoritatively for its users.

The concluding section of the presentation will work from these illustrations to identify possible connections and discontinuities between the life and work of the scholarly and religious communities.

I. *New Approaches and the Study of Numbers 12*

My discussion of Numbers 12 will not be burdened with many details of scholarly argument. Nor do I intend to present a systematic exegesis or even to give you my own conclusions about the interpretation of the text. Rather I hope to show how the approaches to the

Bible that have come to prominence in recent years involve changes in two realms of questions. The first category of questions concerns which passages deserve one's attention. How is a passage chosen for study out of all the pages of the canon? Here there are several possibilities. A scholar may have an interest in a particular method as such (e.g. some form of literary criticism, social world investigation, or structural analysis) and selects a text that appears amenable to the heuristic use of that method. Or, a scholar may have an agenda of subject matter in biblical studies (such as the historical reconstruction of a given period or some specific aspect of Israel's worship) that may lead him or her to focus on a text that contributes to that discussion. It is important for our purposes here to recognize that such bases for selection of a text are not in fact 'neutral' but are grounded in the scholar's 'social location' within particular subcultures of the academic community. Other bases for selection of a text for study also relate to 'social location' in different ways. Prominent among these in the contemporary North American scene are choices of texts based on their focus on women, or on questions pertinent to racial-ethnic heritage or interaction between racial groups, or on issues of economic justice. Such texts may be chosen not only by women or members of under-represented racial-ethnic groups, or poor people, but by anyone whose life circumstances draw the person to a high degree of interest in those texts. To summarize, then, every scholar has social locations both in society generally and in the methodological subcultures of biblical scholarship. Both aspects of social location are leading scholars to focus on many texts that formerly did not receive special attention. Numbers 12 is among these.

The question of which passage will be studied is interlocked with a second question: Which method or methods a scholar will bring to the text? The general history of biblical scholarship has involved the adaptation of methods from other realms of scholarly inquiry to the study of the Bible, and that history continues in the emergence of new methods applied to the biblical text in the past twenty years. The emergence of social world studies, literary criticism of various sorts, and structural studies (also of various sorts) are perhaps the most conspicuous additions to the traditional repertoire of methods. The last two, the literary and structuralist inquiries, may present special challenges in that they seem to many to be the least compatible with (or the least in dialogue with the results of) the previously established repertoire of methods.

Given this general methodological background, let us turn to Numbers 12. This chapter recounts the challenge made by Miriam and Aaron to the authority of Moses. Since this is a part of the Bible that may not be remembered in detail by everyone, a word of introduction to its content is in order. The NRSV of the opening lines reads, "... Miriam and Aaron spoke against Moses because of the Cushite woman whom he had married (for he had indeed married a Cushite woman); and they said, "Has the LORD spoken only through Moses? Has he not spoken through us also?" And the LORD heard it." As the story unfolds, God calls all three leaders to the tent of meeting and gives a speech (the Hebrew of which is difficult poetry) vindicating Moses. Then Miriam is stricken with a disease that leaves her "white as snow." Aaron asks Moses that they not be punished, and Moses asks God to heal Miriam. God decrees that Miriam must be put outside the camp for seven days, but may then return. The people wait to continue their wilderness journey until Miriam returns to the camp.

Certain basic questions to be tackled in studying this narrative have been recognized all along (beginning with the Rabbis and continuing with the earliest critical scholars): Who was the Cushite wife? Where was Cush? What is the heart of Miriam and Aaron's complaint? On what grounds is Moses vindicated? Why is only Miriam punished, not Aaron? What is the nature of her affliction? When, if at all, is she healed?

The degree of scholarly attention given to each of these questions, however, has varied widely. Modern commentaries representing the use of the more traditional tools of biblical scholarship focus on the unique status of Moses as the center of the passage.[2] Scholars

---

[2] E.g. P. Budd in the Word series, A. Noordtzij in the Bible Student's

interested in the history of Israel's religion have concentrated on the probable function of the passage in the era of the monarchy, with some proposing that it was meant to adjudicate a dispute between competing priesthoods (Aaronid and Mushite) during the period of the monarchy,[3] while others argue that the passage addressed a dispute about prophetic authority in relation to Mosaic tradition.[4]

Several new emphases and trends have emerged rapidly in the last two decades, however. We will be looking at four examples of new approaches, which may be subdivided into two broad types: 1) methodological approaches, illustrated by literary analysis and structural analysis, and 2) perspectival approaches, illustrated by feminist analysis and African-American analysis. (The absence of social world studies from the recent scholarly literature on this text may be accidental, or it may reflect the difficulties inherent in relating the questions of that method to this genre of biblical material.)

We turn first to the methodological approaches. Our first example centers on the method of literary analysis and is typified by the work of D. Olson.[5] Olson has emphasized the place of this dispute within the larger narrative of wilderness complaints a challenges to authority. While this observation is not absent from earlier work on this

---

series; G. Wenham in the Tyndale series, J. Sturdy in the Cambridge Bible Commentary series.

[3] See especially F. M. Cross, *Canaanite Myth and Hebrew Epic* (Cambridge: Harvard University Press, 1973), 203-04.

[4] Among many possible examples, see M. Noth, *Numbers* (OTL; Philadelphia: Westminster), *ad loc.*

[5] In his treatment of Numbers in the *Harper's* Bible Commentary, ed. J. L. Mays (San Francisco: Harper and Row, 1988), and more extensively in *The Death of the Old and the Birth of the New: the Framework of the Book of Numbers and the Pentateuch* (Brown Judaic Studies 71; Chico, CA: Scholars Press, 1985). It should be recognized that there are various types of literary readings of texts; among those being used in biblical studies but not yet represented in studies of Numbers 12 are reader-response and deconstructionist analyses.

chapter, it has been unusual to give it specific and highlighted attention in the assessment of a book as seemingly disjointed as the book of Numbers. Perhaps more significant than the treatment of chapter 12 is Olson's effort to take the entire book of Numbers seriously as a coherent literary unit. His proposal that the book be divided into the stories of the first and second generations as paradigms of disobedience and obedience exhibits a concern for the canonical place of Numbers that was all but absent in earlier discussions, which either gave up in despair over the internal structure of the book or else understood it only as part of a pattern involving Exodus and Leviticus as well.

A second new methodological approach to the study of Numbers 12 is structural analysis, a term that has varied meaning depending on the user. R. Culley's use of pattern or structure aims to show "similarity in underlying story frameworks" of a wide variety of biblical narratives, including this one.[6] This story exemplifies the category of "punishment involving a supernatural intervention [as] a central point of the story" (p. 100) and is compared to stories in 2 Kings 2.23-25 (Elisha and the she-bears) and Genesis 4.1-16 (Cain and Abel), as well as other passages in Numbers. Since Culley's interest is in the function of structures in oral story telling, his work should not be classified as 'structural exegesis' in the more technical sense as it is used by D. Jobling.

Jobling[7] uses the method of structural analysis developed in the work of V. Propp, A. J. Greimas and C. Levi-Strauss to make first narrative and then semantic analyses of Numbers 11-12. (He insists that chapter 12 cannot stand on its own, thus confirming in quite a different way the literary design noted by Olson.) Jobling says straightforwardly in his introduction that his analysis of Numbers 11–12 will probably not be accessible (i.e. readily understandable) to

---

[6] R. C. Culley, *Studies in the Structure of Hebrew Narrative* (Missoula: Scholars Press, 1976).

[7] *The Sense of Biblical Narrative: Three Structural Analyses in the Old Testament* (JSOTS 7; Sheffield: JSOT, 1978).

the non-specialist, and as one not schooled in this method, I can confirm that this was true for at least one reader! Jobling points out that part of the difficulty is the intricacy of the analysis, made necessary because it is intended to be "complete" and to "account for every detail," as is required to confirm the results of the method. In brief, he first searches out the "structure of the narrative as such," then turns to a "semantic analysis," defined as "the search for meaning in the discrete elements of the narrative" (p. 27). Jobling proposes that the message of Numbers 11–12 centers in two 'isotopies.' These are: 1) hierarchical organization and 2) communication and knowledge. It may be worth noting here that the isotopies as named by Jobling bear strong resemblance to the themes creating literary unity in this section as analyzed by Olson. But Jobling's structuralist emphasis is on how identifiable 'codes' of 'natural or cultural systems' such as topography, food, or the location of the tent of meeting, function to support these two abstract 'isotopies.' After reading Jobling one has a sense of a variety of bipolar categories underlying this story, but in contrast to Olson or even Culley, the story line as we commonly think of it seems to the non-specialist to have virtually disappeared from the discussion.

Turning now to two perspectival approaches to Numbers 12 in recent literature, we find that one of these, feminist analysis, focuses on the figure of Miriam. This focus is developed especially by R. Burns[8] and P. Trible,[9] whose studies are part of a larger trend in scholarship to highlight texts about women. Both Burns and Trible come to this text out of special interest in tracing all biblical references to a character who has in most other scholarship been only of incidental interest. In the case of this inquiry, as will also be true of

---

[8] *Has the Lord Indeed Spoken Only through Moses: A Study of the Biblical Portrait of Miriam* (SBLDS 84; Atlanta: Scholars, 1987).

[9] "Subversive Justice: Tracing the Miriamic Traditions," in *Justice and the Holy: Essays in Honor of Walter Harrelson*, ed. D. Knight and P. Paris (Atlanta: Scholars, 1989). In this essay Trible mentions that she is preparing a fully documented larger study of Miriam for future publication.

the African-American perspectival approach to be described next, a variety of critical methods may be employed by various scholars. The clustering is not around a particular method but rather around a topic or theme to be explored. The theme in such cases is usually easy to connect with the general social location of most of the scholars studying it; but as has already been suggested, such connections are often more general, not restricted to such obvious examples.

Trible, as is typical of her other work on female biblical characters, uses what I would call a tight yet playful rhetorical method as she traces Miriam's role through a range of texts. She seeks to create a 'portrait' (her word) of Miriam, noting details such as that Miriam appears here for the first time without the company of other women. Here is just a sampling of her observations about Numbers 12. Trible relates the challenge to Moses' prophetic authority back to Moses' own words in chapter 11, "would that all the Lord's people were prophets"; and observes that 'all the Lord's people' here must include women, even though that was not at issue in Numbers 11. Trible notes that God's response "undercuts [Miriam] in gender and point of view," (p.105) and that God's angry words to Miriam are the only words of the deity to her throughout all the Miriam material.

In this (preliminary) study Trible does not ask why Aaron is not punished (though she implies it is because he was a priest). Indeed she treats the text almost as if he were accidental to the narrative.[10] Trible observes (as has been done before) the contrast between the whiteness of Miriam's disease and the blackness of the Cushite wife; for her the parallel has to do with matters of cultic purity, since (like Jobling, p.58) she assumes that Moses' marriage is challenged because of alleged cultic impurity (not further defined) and persons with skin

---

[10] Contrast here Jobling, who sees the separation between male and female and between prophet and priest as important structural features; Jobling's analysis presupposes that "the female Miriam instigates the male Aaron to sin, putting herself thereby on the side of the foreign rabble" and in the category of foreign female seducers. (*The Sense of Biblical Narrative*, p. 48)

disease are cultically impure. More details of Trible's work might be given, but what is most important is to keep in mind her goal: to show that although the "triumphal male voice of Scripture would discredit" Miriam, there are many features of the text which would honor her, features which can be recovered by 'subversive' exegesis (p.109).

At this point let me mention that in an unpublished lecture I also have treated this passage from a feminist perspective in the context of a study of passages about women in the book of Numbers. My focus has been primarily on the 'why' of Miriam's being punished while Aaron goes scot-free, and on the impossibility of resolving a modern woman's sense of 'unfairness' about this situation, no matter what historical or literary theory is advanced to explain the narrative as it stands. At the conclusion of that lecture I tell the story of a chancel drama written by a student of mine that represents what E. Schüssler-Fiorenza has called the "hermeneutics of creative imagination."[11] The drama is a dialogue depicting Miriam's period of purification outside the camp (about which the biblical text itself tells us nothing). Miriam meets a very, very old and very, very disfigured woman who has spent her whole lifetime outside the camp. As their conversations proceed over the seven days, it dawns on Miriam and on the hearers of the dialogue that the old women is none other than Yahweh herself, despised and rejected, yet always present with the outcast. What is remarkable to me is the way in which this interpretation of a silence in the text seems repeatedly to touch a wide range of hearers, particularly people who by their own testimony would never be able to think of the biblical deity in any kind of female imagery. An imaginative elaboration on the biblical text functions to fix the text itself in memory as a touchstone for a new realm of religious possibilities.

A second perspectival approach to Numbers 12 focuses its attention on the location of Cush and on the significance of Miriam and Aaron's complaint about Moses' Cushite wife. These questions,

---

[11] *Bread Not Stone: The Challenge of Feminist Biblical Interpretation* (Boston: Beacon, 1984), p.21.

as I have already mentioned, are very old ones but have now been raised with new intensity by African-American biblical scholars. Contributions to the discussion have been published by D. Adamo, C. Felder, C. Copher, and R. Bailey. Even as feminist analyses are seeking out points of contact with female characters, so African and African-American analyses are giving special attention to references to Africa and Africans in the Bible. The starting point for interpretation of Numbers 12 is commonly the location of Cush, since there is a long-standing debate about whether this geographic term represents an area south of Egypt in eastern Africa or somewhere in northeast Arabia where the Midianites have usually been located. Some African-American analysis suggests that the Arabian theory for the location of Cush is rooted in a deliberate attempt to 'de-Africanize' the Bible, but it is more usual for scholars using this perspectival approach either to presume the African location of Cush or to argue for it along established scholarly lines. The Cushite wife is thus African and presumed to be black, but there is disagreement about whether this black woman is the Midianite wife, Zipporah, known from Exodus 2 and 4 or some other woman. The text itself is silent on this point. D. Adamo[12] (an African who did his doctoral studies in the U.S.) concludes that the woman is not Zipporah, noting particularly that Midian and Cush "were never used interchangeably" (p. 233) in ancient records; he speculates that Zipporah had died or been divorced by Moses. C. Copher,[13] on the other hand, associates the Cushite wife with Zipporah. Two other African-American scholars, C. Felder[14] and R. Bailey[15] do not discuss the identity of

---

[12] "The African Wife of Moses: An Examination of Numbers 12.1-9," *Africa Theological Journal*, 18 (1989) 230-37.

[13] "Black Presence in the OT," in *Stony the Road We Trod: African American Biblical Interpretation,* ed. C. Felder (Minneapolis: Fortress, 1991), p. 156.

[14] *Troubling Biblical Waters: Race, Class, and Family* (Maryknoll: Orbis, 1989), 42-43; "Race, Racism, and the Biblical Narratives," in *Stony the Road*, 135-36.

the woman other than to emphasize the fact that she was a black African.

The significance of the complaint about the Cushite wife is variously assessed by these scholars. Copher indicates that we cannot know what the problem was, except that in his judgment it was not color, since he believes that Moses, Aaron, and Miriam were all black (of Nubian origin) and thus the same color as the Cushite wife.[16] Felder, by contrast, argues that the complaint was based on racial prejudice that is rebuked by God in a symbolic way when Miriam turns white.[17] In this connection it is important to note also that the rebuke of Miriam has been used in South Africa as a key text in the church debate about the permissibility of interracial marriages. Bailey takes yet a third approach to the significance of the complaint. He proposes that Africans were favorably regarded in Israel, rather than unfavorably, and that Miriam was complaining that Moses was gaining extra status with the people by having a high status African wife, whereas the only legitimate ground for status, communication from the deity, belonged to all three equally.[18] In either case, Felder and Bailey suggest that the problem is a racial one, not a cultic one (such as marrying a 'gentile' or marrying outside Yahwistic faith) as previous scholars from the Rabbis to Jobling and Trible have typically supposed. Again these and other details of the views of these scholars illustrate their concern to recover something important that has been ignored or obscured by scholars working in a different social location.

This discussion of Numbers 12 should not conclude without reference to the possibility of a third perspectival approach, not yet developed in the scholarly literature but adumbrated in the work of

---

[15] "Beyond Identification: The Use of Africans in Old Testament Poetry and Narratives," in *Stony the Road*, 179-80.

[16] *Stony the Road*, 156.

[17] *Troubling Biblical Waters*, 42.

[18] *Stony the Road*, 179-80; Felder's essay in *Stony the Road* suggests that he is open to considering Bailey's alternative, 135-36.

womanist (black feminist) scholar Renita J. Weems.[19] In her brief, non-technical treatment, Weems explores imaginatively another silence in the text, as she considers possibilities for the relationship between Miriam and the Cushite wife (sisters-in-law) that could have led to Miriam's complaint. The goal of Weems' essay is not to argue for any particular explanation based on evidence in the text itself. Rather, her work is important because it draws our attention to a *silence* in the text not highlighted by the other four approaches, all of which in their own ways include exploration of other silences in the text.

By now you may know more about Numbers 12 than you ever hoped to, or perhaps you feel that the variety of methods, variety of questions, and variety of proposals concerning possibly unanswerable questions leaves you feeling like you know nothing at all for sure about this text. If you do feel a bit at sea, then this portion of the lecture has accomplished one of its goals. As President Pusey predicted, we are in a period of sharp change, a time of disintegration of the fragile consensus about which questions were interesting and which methods would be helpful in finding answers. At the same time, I hope you have been able to discern areas of overlap in the four examples, despite their very divergent starting points. Despite great differences, I believe a round table discussion with this text as center would be possible, provided that the table could be genuinely round.

Through its history, the American Bible Society has fostered the preparation of accurate and usable translations of the Bible. Will the new approaches discussed here contribute to the improvement of future translations? I think they will, but in ways probably less direct than new manuscript and archaeological evidence. Literary analysis based on the Hebrew or Greek often leads to new translation suggestions, as can be seen throughout Trible's work. Structural analysis is interested in discerning features of the specific culture, as well as in cross-cultural commonalities; its results can lead to new insights into the intent of individual phrases or expressions. To the

---

[19] "In-law, In Love," pp. 71-83 in her *Just A Sister Away: A Womanist Vision of Women's Relationships in Bible* (San Diego: LuraMedia, 1988).

extent that new approaches—such as African-American, womanist, or feminist—involve asking different perspectival questions rather than using less familiar methods, the very act of focusing attention on verses previously passed over lightly may lead to new ideas about their most faithful and effective translation.

II. *Bible Study Methods, and their Implications for Appropriation of Scripture*

We turn now to the matter of the appropriation of the biblical text outside of academia, in the various communities of faith. As I indicated in the introduction, I will describe and comment briefly on three typical methods of group study of the Bible by laypersons in church settings.

The first example of a Bible study method is sometimes called the 'Swedish' marking system and typically offers the following pattern of instructions to the study group: 1) Read the passage silently to yourself. As you read, mark each verse or portion of a verse with one of the following three symbols: An arrow, meaning that "this speaks directly to you, goes to the heart"; a candle, meaning that "this illumines your thinking"; or a question-mark, meaning that "this raises questions and/or doubts for you." In an alternative form of this process, participants may be given a blank sheet divided into three columns headed by the arrow, the candle, and the question-mark. They are then asked to copy each verse or phrase into the appropriate column. 2) When everyone is finished [the instructions continue], read the verses together, stopping to ask how different group members marked each verse. The people who marked a verse with an arrow or a candle may share their reasons for doing so as a way of helping those for whom the verse raised questions.

What are some of the presuppositions of this method for how the Bible is appropriated? First, its structure suggests that the Bible 'speaks' initially to individuals. This initial word may be modified through conversation with others, even though the exercise begins with silent reading. Second, it suggests that meaning/significance/ authority lie in the individual sentence or even in a part of a sentence, not in a larger unit such as a paragraph or chapter. (Each verse or phrase is to be marked or listed separately.) Third, the method values careful attention to the words as they are printed on the page of the translation being used by each group or individual member. Fourth, since this method either compresses or splits reactions to the text into pre-set categories of feeling (heart), intellect (thinking), or questions/doubt, it suggests that these are the only options for reaction and that they are mutually exclusive. Sometimes participants will balk and use more than one mark or insist that none fits, but the method presupposes limited choices. Fifth, the method views doubt/questioning as an appropriate initial reaction but still as an ultimately undesirable response to anything in the Bible. This is seen by the instructions in step two that the responses of arrow or candle are to be used as 'help' by those for whom the verse raised doubts or questions. Finally, no specialized knowledge is presumed or required, either in terms of an 'expert' leader or in terms of secondary literature, although such knowledge is not precluded if a group member happens to bring it to the discussion.

In the second method of study, once more all participants read the assigned passage silently. But in this second method they are instructed to rewrite the passage individually in their own words, trying to avoid using the words of the printed scripture text.

After rewriting individually, participants pair off to read each other what they have written and discuss what they have said. If time permits, as a final step the group may attempt to re-write the passage together.

What are some presuppositions of this second method? 1) The authority of the text is not inherent in the words printed on the page. The focus on restating the content in one's own words suggests that the ideas (concepts) in the text are more important than the words themselves. 2) Although the procedure begins with the individual, it values the perspectives of others on the meaning of the text. The activity of discussing various restatements of a written text functions to highlight the variety of meanings possible in it. The attempt at the end of the exercise to agree upon a group paraphrase suggests the possibility of a common conclusion about the text, but in practice it is often very difficult to achieve consensus on wording. 3) Thus, those using the method might infer that there is no one 'correct' or 'true' meaning of the text. Alternatively they might infer that one correct or true meaning does exist, but that it can be discovered only by getting further human information or Spirit guidance to adjudicate disagreements in the group. Whether individual learners will assume that there is or is not a single correct or true meaning will depend largely upon what kind of book they believe the Bible to be and upon how the leader or organizer closes the study session. This method 4) legitimates the participants' own wordings as valid expressions of biblical content, and 5) like the first, does not presume special knowledge on the part of the participants or require special preparation on the part of the leader. The Bible can function authoritatively without presumed or necessary reference to 'scholarly' literature.

The third method for our consideration proceeds as follows: Each person reads the assigned text silently, and/or some one reads it aloud. Participants discuss together the meaning of the passage using some or all of the following questions: 1) What is known of the context of these verses? In what circumstances were they written? To what situation or issues do they speak? 2) What is the general teaching of these verses? Is it more applicable to individuals or to the church or to society at large? 3) What connections with today's life are evident? 4) What parts or ideas seem irrelevant to life today?

This third method of group Bible study, by contrast to the first two, bears explicit relationship to the questions those of us schooled in the historical-critical method have been taught to ask. Its opening questions about context and history presuppose first of all the need for and the value of information from other parts of the Bible, from cognate literatures, and from archaeology that have been discussed in other presentations at this conference. It presupposes that such information has been important to the translation of the Bible but that not all the needed insights are conveyed by the words themselves. Pedagogically the method therefore also presupposes 'expert' knowledge and leader preparation or resource books in order for the mean-

ing/significance of the text to become known to the participants.
Second, this method presupposes that the Bible is both distant from
as well as near to the readers/hearers. This is seen not just in the
lifting up of its historical distance from the modern era, but also in
the discussion questions about connections and irrelevancy. The wording of the questions suggests that 'irrelevance' is a category of
response that might properly be simply acknowledged, not something
that must necessarily be overcome. Third, this method offers a different option from the other two in terms of its view of the words on the
page. On the one hand, unlike the view of method one, the words are
to be discussed and understood as a whole, not as isolated sentences
or phrases. On the other hand, in contrast to method two, the focus
is on understanding the meaning of the text rather than on restatement of it in similar but different words. The implication is that
something would be lost or altered by attempting to restate the text.
Finally, by explicitly raising various spheres of applicability of the
passage (individual, church, society), this third method pre-supposes
a variety of spheres for proper appropriation of the biblical text. The
previous two methods, by contrast, tend to focus much more on
individual or private study group appropriation.

Several general comments about these examples are now in order.
First of all, they are of course only illustrative. Christian education
handbooks are full of dozens of other methods and variations.[20] My
limited knowledge suggests that quite different approaches to biblical
passages are taken in Jewish religious education, with much heavier
exposure to teachings of Rabbis over the centuries. Second, all three
methods described here presume the Bible is of life-affecting significance to its present readers. Third, all are designed to cover small
blocks of text, perhaps a chapter at most, often less in the first two
methods. Of course a study could be extended by dealing with a

---

[20] One might do a similar analysis, for instance on some of the current
highly appreciated programs of Bible study, such as Kerygma or the Bethel
Bible program. I have chosen to use these three simpler examples for the
sake of clarity in a brief discussion.

sequence of passages over a series of lessons, but the methods presume that significance/meaning comes from small units. Fourth, only the last of the three methods shows any inherent interest in the text as distant in time, geography, or culture from the present readers. And finally, only the last method moves beyond the boundaries of the passage to press questions of its literary contextual setting.

For most of us scholars trained in historical-critical methods, the notion of ignoring distance and context seems irresponsible, or even unimaginable. What we have learned about the Bible cannot be just erased from memory. And yet, some of the developments in biblical scholarship in the last twenty years, even as we have seen them briefly illustrated in part I of this lecture, might push us to reassess this view. As I think about the three methods of Bible study and then the recent scholarly approaches to Numbers 12 that I have reviewed for you, I am struck by how little of the methodology in which I was trained, which forms the basis for the third bible study method, comes into play in the recent work on the Numbers passage. Adamo's use of other Ancient Near Eastern documents in identifying Cush is the one major discussion that conspicuously represents the methods I learned, beyond general techniques of inner-biblical comparisons in exegetical work. To some extent, this may be 'caused' by the text itself, which is arguably less amenable than many others to analysis by historical-critical tools. And yet older scholarship certainly tried to work with categories such as source or redaction criticism, schools of tradition transmission, and the like in the analysis of this chapter.

Yet, there may be some elements of connection that can be observed between the newer scholarly approaches and aspects of the strategies of the first two methods of lay Bible study. For example, the feminist focus on Miriam and the African-American focus on the Cushite woman [also a woman, note, but nameless and narrative-less in the text] suggests to me a possible parallel with the first study method. It is as if each group has drawn an arrow next to a selected portion of the passage, indicating that this portion of the text 'speaks to their heart.' The text is much less likely to elicit an 'arrow' anywhere in particular for North Atlantic white males, so their approaches tend to take up the text as a whole.

There are also elements of the newer scholarly approaches to Numbers 12 that may bear some resemblance to the second group study method and its restatement of the text. The scholarly restatement is of course not as direct as one might get in a lay Bible class, but it seems to me that Jobling's elaborate diagrams of the structure underlying the narrative are one kind of restatement, while Culley's abstraction of the outline in common with other stories is another restatement. Trible's portrait of Miriam restates it in yet a third way. To be sure, each of these efforts is guided by certain methodological controls that would not be likely to be known or used by most lay students, but the general goals are not so radically different as might first appear.

As to how the results of our scholarly inquiry get incorporated into the thinking of the 'grass roots,' I have no magic formula. What is important for now is to realize that the new scholarly horizon may call us to reassess—and in some respects view more positively—the less historically-oriented methods of lay Bible study.

III. *Conclusion: How Do We Move Ahead?*

Twenty years have brought sharp changes, and the jury has scarcely begun to assess the interrelationship or long-term contribution of the move toward new scholarly agendas in biblical studies. In this time of transition, I believe that the most important goal for all of us should be to adopt a stance of mutual listening rather than of mutual denigration. I remember a number of years ago a conversation with a colleague from another school who felt strongly that the new literary methods were being touted by people who were too lazy to put in the time required to learn sufficient cognate languages and ancient history and culture to be able to do the job right. Of course scarcely a one of us could ever control all the languages and cultures needed for historical-critical inquiry. At the time I was inclined to agree with him, but I have since been humbled by awareness of the vast technical literature that undergirds each of the newer methods in the field today. Let us practice listening for a while to the results of others' specialties, even if their methods will never be our own. One can read and learn from the results of structuralist analyses or of various types of literary analysis, whether or not one adopts these methodological approaches in one's own work.

This kind of mutual listening must be fostered not only among those using different methodological approaches however, but also with those sometimes called special interest groups, such as feminists or African-American analysts, who bring new perspectival approaches to the Bible. Scholars in any field tend to be quick to label new ideas as 'impossible.' The tendency is only compounded when it is noticed that those with the new ideas have some identifiable personal interest in their results. I believe we need first of all to realize that every scholar has a social location and that every scholar has a personal interest in the results of his or her work. Then we need to discipline ourselves to listen long and well to those whose social locations are most obviously different from our own before we assess their work. Perhaps we might even try devoting our initial energy to finding additional support for a new and surprising or uncomfortable interpretation of a text put forward out of a different approach (whether perspectival or methodological), before we marshal our arguments against it. This is not easy for any of us, but it would open doors of communication. Not long ago I asked two African-American clergy-women for their assessment of Bailey's interpretation of the Cushite wife. They could scarcely grasp my question, since in their churches they had been taught since childhood to admire this black biblical character and they did not perceive a radical departure from the familiar in what Bailey had written. I was surprised and also chastened by my ignorance of the significance of the Cushite woman for persons I counted as friends. The gulf between our worlds was made evident, even as it was narrowed just a bit by that encounter.

I conclude this presentation with a word about the role of the Bible in our faith communities. None of us would advocate fostering ignorance or allowing patently impossible interpretations (whatever we think those to be, and we would not all agree) of biblical texts to go unchallenged. But for myself I am learning to take a longer view and to worry a little less about the havoc that may be wreaked for lack of sufficient scholarly information. For insofar as I regard this book, the Bible, as sacred, I trust that the ultimate guardian of its meaning and of its place in human life is God, not the scholar (who may or may not interpret wisely), and not the non-expert group or individual (who may or may not have access to the wise or not-so-wise words of the experts). Trusting God to make meaning in the long haul despite the technical disputations of scholars and despite the naiveté of non-specialists does not, however, mean appealing to a *deus ex machina*. Rather, the long and varied history of biblical interpretation in Judaism and in the Church bears witness that no method has ever obscured everything that might be known by the communities that read this book, and likewise that no method has ever made manifest everything that might be known by the communities that read this book. That mix of obscuring and making manifest the meaning/meanings of sacred text will surely continue with new approaches in a new millennium. We should rejoice to be living and working in such an exciting time.

RESPONSE: Melvin K. H. Peters

First of all, my thanks to Professor Sakenfeld for her presentation. I intend neither to recast her paper in my image nor to comment on everything that I deemed right or wrong with the presentation. Rather, three simple interrelated questions to which I would offer slightly different answers from those implied or stated in the paper, serve as organizational foci for my response. I hope by this means to stimulate a helpful discussion. The questions are: "What constitutes a new approach to/method in the study of the Bible?" My answers will not necessarily follow that order.

Professor Sakenfeld begins with a reference to her final days as a graduate student at Harvard in 1971. Her experiences in that setting undoubtedly helped shape her vision of her task for this symposium in much the same way as mine did some four years later in the Graduate Department of Near Eastern Studies at the University of Toronto. Hers was a setting in which (and I quote) "scholars from different religious traditions ...could at last study the Hebrew Bible in common and in conversation"; in my situation, the religious traditions of faculty and students were never raised nor deemed important. We studied the Hebrew Bible, the most visible and well-known literary artifact to emerge from the ancient near east, alongside several other bodies of literature in their original languages, with a view to understanding and analyzing critically the historical, cultural and linguistic features of this important region. Since then, the bulk of my professional life has been spent in secular university environments which have further sharpened, shaped and challenged my perspective. My reaction to her presentations should be understood against this backdrop.

While I understand and applaud the direction taken in the paper, I felt somewhat distanced from it because it seems to be written with,

---

MELVIN K. H. PETERS is Associate Professor of Religion at Duke University, Durham, NC.

and targeted to an audience that shares, an exclusively protestant Christian definition of the Bible and world view. It does not sufficiently recognize the diverse community which continues to use the Hebrew scriptures for reasons other than faith; nor indeed those other confessions for which the Hebrew scriptures hold religious meaning—Catholics, Jews and Muslims immediately come to mind.

The Bible as an icon of western culture is constantly being analyzed and understood. Some of the more popular courses on the Bible at universities nationwide are offered in English departments; like other colleagues in Religion, I teach highly subscribed courses on the Hebrew Bible to students of all persuasions whose interests are primarily educational not confessional, and I am sure that in state universities and high schools, courses on the Bible attract similar kinds of students. From my perspective, the exclusion of this audience seemed unfortunate.

Perhaps the clearest example of the limitation of the paper in this respect is the uncritical use throughout of the noun God. Although Professor Sakenfeld cites the NRSV accurately in the quotation "Has the LORD spoken only through Moses?..." etc., she suggests in her synthesis of the subsequent narrative, that it is *God* who calls the leaders to the tent of meeting; that Moses asks *God* to heal Miriam; that *God* decrees that Miriam be put outside of the camp, and so on. In point of fact, it is the divinity Yahweh, the god of Israel, to whom, properly, all this activity should be assigned. Those who accept the equation of Yahweh with God (however defined) might find the synthesis acceptable; to those for whom God is defined in other ways, such an equation would be unacceptable, even more so in light of the author's later statements which seem to suggest that God for her is not limited to Yahweh. She writes, for instance: "I trust that the ultimate guardian of its [the Bible's] place in human life is God, not the scholar who may or may not interpret wisely," or "Trusting God to make meaning in the long haul..." and so forth.

I cannot quarrel with the decision to 'sketch' newer approaches or 'suggest' novel ways in which the Bible is being used. I entirely concur that in the best of circumstances either of these tasks would be daunting; together they are well nigh impossible. Nor would I question the pragmatic decision to argue from the particular to the general. Having just completed a critical edition of the Coptic text of Numbers, I was in fact pleased that the specific text chosen for discussion was one I had recently studied in some depth. However, one could dispute the labels *conspicuous* or *new* for methods such as literary criticism, social world investigation and structural analysis.

Other methods could just as easily be highlighted. Social science methods for instance are being constantly employed these days to help make sense of the Bible. I think of the adaptation of techniques from anthropology in the understanding of the prophetic corpus or the utilization of various sociological techniques, or Marxist ideology in making sense of the group dynamics in the Bible. In the last twenty years the use of the computer and related devices has revolutionized the analysis of texts.

But granting the categories used in the paper, the strongest objection that can be raised is this: two of the four examples of new approaches from new social locations—femininity analysis and African-American analysis are not approaches at all, but are, to my mind, examples of particular audiences using the Bible to meet their own perceived needs. The other two approaches—literary analysis and structural analysis—were labelled earlier in the paper as methods, not approaches, and I would be hard pressed to call one of these—literary analysis—new.

The self-serving use of the Bible by particular individuals or groups, while entirely justified and appropriate, is equally not new. Within the biblical corpus itself, we see examples of this already in the books of Chronicles which recast and retell a particular story with a distinctly political agenda. Paul quotes the Hebrew Bible without regard for context, or reshapes the quotation to fit the theological point he seeks to make. Scores of special interest groups in the history of biblical interpretation have chosen to appropriate portions of the Bible to suit their own needs. Were we to count all the current ones—many of which, by the way, are led by or include persons with advanced academic degrees—we would indeed have innumerable new methods for interpreting scripture. But beyond that, the singling out of feminist analysis and African-American analysis as special approaches would seem to imply that persons within those groups could not/do not use literary-critical or structuralist approaches to understanding the Bible. Furthermore it would seem to preclude the possibility of a feminist African-American analysis of scripture or, for that matter, that males of any kind could produce a feminist analysis. I hope, by the way, that African-American analysis was discussed last only by accident.

At another level, the specific methodologies identified with feminists and African-Americans are not really new or exclusive. Thematic or topical studies of the Bible, or even approaches emphasizing the development of biographical profiles have been practiced for centuries. Most of the biblical discussions of feminists and African-American groups seem rather to be grounded in the desire to rearrange the structures of power within the scholarly or believing community. There is a consensus within those discussions, that what has passed, and is passing, for dispassionate, objective, scholarly biblical study has been, and continues to be in fact, only a carefully disguised foregrounding of the concerns of one particular population group— white males from European-American culture. Thus the efforts of African-Americans and feminists seem generally to be corrective, retributive, or compensatory in nature. But such efforts to 'level the playing field' reveal only that both traditional and the more recent interpreters are in agreement on one thing: the Bible is a powerful source of authority to be manipulated to one's ends. Or, to expand the sport metaphor, the Bible is the *only* playing field on which the drama of human activity unfolds, not one of many fields. The propriety of such a view of the Bible is a matter about which persons of goodwill will differ, but I must stress, such political use of scripture is in no way new.

This leads naturally to the question "What is the Bible?" and takes us back to the differences in perspective with which I began this response and, in a way, takes us to the purpose of this entire Symposium. I do not think there would be much variance among us with respect to the denotative meaning of the term Bible. Sure, purists like myself would argue for the recognition of the various canons and the plethora of divergent witnesses to the biblical text in ancient languages; we would caution against the widespread tendency to consider English translations equivalent to *the* Bible and so forth. But we would all agree that, in general, the term Bible at its core denotes a body of literature collected, transmitted and used by Jews and Christians.

However it is at the connotative level that greatest variance would develop among us, and the debate would cluster around two nodes. I would venture to suggest that a large majority would see the Bible as *more* than a simple human document. If viewed only as a human product, the Bible would not be very difficult to understand and frankly not terribly interesting to many people. But the reason new approaches are constantly being sought and tried is related to a persistent conviction shared by a wide range of interpreters and captured in this quote by Professor Sakenfeld.

"For insofar as I regard this book, the Bible, as sacred, I trust that the ultimate guardian of its meaning and of its place in human life is God, not the scholar who may or may not interpret it wisely and not the non-expert group or individual who may or may not have access to the wise or not-so-wise words of the experts."

Various formulations of this conviction consciously or unconsciously undergird the professional activity of a broad spectrum of biblical scholars and lead to the kinds of political bickering about intention and meaning to which I alluded earlier.

But many other scholars would see the Bible as a human document and nothing more. There is no particular authority that resides in it and nothing terribly complex to understand. There is only one task: establish as well as possible what the materials *meant* in their original setting so that as modern humans we can be enriched by the lives, or freed from the foibles of ancients. Members of the first group—the majority—only make things more fuzzy when they try to merge their activities with those of this second group, seeking, as is frequently asserted, to determine both what the Bible *meant*, and also what it *means*.

I will not try to resolve this impasse or to pronounce on its virtue or value. I only would suggest that, as we approach the twenty-first century, we should celebrate as most useful those new approaches to the Bible that any one so minded could embrace; those that require no special qualifications—not even faith—to adopt. The task may be daunting in this current climate of tolerance, but it is achievable.

At different times in my teaching career, I have had students drop my Hebrew Bible course, because for some I was not Jewish (certainly not Jewish enough in my sympathies) and therefore un-qualified to teach Jewish scripture; for one other young man, the son of a Methodist minister (who I suspect persuaded him that the university was a Methodist institution) I was not Methodist enough in my approach to the Christian 'Old Testament' which, for him, pre-figured the activities of Christ. In one other instance, a student was disappointed and wished to drop because I was not bringing enough of an Afro-centric world view to the Bible. This kind of disputation about the meaning of the Bible is inevitable so long as we continue to endorse and validate equally all efforts to interpret it. In my view not everyone who reads the English, or even the Hebrew Bible is qualified to interpret it and certainly not everything that is published concerning the Bible is scholarship. But there are ways for people with different presuppositions about the Bible to find common ground for dialogue and these integrative, non-divisive techniques should be explored and treasured.

This leads me to raise another basic cluster of questions. Who is a scholar? How widespread should a viewpoint be disseminated within a given academic population group for it to be identified with that group? With the easy availability of graduate degrees from widely divergent institutions, is it fair to label everyone holding a final degree a scholar? The majority of the African-American scholars specifically identified in the paper, happen also to work in institutions with predominantly African-American populations. Does that make their view-points more or less valid than those of African-Americans working in other contexts, or of African-American clergy? Is everything published, even in refereed journals, to be considered scholarship, and who decides? Are the views of the published scholar, however defined, more valid than those of the masses? Time does not permit me to offer nuanced answers to each of these rhetorical questions but the direction of my sentiments should not be in doubt.

Clearly, African-Americans of all viewpoints continue to read and interpret the Bible, coming to quite different conclusions about its meaning. But there is not, indeed cannot be, any such things as an African-American biblical analysis any more than there is a European-American biblical analysis—the population groups are too diverse to be characterized in any single way. I would guess too that not all feminists (and certainly not all women) would concur in their approaches to biblical interpretations, nor specifically with the work of Burns and Trible.

Sakenfeld on the one hand calls for mutual listening not only to those using different methods but to special interest groups. We need to realize, so she urges, "that every scholar has a personal interest in the results of his or her work." On the other hand she would not "advocate fostering ignorance or allowing patently impossible interpretations to go unchallenged." Quite apart from the fact that the first assertion "every scholar has a personal interest in the results of his or her work" is not always or necessarily true, it would seem, frankly, that she cannot have it both ways. Interpretations may be deemed "patently impossible," only when there *are* accepted standards of interpretation. Interpretations which fall outside of those standards *are* impossible whether advanced by persons with or without final degrees, regardless of gender, appearance or any other classification, and should be vigorously challenged. On the other hand, if everyone does what seems right in his or her own eyes because the Bible is amenable to all kinds of interpretation, there can be no such thing as a "patently impossible" interpretation.

But I would be remiss if, as one whose research interest is textual,

I did not respond to the passage around which much of the presentation was woven. The passage seems to be of existential significance for African-Americans because of an unarticulated assumption which to my mind is crucial to any discussion of it. That assumption is this: there was a physical, visible, complexional difference between Moses and the Cushite wife, not merely a cultural or religious one. A concomitant of this assumption is that Moses' complexion was lighter—significantly lighter—than that of the Cushite wife.

None of these assumptions is derived from, or necessary to the understanding of, the text as it stands. They are usually brought to the text because of at least two factors: 1) interpreters have read modern conceptions of race back into the ancient demographic picture, and 2) interpreters accepted the idea of a geographical disjunction between Egypt and the rest of Africa. A mounting body of evidence is making quite clear that any such disjunction, especially in early times, is entirely unfounded. The culture of Egypt was influenced by the region south of it as much as or more than by any other region. It is quite another matter that the origins and identity of the group that later became known as the Israelites is a matter of hot debate or, to widen the picture, that the origin of all humans is now being traced to Africa by some scholars. If we do not know what the Egyptian Moses looked like, (and Egyptian he was, as the comments of the seven daughters of the priest of Midian concerning the man who helped them combat the shepherds in Exodus 2.19 would suggest) why presume that he was light complexioned?

With respect to the contrast of the whiteness of Miriam's leprosy and the blackness of the Cushite wife, it need only be said that the same phrase "leper as white as snow" is used to describe the leprosy of Elisha's greedy servant Gehazi in 2 Kings 2.27, but no racial point is made in that story. Or again, many commentators, with no grounds whatsoever, determine that the unnamed Cushite who brings the accurate news of Absalom's death to David in 2 Samuel 18.19ff, was a slave. Those kinds of interpretations, from whatever source, reflect more often than not the private, contemporary, racial politics of commentators, not careful biblical exegesis.

On a more scholarly note, it may be entirely accidental but noteworthy nonetheless that the explanatory gloss, "for he had indeed married a Cushite wife" does not appear in the existing Coptic versions of this text. While the variance between the Coptic and the majority tradition could have occurred in the course of textual transmission, what seems clear is that in traditions coming out of Egypt, the marriage of Moses to the Cushite was not an incredible or unusual event and did not need reiteration. Racially, Moses was not distinctly different from the Cushite wife.

This last observation provides me with the pretext to make my concluding point. One of the most exciting new approaches to biblical study, in my view, is the increasing recognition of the value of versions in general and specifically the recognition that textual criticism can no longer be separated out as a cocktail hour, before the main meal of biblical interpretation begins. The gulf between so-called higher and lower criticism, which ought never to have been there in the first place, is rapidly evaporating. More and more scholars are recognizing that even the very term 'the Bible' needs to be rethought. The rubric 'Biblical Archaeology' for example, has already fallen out of favor in some circles, and the scope of the canon, the proper place of the so-called apocrypha and the pseudepigrapha are subjects of thoughtful reconsideration. The assault on the hegemony that one Hebrew manuscript—Codex Leningradensis—has had on our definition of what is the Bible, will and should only become more intense. As we decode more of the Dead Sea Scrolls, and as we understand even better the relationship of the readings in versions other than Hebrew and manuscripts other than Codex Leningradensis to the so-called received text, the tendency to see the Bible as a monolith will be attenuated. In twenty-five years, the bicentennial of this great Society may well be celebrated with sessions such as New Approaches to Understanding and Interpreting the Forms of Biblical Texts not simply the Bible. I hope to be alive and well enough to enjoy that day.

What is meant by 'New approaches' in relation to biblical studies? 'Approaches' can be methods, presuppositions, priorities, theories, or even theologies or ideologies. Part I of Katherine Sakenfeld's paper illustrates four such 'new approaches' (new at least since 1971) with reference to the twelfth chapter of Numbers. Part II discusses the presuppositions underlying three popular methods of 'Bible Study.' Sakenfeld then raises the intriguing (and hopeful) possibility that 'Bible Study' (in the church) and 'Biblical Studies' (in the academy) have drawn closer together in the past twenty years—not because small group leaders in religious communities have been learning more of the historical-critical method, but because the historical-critical method is no longer the only option in the scholarly community.

Sakenfeld rightly makes the point that the choice of passages to be studied is a matter of great importance, and in recent years a significant index to change in the world of scholarship. Why, for example, did she choose Numbers 12 for her own case study? It is not a perfect choice, because (as she observes) social world studies have not been consciously brought to bear on this passage. Sakenfeld surveys four other 'new approaches' that have been applied to it in the past twenty years: literary analysis, structural analysis, feminist analysis, and African-American analysis.

My first impression was that the four 'new approaches' are a mixture of apples and oranges. The first two are methodological in the strict sense. The latter two are ideological, in much the same way that a 'biblical theology' or 'convenantal' approach to the text would be ideological. Sakenfeld uses the term 'social location' to explain the appeal of these varied approaches to individual scholars. She attributes 'new approaches' to "new social locations, whether in the subculture of scholarly method or in the more general society." In the

---

J. RAMSEY MICHAELS is Professor of Religious Studies, Southwest Missouri State University, Springfield, MO.

NEW APPROACHES TO STUDY OF THE BIBLE   155

case of both literary and structural analysis, I would be at a loss to identify the 'social location' of their proponents, and Sakenfeld does not attempt to do so.

The term 'social location' is more appropriate for feminist and African-American analyses of Numbers 12. While it is not true that only women and blacks respectively will look at the text from these perspectives, it is true (as Sakenfeld suggests) that women and men, white or black, are likely to be drawn to this kind of text and these kinds of analysis out of personal or social 'life circumstances.' And it is probably also true that such motivations have become more common in the past twenty years than previously. Yet caution is necessary. If I might share a bit of personal history, I first encountered this text as a young fundamentalist, in a fundamentalist seminary in the fifties. As a white male primarily interested in the New Testament, I was not drawn to the text by my 'social location.' Yet being a literalist, I interpreted the passage along the lines of what Sakenfeld now calls 'African-American analysis' (especially Felder), and derived a gleeful satisfaction from pointing out to my contemporaries—including some faculty, as I recall—that not only is racial intermarriage not forbidden by Scripture, but those who tried to forbid it were rather severely judged. In this case, the brashness of youth was every bit as strong a motivating factor as ideology or racial sensitivity.

I still think there is much to be said for the interpretation I espoused back then. I am still a white male, still specializing in the New Testament, and probably more of a literalist than I care to admit. Of course I missed the feminist angle completely. I never asked why Miriam was punished and Aaron was not. I knew nothing of 'deconstruction' or 'subversive exegesis.' I did know that some people 'explained away' some texts (that's what we called it then: 'explaining away'—not 'deconstruction' and not 'subversion'). I learned how to do it myself. Back then our theology was our ideology, and we tried to bring all of Scripture under its control.

Most of us today are far more willing to acknowledge that there are many voices in Scripture. The text Sakenfeld has chosen for us is a fascinating one, with two agendas or two 'social locations,' which are at cross purposes. At least on a literalistic reading, 'African-American analysis' seems to win hands down. This is the case even if the Cushite woman is Midianite, and not black or Ethiopian. Either way she is an outsider, representing (like Ruth) a marginalized race or tribe. Because Miriam rejected the outsider, she herself is made an outsider (temporarily) and the authority of Moses is vindicated.

'Feminist analysis,' as Sakenfeld describes it, takes up the cause not of the Cushite woman, but of Miriam. Is this because there is too little information about the Cushite woman—obviously there is more if we identify her with Zipporah—or is it because 'feminist analysis' is a methodology used mostly by whites? Whatever the reason, the spotlight is on Miriam in the work of Trible and of Sakenfeld herself. Three options—not mutually exclusive—present themselves to the feminist interpreter: first, to underscore the unfairness and the limited perspective of the text; second, to spot contrary or mitigating factors in the text or context which honor Miriam in some way; third, to deconstruct or even re-write the text in light of truths that emerge from the rest of Scripture. Both Trible and Sakenfeld adopt both of the first two options. The third option ('creative actualization') is represented by the chancel drama about the old disfigured woman outside the camp—which strikes me as a way of looking right through the text as though it were transparent and reading behind and beyond it Matthew 25.31-46 ("Inasmuch as you have done it for one of the least of these my brothers or sisters, you have done it for me"). In short, it is an appeal to what theologians call 'the analogy of Scripture.' The testimony of the Bible as a whole is allowed to take precedence over any one text, even the one under discussion. And if that is the case, the 'new approach' may not be so new after all. All that is new is that a more reader-oriented approach makes it easier to do what theologians have done all along.

Re-reading Sakenfeld's paper, I kept coming back to the same conclusion. As the French like to say it, the more things change, the more they stay the same. I don't want to sound naive, and I certainly do not deny that literary analysis and structural analysis have had a significant impact on biblical studies in the past twenty years. Yet *in relation to this passage*, is Olson (as Sakenfeld represents him) proposing anything more startling than careful attention to the larger context? Isn't his recurring 'genre' (if that is the right word) of "wilderness complaints and challenges to authority" just another sort of traditional form-critical classification? Isn't the same thing true of Culley's category of "punishment involving a supernatural intervention"? Jobling, admittedly, *is* different, but is a structuralist analysis that makes the story line disappear helpful to translators or 'Bible Study' group leaders? I can't help but be reminded of Krister Stendahl's story about a professor who told a Ph.D. candidate, "Your dissertation is both good, and new; unfortunately the parts that are good are not new, and the parts that are new are not good."

If I had to classify according to this stark alternative, I would characterize Trible's appeal to Moses' words in Numbers 11, "would that all the Lord's people were prophets" as 'good' rather than 'new.' Even if the point has not been made before in just the same way, it is the kind of point that *could* have been made without the benefit of 'new approaches.' The same is true of Sakenfeld's own curiosity about "Miriam's being punished while Aaron goes scot-free." On the latter question, an Old Testament colleague reminded me that Aaron led a charmed life on at least two other occasions, when Miriam was not in the picture: first, when "the Lord sent a plague upon the people, because *they* made the calf which Aaron made" (Ex 32.35), and second, when Aaron's sons, Nadab and Abihu, were destroyed by fire, "and Aaron held his peace" (Lv 10.3). In some sense these punishments, like Miriam's, are viewed as punishments of Aaron as well (cf. Nu 12.11, "Oh Lord, do not punish *us*, because *we* have done foolishly and have sinned"), yet Aaron himself remains untouched. I have also wondered about other things: e.g. the use of leprosy on another occasion as a validation of Moses' authority (i.e. on Moses' own hand, Ex 4.6-8); also, Aaron's strange comparison of Miriam to an aborted fetus (Nu 12.12), where in the LXX the same word (ἔκτρωμα) is used that Paul applied to himself in 1 Cor 15.8 ("as to one untimely born"); also the subordination of Moses to Christ in He 3.1-6 with explicit reference to our passage.

Such observations only bear out Sakenfeld's point that we all bring our own questions to a text like this out of our varied life and professional experiences. Because I never believed, even twenty years ago, that the historical critical method was the *only* way to study the Bible, I am not as aware as Sakenfeld of radical changes since then. I suppose in this respect I am a little like the two African-American clergywomen in her illustration. There have always been those who approached the Bible historically, those who approached it theologically, and those who approached it as literature. Many of us, however, tried instead to select or combine these approaches depending on our audience and our goals—i.e. whether we were in a graduate seminar, a college or seminary classroom, or the church. I am not convinced that the situation is basically different today.

Two things *are* different: first, theological interpretation has now been broadened to include ideological concerns, especially in relation to gender and race; second (and this is a major contribution of Sakenfeld's paper), more of us are realizing that the historical-critical study of the Bible, while valid and worthwhile, always was a rather low-yield procedure compared to a careful, perceptive reading and re-reading of the text. Now that the accent has shifted from the author to the reader, this is even more true than before. Those who engage in traditional historical-critical research, therefore, should do so because they love it. Their love affair with the past should not be dependent on some imagined relevance to whatever issue may be current in the church or American society. If it is, they will be disappointed more often than not, for at most their discoveries will fine tune the insights of the Bible study group, not generate them. It is no accident that the art of Bible translation has been linked more closely to the church than to the academy. For good or ill the translator actually *writes* the Sacred Text that individuals and faith communities will read. Translators normally are, and should be, part of those faith communities. Even though they have always been substantively informed by the findings of historical scholarship, their goals are, and should be, the goals of the Bible study group, not of the biblical studies faculty.

NEW MEDIA FOR COMMUNICATING THE BIBLE: THE POTENTIAL AND THE PROBLEMS

Richard M. Harley

Perhaps no technological development raises more hope or more ambiguity for those involved in Bible translation than today's electronic media, and the brave new information world those media have wrought. Through computers, sound recording technologies and television we find ourselves empowered with astonishing capacities for producing translations and for sharing them with others. Along with the euphoria we feel, most of us also have questions and, perhaps, reservations about where the new media are taking us. For those of us who received our basic training in biblical language during the pre-computer period, some reservations seem to spring from assumptions we gained back then about learning, when the ways we learned were tied to the printed text, and 'bits and bytes' were still the dreamy notions of laboratory researchers. Some of our questioning today may also spring from the sheer joys we recall in exploring the text of Scripture, explorations so memorably formative as to make it hard for us to conceive of working with the Bible in any other mode.

One such expression of the joy many of us have felt is captured so well in J.B. Phillips' recollection of his own first encounter with the text of the Greek New Testament. The description is found in his book, *Ring of Truth*. Phillips was an Anglican pastor who came to Biblical Greek after deep immersion in the classical Greek of the philosophers and poets. At first, he wrote, turning from the high style of the classics to the common Greek of the New Testament felt a little like shifting from the grandeur of Shakespeare to a newsletter from the local priest. Yet as he pressed on with translation, Phillips began

---

RICHARD HARLEY is President of World Development Productions and trustee of the Foundation for Biblical Research, Boston, MA.

to find the texts under his hands, as he put it, "strangely alive." They produced, he said, "an effect of inspiration which I have never experienced, even in the remotest degree, in any other work."[1] At the time I first read Phillips' account, I was myself launching into Biblical translation and finding the original texts very 'alive' indeed. Part of the wonder lay in the sheer *tangibility* of the process—the feel of original text under one hand, a pen in the other, its point touching clean paper. Part of the wonder also lay in the simple awareness of being poised for the act of writing, not unlike those who first wrote the text itself. Somehow the trappings had the right *feel*, readying one to receive what our biblical forefathers and foremothers were trying to say.

Decades later, I confess, the encounter with original text still produces for me an effect of wonder. But as our world is transformed by the wonders of electronic communications, it's inevitable that all of us nurtured on the printed Word must now square with new realities that modern media have thrust before us, and the questions they raise. When people are getting so much information through *nonprint*, electronic media, is the once text-oriented enterprise of Bible translation destined for radical change? Does our very concept of 'original text' need to change, as hard copy increasingly moves from print into the world of bits and bytes? And if, in the long run, we get more used to exploring scripture with our hands on a computer than the pages of a book, can we still know what it means for the text to come 'strangely alive' under our hands, full of that familiar ring of truth? Moreover, what about the implications for the *readers* of translations, and public concern over the decline in literacy? Should those charged with transmitting a text-based tradition *resist* the new media, in hopes of stemming further decline? Or should we open ourselves to the possibility that electronic media might actually do some good?

For those of us who are now working with ABS, sifting through the questions and possibilities, the new communications technologies do indeed appear to hold real promise. And it is important, in any

---

[1] J.B. Phillips, *Ring of Truth: A Translator's Testimony* (New York: The Macmillan Company, 1967), pp.24-25.

assessment of where the media are taking us, to recognize the potentials at hand. There has already occurred a rapid transition toward making Scripture available in computer form. The original texts, as well as entire translations, can be obtained for use on affordably-priced computer systems. The benefits for translator and student alike are dramatic. It used to be, for instance, that the only way to compare different translations was to open books and spread them out over a large surface, or to search a parallel Bible, again in book form. Now comparisons are aided by the increasingly familiar 'windows' environment of computers. While holding the words of original text in one window, today's translator or student calls up to the screen parallel windows in which different translations appear.

Searching for passages—a process that once required painstaking exploration of concordances in book form—is now easily and almost instantly handled by the powerful search capacities of computer programs. Meanwhile, advances in the storage of data put whole libraries of biblical research materials at our disposal in computer form. The same compact disk technology that revolutionized the music industry makes this possible. The data stored on compact disks—CDs—can now be accessed on computer screens through the increasingly affordable CD-ROM systems.[2]

Technological changes, of course, not only change our world but the way we *speak* about it, including Scripture. Gone are the days, it seems, when we would speak in all simplicity about 'the Word' and have just the familiar printed Book come to mind. With new Biblical products hitting the CD market, we now start to accommodate names and slogans wrought straight out of computerese—on one side, 'CD Word;' on another, the 'PC Study Bible'; on still another, new products from a company called 'Biblesoft.' And don't forget the hype

---

[2] CD-ROM technology provides the capability for massive storage of information on single disks (at present state of development approximately 300,000 pages of text can be stored on a single 5" disk) and for making instant searches for words and word combinations.

of advertising. In the memorable words of one brochure: "After 2000 years, the ultimate Bible!"

Still, for all the sloganeering, the amazing CD research libraries put at our disposal the resources that once required time-consuming library lookups and book handling—all on a single 4½ inch compact disk, accessible by the push of a button. Researchers like Robert Kraft of the University of Pennsylvania are taking advantage of the new storage and retrieval capacities to develop new texts that aid Biblical understanding, such as his text of the Greek Old Testament, set in parallel with the Hebrew Scriptures and grammatical study aids. Such computer-aided work becomes that much more impressive when sophisticated computer imaging techniques are applied to reconstruct texts that are fragmentary or visually unclear.

A striking thing about the technologies pioneered by researchers like Kraft is that textual study materials once accessed by only a tiny few can now be accessed by the many. Translators and students of the Bible, including non-experts, are all potential beneficiaries. Kraft himself was aided by the democratization of information made possible by the opening of data banks of Greek literature at the University of California, Irvine—the so-called TLG project (Thesaurus Linguae Graecae). Before long, democratization is likely to reach beyond the availability of texts, to *image* and *sound* as well. Projects like the Perseus Project at Harvard University have shown that packages of text, still pictures and moving pictures, along with the voices of expert commentators, can be assembled to assist students of ancient Greek. The principle is one that is well-known to Bible scholars: ancient texts are better understood when seen in the context of the life setting that produced them.

Of course, it is hard yet to know how much these multimedia programs will reach the public at large. And it can be just a little daunting to ponder what effects the new multimedia powers might eventually have on the personal research styles of those of us who do Bible translation. We get some clues, if I may speculate just a bit, from the impact already felt by people like Greg Crane of the Perseus Project at Harvard. Sitting in his media research center, Greg looks a little like a transmediated version of Albert Schweitzer who, when doing his famed study of European New Testament scholars, sat like a jungle explorer amid a forest of books. With Crane the forest around him is *technological*—the computer screens displaying video images, intermingled with larger high-resolution TV screens, CD-ROM machines and video-disk players—all of them working in sync to aid the study of ancient Greece. Seeing Crane some months ago, I couldn't help wondering if those of us involved in Bible translation will also be swallowed up by the new machines, yearning for the simple joys of the books we once loved to pile up, or the page of printed text that seemed to tell our fingertips the meaning was about to burst through. Or will we, like Crane, feel astonishingly empowered with new exegetical prowess?

Perhaps the main promise of today's experimentation in multimedia lies in their potential to open new approaches to *learning* that were not possible before. The code word for the new learning approaches is the word 'interactive.' It's not just that Bible translations can be placed on computer, along with notes in the form of moving pictures and sound; the users of these materials can also be encouraged to 'interact' with the Biblical stories, pausing from analysing textual materials to examine related background in displays of image and sound. As questions arise in their reading, users can find answers at the push of a button, calling up reference materials to the screen, then turning back to textual materials to read on. In short, the new effort to make media work interactively with users opens real possibilities for people to engage for the educational process, becoming more creative in their use of media, rather than just sitting before electronic screens, dazzled by hypnotic and titillating imagery. It all brings to mind the dialogical elements that—from early centuries—accompanied Jewish religious study. Students of sacred texts were encouraged to ask questions of those texts, challenge them, and be challenged. Oral discourse and interaction were seen as a natural activity alongside the written. Even the engagement of printed Scripture could be seen more as dialogue than a one-way movement of messages moving from print to eye.

The other promise of multimedia lies in reaching people for whom the written Word is not accessible. Either they cannot read it, or can but don't do much of it. Among adults worldwide, we are now told, an estimated one third are now illiterate,[3] most of them living in the developing world. Yet many of the world's illiterate, though poor in education, are rich in biblical interest. Even in this country we hear about widespread illiteracy, some hidden, some out in the open.[4] We know that a large number of American youth are more attuned to television than to the world of print. The question naturally arises: can more of these persons have a chance to encounter Scripture, albeit in non-print forms? As many of you will know, the United Bible Societies is exploring on an international scale the production of new oral versions of Scripture to serve illiterate people abroad. The American Bible Society, meanwhile, is exploring the use of multimedia for presenting Scripture here at home—an effort I will describe in more detail in a moment.

I. *The Theoretical Backdrop*

But first, a word about a larger struggle that sets the stage for today's exploration of new media for Bible translation. It is a struggle to understand where our media changes are taking the culture at large, and what that means for access to Scripture. There is widespread agreement among observers of the new media that electronic media have changed what Neil Postman calls the 'symbolic environment' in which we live. Postman, a scholar on communications at New York University, describes it like this: "We have reached, I believe, a critical mass in that electronic media have decisively and irreversibly changed the character of our symbolic environment. We

---

[3] Hans Rudi-Weber, *Experiments with Bible Study* (Geneva: World Council of Churches, 1981), p.10.

[4] See, for instance, Carl Kaestle et al., *Literacy in the United States: Readers and Reading since 1880* (New Haven and London: Yale University Press, 1991).

are now a culture whose information, ideas and epistemology are given form by television, not by the printed word."[5]

As a practical matter, many who have studied the shift in ancient times from orality to literacy—Ong, Havelock, Kelber, and others—have claimed that such shifts in a culture's symbolic environment also bring a shift in the ways people think. The great transition to writing, Ong argues, brought a surge in the "analytic management of knowledge."[6] Working with written texts, many would agree, promotes linear reasoning, a testing of propositions for logical coherence, and a focusing of arguments for testing them against others. Today's shift into electronic media may also be encouraging new modes of thought, in some cases *breaking* from the tight analytic reasoning encouraged by print culture. Television programming, for its part, caters more to the values of amusement, situational drama and titillating visual effects than to the enrichment of the mind's analytical powers or skills in linear argument. There are, of course, notable exceptions on TV.

Meanwhile, trends in the display of images on TV involve a piling up of images in dazzling montages of visual stimulation, rather than emphasizing sequence or linear logic. The trend is epitomized in the music videos that pervade youth culture and now influence all kinds of presentations on TV. Even the nightly news programs present their segments in rapid-fire succession. There is no particular order or overall context. They play to our growing appetite for a rapid consumption of endlessly shifting scenes, and our intolerance for items that last more than the standard 45 seconds. As every politician knows, the popular mind that once craved the well-crafted reason of a Lincoln-Douglas debate will now tolerate only the titillating quick image, dialogue reduced to an exchange of one-liners, the knock-out punch of the mind-convicting 'sound bite.'

---

[5] Neil Postman, *Amusing Ourselves to Death* (New York: Penguin, 1985), p.28.

[6] Cited by Postman, *op.cit.*, p.51. See Walter Ong, "Literacy and the Future of Print," *Journal of Communication* 30:1 (Winter, 1980); and *Orality and Literacy* (New York: Methuen, 1982).

Perhaps most important for the future of Bible translation, the electronic media can dramatically change the way even well-constructed texts are read, particularly on computer. At the forefront of these changes are the powers of *hypertext*. Hypertext makes it possible for someone reading the text of one author to stop, then call up on the screen a window of text from another author, then return again to the original. The control an author used to have over centering reader attention and holding the flow of his or her thought is broken; now readers are encouraged to explore materials in any way they like.

Compared to the normal thought processes involved in reading a novel or following a Biblical story in print, the perceptual shifts of hypertext are astonishing. As George P. Landow of Brown University summarizes it, with hypertext we are dealing with a linking of blocks of texts across different documents, making computer access to literature 'intertextual' and what he calls 'infinitely re-centerable.' Readers are given unprecedented control of what—and how—they read. Hypertext overthrows the author's usual preeminence, since the text is 'atomized' into blocks of text, and these are again dispersed and reconfigured with other texts. As a result, the linear drive of the printed page gets disrupted as readers choose among a virtually endless number of paths along which to work and think nonsequentially. The interdisciplinary study of texts is potentially enhanced as hypertext links materials that are usually separate and offers the 'virtual presence' of teachers in various disciplines—called into view from other documents, either in the form of printed comment or moving picture. Argues Landow, all kinds of hierarchies of status and power that were once in force become irrelevant. For writers and readers hypertext creates stunning possibilities but also raises challenging questions.[7]

---

[7] For elaboration, see George Landow, *Hypertext: The Convergence of Contemporary Critical Theory and Technology* (Baltimore: Johns Hopkins Press, 1992). See also George Landow, "Hypertext and Literary Education," *Computers in the Humanities*, June 1989; and Paul Delaney and George

For some media observers, the rise of computers and TV portend an ominous decline in the printed word, and especially the qualities of thought once encouraged by it. Writes NYU's Neil Postman: "As typography moves to the periphery of our culture and television takes its place at the center, the seriousness, clarity and, above all, value of public discourse dangerously declines." To be sure, he concedes, even the most disruptive new technology is capable of making positive contributions. Still, he feels, what the electronic media contribute to culture—mostly by entertaining us—will pale in comparison with the joys of literary thinking it takes away.[8]

Other observers, including Biblical scholars, are not so negative on the potential of electronic media. They favor *harnessing* the new media for what they can do in the communication of Scripture. Members of the Bible in Ancient and Modern Media group of the Society of Biblical Literature, spearheaded by Tom Boomershine,[9] are convinced that the influx of new media has brought a shift in human consciousness no less dramatic than the transition from orality to print-oriented literacy. It is a shift, Boomershine argues, that requires efforts to understand the new communications, and to adapt translation work to address those realities.[10] The new media, in this view, actually hold the future, if only we will be open to them.

Still other sympathetic observers argue that there are huge stakes in the media issue for the place of churches and translators in our culture. Without mastering and employing the new media, they say, the churches could turn over the sacral mythmaking of today to the

---

Computers in the Humanities, June 1989; and Paul Delaney and George Landow, editors, *Hypermedia and Literary Studies* (Cambridge, MA: MIT Press, 1992).

[8] Postman, *op.cit.*, p.29.

[9] See Boomershine's response on pp. 181ff.

[10] Thomas Boomershine, "Biblical Megatrends: Towards a Paradigm for the Interpretation of the Bible in Electronic Media" (see Appendix).

secular imagemakers of Hollywood. Gregor Goethals,[11] for one, says that the creation of sacral space—and the communication of myths that interpret the meaning of life—has increasingly been usurped by the captains of the media, in particular TV. Artists, theologians and translators, she says, must not shy away from engaging the new media world if the noble myths of biblical religion are to maintain a presence in public discourse.[12]

Partly, the advocates of media engagement perceive an opportunity not just for keeping pace with society, or reaching more people, but for enriching translation itself. Research has increasingly brought to light those features of oral and rhetorical presentation which underlie the original texts, and are still embedded in them. For some time now, the likes of Ong, Kelber, and others, have been telling us that our text-based definitions of Scripture have obscured the fact that the Biblical materials were recorded largely, if not primarily, to assist oral presentation, only secondarily for personal reading.[13] If more can be learned about a text's original meaning by studying its *oral* and *rhetorical* features, the argument goes, translators could be greatly aided in their work. To some, the argument must lead even a step farther—that *only* by using the oral and visual powers of the electronic media can the original oral thrust of many passages be conveyed in their truest import.

II. *A Journey into the Electronic Media*

No doubt this last position, and the more general debate over media, will spark controversy within the translation community for years to come. Positions will be staked out as diverse as the variety

---

[11] See Goethals' response, pp. 187ff.

[12] Gregor Goethals, *The Electronic Golden Calf: Images, Religion, and the Making of Meaning* (Cambridge, MA: Cowley Publications, 1990).

[13] Walter Ong, *op.cit.*; Werner Kelber, *The Oral and Written Gospel: The Hermeneutics of Speaking and Writing in the Synoptic Tradition, Mark, Paul, and Q* (Philadelphia: Fortress Press, 1983).

of religious styles in America, and as far-ranging as the views different communions hold on the place of the printed Word in church life. I shall not try here to predict the outcomes. But I will conclude by giving you an inside look at what happens when translators *do* make that radical move to engage the media, loosening for a moment their attachments to the printed page, putting aside all reservations, and stepping forth into the world of bits, bytes and video. Personally, I was propelled into this world at the request of Fern Lee Hagedorn who manages the multimedia translation project for ABS. So far as I know, the ABS project is the first attempt at genuine translation using the electronic media. As now planned, Tom Boomershine would be serving as Chief Consultant, Gregor Goethals as Director of Art. My own role would be to muster my experience in journalism and biblical studies to assist in research for design of the interactive computer package.

The project began with an experimental rendering of a story from Mark 5—Jesus' healing of the Gerasene Demoniac. The aim primarily was to reach young people, and teenagers in particular. The new translation would embody exactly what its name implies—multimedia. It would be housed in an interactive computer format. To interest teenagers, a music video would be produced. This would be available separately as a simple video, but also as one part of a larger computer package. In addition to the video, there would be examples on the screen of storytellers rendering the demoniac story in different oral styles.

Importantly, the product would utilize the 'windows' capacities of computers. These were to be delineated sections of the computer screen where, at the push of a button, users could explore the background of the story and learn more of what the story meant to those who first heard it. This section came to be dubbed the LEARN section of the translation (later EXPLORE). Here scholarly perspectives would be drawn together and packaged in user-friendly forms. With these perspectives at hand, and the powers of hypertext at work, users would be encouraged to encounter the story in an interactive way, exploring the various sides of its features and meaning. In addition to the LEARN section, finally, there would also be materials in still another window inviting teenagers to think about how the story could apply to them and their world today. The distinctive feature of the ABS multimedia translation project, compared to others, would be its attempt to stay close to the meanings scripture had for the original receptor audiences. Other projects have tried to put the Bible on TV, incorporating dramatizations of sandal-shod characters, thousands of cheering extras, stylized in the imaginative modes of a Cecil B. de Mille. More recently, Franco Zeffirelli's *Jesus of Nazareth* drew together elements from across the gospels to tell, in a single story line, the story of Jesus. But the ABS project, as David Burke puts it, takes a different tack. "It is based on a message-dominant principle," he says, "in contrast with those Bible bathrobe epics where the main attraction is a movie star like James Mason playing the high priest, or the muppet-like presentations, or the Hanna-Barbera cartoon fantasy adventures in which modern-day kids are shown going back into Bible lands to mingle with the characters. So much on television is done with the motive of entertainment or profit—not with the firm grounding we want on text and translation. We want the message to control the medium, not the medium to dominate the message."

In short, the multimedia translation aspired from the outset to be genuine translation, not adaptation. The now well-known concept of functional or dynamic equivalence, developed within ABS, remains very much at the center of this effort. As Eugene Nida and Jan de Waard defined it, genuine functional equivalence must enable people today to understand—in modern idiom—what the original receptors understood in their day.[14] Applying this definition to our project, ABS chief translator Barclay Newman recently tried to sum up what a multimedia translation should be. "A multimedia translation," he said, "combines a faithful functional equivalent rendering of the source text with supplementary audio-visual features that maximize

---

[14] Jan de Waard and Eugene Nida, *From One Language to Another* (Nashville: Thomas Nelson, 1986), p.36.

the potential for both a proper understanding of and an appropriate response to the message of the source text."[15]

Some people, on first hearing of this experiment, may wonder why the Gerasene Demoniac was chosen for the pilot translation. Here, after all, is a rather strange encounter of Jesus with a demon-possessed man, a man who wandered among tombs, slashing himself and breaking the chains people had used to subdue him. Jesus casts out the 'Legion' of demons which had troubled the man, giving them leave to enter a nearby herd of pigs, which violently stampede off a cliff and drown in the sea. While we learn that the once troubled man was healed and asked to follow Jesus, we also learn the surprising response of townsfolk—troubled by what had occurred so close to home, asking Jesus to leave. In some ways, it's all very strange. Yet the narrative's features of lively storytelling and powerful compassion combined to make it attractive. Surveys of young people also showed that the story evokes real interest, including its stress on crossing boundaries and the authority of Jesus. Scholarly analysis revealed potentials for conveying some of the central themes of Mark.

My own work, along with some others, focused on researching the meanings this story would have had for the first hearers, and finding ways to embody that research in the computer part of the translation. We were aware that the meanings this story had for its first receivers can only be determined imperfectly, given uncertainties about the original settings. But we had confidence that close study of the original texts, along with a thorough review of published research, would go far to reveal how early audiences understood the storyline, idioms, cultural norms, religious context, and so on. While our findings on original meaning would ultimately be used in the computer interactive, they were also meant to assist in new rendering of the story's text, to help storytellers make their oral presentations, and to assist producers who would design the music video. In this way, it

---

[15] ABS internal memo, September 17, 1990, for the Multimedia Translation Project.

was hoped, the story's own message would drive the design of media presentations, not the other way around.

What, then, happens when the well-meaning translator marches forth into new media terrain? We began our well-meaning task with probes into the story's original import, and by coordinating with an equally well-intentioned team of computer experts. The computer team would ultimately develop our program's software. We had hardly stepped into the new media world when the spirits of that world fired back some rather brash response. Our computer colleagues presented what seemed a ferocious timetable for completing the project. It was based on other projects the company had done. They assumed it would work again. Unfortunately, it would require a drastic compression of our textual research into the intent and content of the text, jeopardizing our base of understanding.

The computer team also assumed that they would direct product design, incorporating whatever they found intriguing in the story of the Gerasene Demoniac and whatever 'facts' we might put at *their* disposal. They rapidly pushed forward visions of what the music video might do, as well as textual materials that would go into the computer interactive package. To compound our dismay over these developments, the computer team entered into discussions with one of the country's best-known manufacturers of computer software—which I will call, simply, 'Software America.' This computer giant just happened to have an interest in developing a Bible-related study program to showcase its new windows software. As executives at Software America heard from our computer team about the multimedia translation, they started to see a good candidate for their own biblical showcase. Our computer colleagues, we suspected, were starting to see stars over the possibility of longterm, lucrative contracts with Software America.

Needless to say, for those of us working on core research, the media forces bearing in on the project appeared less than helpful. Rather than opening new space and possibilities, these forces introduced artificial pressures keyed to production of something that would work for Software America, but not necessarily our translation.

It was as if we had crossed over into a world stranger than we had thought, only to be met by the more aggressive spirits of that world, rushing forward to embrace our story and make it their own. Fortunately, firm stands taken by Fern Lee Hagedorn and her colleagues at ABS-New York turned back these pressures. New understandings were reached with Atlanta, and the proper research into the original texts has gone forward as hoped.

In our role of gathering the relevant scholarly perspectives, my staff and I did the usual exegetical legwork, draining all commentaries and related materials on Mark from the libraries of Harvard University and the nearby Episcopal Divinity School. In gathering materials we felt reassured that all was indeed well. Yes, the new media translator could still feel all the safety and comfort of the 'Schweitzer effect,' nestled in his or her forest of printed books. Only again, like Greg Crane at Harvard, we were aware that our forest grounds had come to be shared by beasts prowling on electronic feet. The data we would gather from books would now be entered directly into high-tech computers. And electronic communications would make it possible for the forest-dwellers in one location to link up with others around the country—something Schweitzer could scarcely have dreamt.

More important in the research, however, was the priority given to research perspectives that could serve us and other translators working in multimedia. What perspectives from scholarly research would shed light on how the first receivers heard and visualized the story? Put another way, in our particular story, what did the features of image and sound reveal about how the story was told, and the reactions of people who first heard it? The more we looked, the more special answers came. And once these insights were in hand, we had a body of practical guidelines that could assist those colleagues designing other parts of the translation—the sections in video and sound. Our 'meaning guidelines' would also inform the design for the interactive portion of the computer package. It was here—in design of these non-video portions of the translation—that I would devote the rest of my efforts. I will call these portions the 'Computer Notes,' for want of a better name.

But how can one design such Notes in a way that might inspire users to dig deeper into the story? How do you encourage teenagers to *want* to see what the story meant to those who first heard it? We had to recognize that many teenagers have little, if any, exposure to Scripture. Done properly, notes could help to set them in context. In addition, the story we were telling had elements which often sound strange to modern listeners—the demons, the fate of the pigs, and so on. Without helping our users to understand these elements properly, they could jump to wrong conclusions about the story, and translation would fail to convey functionally equivalent meanings. Here again, the powers of computers to store and retrieve information—if properly arranged—might do much to help the story's meaning come through.

Imagine several teenagers who have just viewed the music video or a storyteller's oral rendering of Jesus' encounter with the demoniac. The story line has now come into view. They are intrigued by various features, perhaps confused by others. At the push of a button, they refer to the menu in the Computer Notes. Here they see a topic that needs explanation—for example, the fate of the pigs. At the push of a button, explanations come to the screen on pigs, how people of the biblical world viewed them, and their symbolism in the story. The window of information appears on the screen next to windows carrying the video and the written text. In the spirit of multimedia, the teenager finds the notes presented in various ways—some through young people's conversation, some through scholars speaking, some with charts, some moving pictures, some interesting texts. At any point, the teens can refer back to the story's text, and as other questions come to mind, come back to the Computer Notes, then return to video or audio presentations. In theory, at least, every step in the search and discovery process becomes more satisfying, for the teenagers realize their questions are being answered. The story starts to have real meaning for them.

As those of us on the translation team increasingly viewed biblical encounter in terms of this multi-entry access and broad freedoms of enquiry, we started to see just how crucial the Computer Notes would be for multimedia translation. Often such notes figure into print translations as secondary elements to help clarify the main text. Here they would be crucial for stabilizing and anchoring the presentations of image and sound, and more generally to ensure that dynamic equivalence was reached. In other words, the Notes would need to be seen not as an add-on, but an integral part of the translation itself.

Assuming, then, such an integral role for the Notes, how would the *content* of the Notes be selected and organized? The team first identified ten aspects of the story which had special significance for listeners in the first century. One section of the Notes would be devoted to the symbolism of Jesus crossing the Sea to what Mark calls 'the other side.' Another section would deal with first century views of demons and illness. There would be another section on the identity of Jesus as deliverer, the name 'Legion,' pigs, the practice of casting out demons, and the sea as a place where the pigs drowned. Finally, there would be sections on the transformation of the man to soundness of mind, on the fearful response of those living in the area, and Jesus' refusal to have the man follow him.

With these ten selections, a computer menu was born. When teenagers looked at Computer Notes, they would now have ten topics at their disposal, and a glossary as well. Each section could be retrieved at the push of a button. As we created materials for each section, we would need to ensure acceptability to the broad spectrum of churches, keeping our presentations as free as possible from theological or doctrinal slants. The information of each section would also be tagged to link to other sections, so that users could instantly move between Notes, seeing how all elements of the story hang together—again, a capacity made possible by hypertext.

Pondering the freedom of exploration we were building into the interactive computer use, we began to realize how differently this translation would work from the customary reading of Biblical stories on the printed page. There would be all the power for users to follow their own leadings as they walked around our subject. They would see it from many angles, and happily, get answers to their questions as those questions arose. But for all the advantages of the freedoms and control, there could also be drawbacks if we were not careful—if we were to cut the user so free from the narrative line intended by the author that the story would not cohere, and dynamic equivalence be lost.

As a final task, then, could ways be found to ensure that this narrative line—so important for the author's intention—not fall away but be maintained? One safeguard would come in the approach taken by Tom Boomershine and those designing the music video and oral presentations. They were determined to keep the story line very clear in those presentations. As many of you will know, maintaining a sequential story line is not always done in music videos; the very nature of music videos is almost *anti*-linear by definition, comprised as they are of fast-changing montage, loosely-knit images that may have no sequence whatsoever. But planners of the video portions of the ABS translation were determined to hold fast to the Bible's own sequence and story.

Meanwhile, those of us focusing on the Computer Notes, would keep the story line in view in other ways. We would support the use of visual cues that keep users of Notes apprised of where they are in the story—somewhat like flags placed along the roadways on a map. We would also attempt to word the Notes so that users are keyed back to the story's context, avoiding detours and distractions that could take away from the story's own flow.

III. *Retrospect and Prospect*

As the pilot phase in the multimedia translation now approaches completion, much has been learned, and many questions remain. None of us has been able yet to stand back and make a final evaluation. But I have described for you the process of developing Computer Notes partly to show how multimedia translation surfaces a range of new questions. They are questions not only about how to present the biblical materials afresh, but also how to understand the idea of translation itself. For centuries, in print cultures we have thought of a Bible translation as a book with text printed on its pages. Can a computer interactive package—with a mix of video, oral and print components—be thought of as a 'translation' too?

Perhaps the answers we reach—and I deliberately speak of *answers* in the plural—may depend on how we feel about the implications of hypertext, and our ability or inability to make it serve Biblical meaning. As Landow reminds us,[16] with hypertext, people move back and forth between texts and other stored information, bringing into view new information that wasn't specifically included by the original author. The new media portend an extraordinary degree of freedom in textual encounter. As people get used to the powers of hypertext, they may develop more inter-textual habits of thinking and reading, seeking to encounter subjects in a more multi-angled way, like a person who walks around a sculpture, viewing it from many angles, withholding judgment until the whole finally comes into view. So with Scripture, we may need to have definitions of Biblical encounter which accommodate this dancing in and out of the stories, an approach wide open to all kinds of detours for reflection and observation. If so, the idea of what a translation is may itself need to expand, accommodating a fuller range of components than those afforded by the printed text alone.

Of course, which components are ultimately selected is a wide-open question. Broader definitions of translation need not incorporate the new media in all their varied forms. But if we are to know how to make intelligent choices, we must be prepared to test the possibilities, reaching beyond mere speculation about what *might* be the implications of new media to an understanding of what *actually* happens when they are used. The experimentation will, no doubt, be fraught with uncertainties, even perplexing confusion at points. Still, we must walk out into the arena and wrestle with the potentials and the doubts. In the end, all of us will ask: Do the new media translations have the right *feel* to them? Do they resonate with that old familiar 'ring of truth?' Do they allow us to engage the original excitement, to feel the Bible—once more—'strangely alive' under our

---

[16] See footnote 7.

hands? This will be our final test. We may say of some results that they don't measure up. Yet with other results we may be very strangely pleased indeed.

RESPONSE: Thomas E. Boomershine

Richard Harley has given an excellent overview as well as an inside view of the inner workings of the American Bible Society's newest project, the production of audio/video and multimedia translations of the Bible. Historic events can actually only be identified in retrospect, but let me risk a prediction. These days, October 11 and 12, 1991, may well be recognized as historic days in the history of the translation of the Bible. As we have been meeting to celebrate the founding of the American Bible Society, we also have begun the filming of the first video translation of the Bible in history.

Yesterday the filming crew overcame great ecclesiastical barriers with the help of Jimmy Breslin and filmed the first scene of the Gerasene Demoniac in Calvary Cemetery in New York. Based on months of source research on the sounds and images of Mark's story by a dedicated and diverse community of scholars, and after months of target research working with creative and committed producers who have given themselves wholeheartedly to this work, yesterday we began the production of the first biblical video that seeks to present a functional equivalent translation of the Bible in the electronic media of the 20th century. The aim is to make the Bible available in a vital and relevant translation to American teenagers in the medium in which they live.

This work is a continuation of the tradition of the translators of the Bible throughout its history and of the founders of the American Bible Society. We have gathered here to celebrate, remember and reflect upon the establishment of the American Bible Society in 1816. In responding to Richard's talk I would first like to call our attention to the relationship between the original character and purpose of the Society and the systems of mass communication in the early 19th century. Then I would like to address the implications of this for the

---

THOMAS BOOMERSHINE is Professor of New Testament at United Theological Seminary, Dayton, OH.

mission of the Society today in the context of the systems of mass communication 175 years later.

The story of the founding of ABS that I am about to tell you is based on the research of David Paul Nord. He is a professor of the history of journalism at Indiana University and has done extensive research on the American Bible Society and its sister, the American Tract Society.[1] We should invite him to address the Society at some other historic moment soon.

Elias Boudinot was a pious Christian, a prominent Presbyterian layman, and a leader of the Federalist forces in the new House of Representatives in the 1790's. For the Federalist forces with their pro-British and anti-French political leanings, the victory of Thomas Jefferson and his democratic forces was ominous. With the Unitarians and radical Republicans in power, orthodox Christianity and the forces of traditional civil authority were under assault. Hence, Boudinot's first book in 1801 was an attack on Thomas Paine's *The Age of Reason*, and was called the Age of Revelation. In the preface, he states that he was shocked that thousands of copies of Paine's book had been sold for a cent and a half in the streets of Philadelphia. He decided, in the context of the power of this kind of mass printing, to establish a counter-fund and a counter-organization: in 1809, the New Jersey Bible Society, and in 1816, the American Bible Society. The men whose portraits grace the rooms at ABS offices in New York were Boudinot's political and ecclesiastical allies.

These men founded an organization that within fifteen years established the origins of modern mass media through the unprecedented use of new technological developments for the distribution of the Scriptures. These men were media pioneers. It took American business decades to catch up to the level of media sophistication and power that they generated. As Nord outlines, four elements came

---

[1] David Paul Nord, "The Evangelical Origins of Mass Media in America, 1815-1835," *Journalism Monographs,* Number 88, Columbia, SC: Association for Education in Journalism and Mass Communication at the University of South Carolina, May 1984.

together to make this possible: stereotyping, power printing, machine papermaking, and systematic organization.

Stereotype printing was a new technology in which a facsimile of a page of standing movable type was cast in a solid metal plate. While requiring a large initial capital outlay, this made possible mass printing of fixed works. The first major customers of stereotypers were the Bible societies. Immediately after its founding in 1816, the Board of Managers of ABS procured stereotyped plates of the Bible at the high cost of $4000. By 1820, the ABS owned eight sets of stereotype plates of the whole Bible and another two of the New Testament and was one of the largest publishers in America.

The ABS was also the first publishing house in the Americas to install steam powered presses. Developed by Daniel Treadwell of Boston, the steam powered press made it possible to print much more rapidly than the earlier hand presses, one of which now sits in the ABS library in New York. The first power press was installed in 1826 and by 1829, ABS had 16 Treadwell presses.

Machine papermaking was the final technological development of which the Bible Society was the pioneer supporter. Prior to 1800, papermaking was slow and costly with each sheet of paper being made separately on a screen frame dipped into a vat. The development of papermaking machines was led by Henry and Sealy Fourdrinier of London. The buyer of the first Fourdrinier papermaking machine built in America was Amos H. Hubbard, who ran a handmade paper mill. He was an active member of the Norwich Bible Auxiliary and soon became a Life Member of the ABS Board of Managers. His contribution to ABS was in reams of paper rather than money.

And finally, these media entrepreneurs developed the first systems of mass distribution through the training of traveling book agents and the organization of a network of auxiliaries around the country. With the support of large donations from the evangelical financiers of the emerging benevolent empire, the American Bible Society in the period from 1829-1831 printed over a million volumes and distributed them throughout the new country. Thus, the American Bible Society was the first organization to establish the possibility of true mass media communication in American history. Thus, a major dimension of the founding and early history of the American Bible Society was energetic innovation in the use of communications technology in the service of the communication of the Word of God to the masses of America. When seen from the perspective of the history of communications technology, this development in American church history is in continuity with the history of biblical translation. In every culture and in every period of major change in communications technology, the community of biblical translators has found ways to make the Word of God available in the new means of mass communication. In the oral culture of ancient Israel, storytellers and prophets organized networks of oral distribution of the stories of God through the tribes and families of Israel. The first translations of the Bible into Aramaic and Greek were done in the context of the emerging culture of literacy. Indeed, they were needed because the original sounds of the Hebrew had been recorded in writing and were broadcast by public readings of the manuscripts in places which came to be called synagogues. But, increasingly people did not understand the Hebrew and hence the need for translations and new forms of distribution of the Word of God.

The transition from orality to literacy has been an ongoing process in the history of translation. Early Christians were pioneers in the development of the codex[2] rather than the scroll as a more economical and efficient way of copying and distributing writing. Jerome's Latin translation, the Vulgate, made it possible for the reading of the Scriptures to become the major media event of the medieval world.

At the time of the development of the printing press, biblical scholars first in Germany and then in England again produced new

---

[2] A codex is formed from several sheets folded and sewn together at the fold—what is now known as the book form—in contrast to what was then the usual practice of writing on a continuous scroll composed of as many sheets pasted end to end as might be necessary for a document, sometimes extending to several yards in length.

vernacular translations which made the Bible available in this new communications culture. And, in the modern era, as we have heard in this conference, a veritable flood of translations of the Bible has been produced in order to make texts of the Bible available to people all over the world.

We now live in an age in which the development of electronic communications technology—telegraph/telephone, radio, film, television, computers—has transformed the world. But, apart from the electronic processing of texts about which I have heard a lot of conversation here, the community of biblical translation has been slow to respond to these new potentialities.

These are the needs.

In the world, at least 1 billion of the 5 billion persons on the earth are totally illiterate. In Africa and Asia, approximately 50% of the population, 70% of those over the age of 45, and 85% of women are illiterate. Add to these figures the semi-literate who can barely read and the numbers double. And then add to those numbers, the post-literate populations of the electronic media age who can read but who get most of the information on which they base their faith and commitments from electronic media. We face a radically new situation as a community of biblical translators. For the majority of the world's population, printed Scriptures as the technological means for the translation and distribution of the Bible are now and will be increasingly irrelevant.

From the point of view of the goal of the communication of the Word of God to the human family, we have until now been wholly dependent on the technology of writing to make the Word of God available to people. But that is no longer the case. Via electronic technologies of communication, it is now possible for us to make audio and video translations of the Bible available to everyone in the world in a manner that they can perceive and understand. The limits imposed by the requirement of literacy are no longer present. When combined with printed texts and computer interactive programs, the community of biblical translation has a whole new set of potentialities laid out before our eyes.

In order to do this, we need new translations based on an analysis of the sounds and images of the original texts that will translate the Bible into audio and video. Audio and video are the electronic media that have the greatest potential to make the Scriptures available through electronic communication technology. In order to do this, we will need new systems of critical analysis, translation process, and production. For example, we need to investigate the images that were evoked by the biblical texts and the images that would be functional equivalents now. We need to explore the musical dimensions of the sounds of the original texts and appropriate functional musical equivalents. The accomplishment of this task, if the community of biblical translation undertakes it in a systematic way, will require the reorganization of the methods and communications systems of biblical scholarship and translation and the development of new systems for the production and distribution of the Scriptures. To conclude, when seen in the context of the history of the pioneering work of the American Bible Society in developing new techniques and strategies for biblical translation, it is appropriate that the Society has once more launched a new translation in a new medium.

RESPONSE: Gregor Goethals

Images in the service of religion have been viewed with suspicion from the beginnings of an American culture dominated by a Protestant ethos. Yet, ironically, over time we have become perhaps the most image-saturated nation in the world. Moreover, in their use of mass media technology, secular institutions, *not* religious groups, have transformed the religious forms of communication—ritual and icon, appropriating them for a variety of purposes.

Before speaking of the positive dimensions of audio visual and multimedia translation, I want to review some of the things that frequently turn people off about the mass media. Richard Harley has alluded to these already, and I want to build on his observations. Then, against that background of criticism, I would like to project some of the radical departures from current cultural use of the electronic media—in form, content and function—involved in the translation project currently underway.

A. First, then, in response to Richard Harley's observations let me focus on some *troubling motifs* in contemporary mass media, especially television. I want to briefly consider three: 1) Power and the Mass Media, 2) the Pervasive Mode of Entertainment, and 3) the 'strobe light aesthetic.'

1. *Power and Media.* We must take seriously the critiques of Neil Postman and others. Yet, we must push them far beyond the discussion about literacy, beyond the debate about the ways that print or moving images instruct, enrich us, or hinder our capacity for knowledge. The symbolic universe of electronic images in which we live is a costly one to produce, and we should be looking at the co-dependency of major corporate economic interests in creating that

---

GREGOR GOETHALS is Professor and Dean of Graduate Studies at Rhode Island School of Design.

symbolic world which for many has become as real as ordinary life.

Researcher and critic, Ben Bagdikian, in his book *Media Mono-poly,*[1] warns of a threat to the democratic principles of a genuinely free and open information system. This cannot be grasped, he says, simply by criticizing the symbolic forms of the mass media. Bagdikian examined the concentration of power which has been building as diverse ownership of media corporations declines. In his first studies, in 1982, he found that half or more of all the media in the United States were controlled by over fifty corporations. Five years later, the number had dropped to twenty-nine. In his most recent study he cites Wall Street predictions that in the 1990s as few as six companies may control all media—newspapers, magazines, books, radio, film and television, all the major forms that fabricate our symbolic world.

Complicating this power complex still further is the fact that corporations which depend upon newspapers, magazines, and broadcasting to sell their goods also need them to maintain their economic and political influence. Now, Bagdikian points out, the media institutions are not simply needed by them but, increasingly are owned by the corporate giants. His fear is that both print and electronic media will find it difficult to be neutral agents displaying consumer goods. There will be growing pressure to become instruments of power for major corporations.

2. *The Pervasive Mode of Entertainment.* As critics of contemporary mass media, I think most of us have written, in one way or other, footnotes to Jacques Ellul and George Orwell. Both men understood the power of an environment of symbols.

Long before this contemporary explosion of mass media, Jacques Ellul, in his book *Propaganda* called attention to what he identified as a horizontal and vertical propaganda that comes from within society itself, particularly information. Modern information mecha-

---

[1] Ben H. Bagdikian, *The Media Monopoly* (3rd revised edition, Boston: Beacon Press, 1983), p. 152. See also Bagdikian's article, "The Lords of the Global Village," *The Nation,* June 12, 1989.

nisms, he says, "induce a sort of hypnosis of the individual, who cannot get out of the field that has been laid out for him by the information."[2]

Orwell, in his book, *1984*, gave a fictional account of such vertical and horizontal propaganda. The Ministry of Truth, you recall, provided all forms of entertainment and diversion: "newspapers, films, textbooks, telescreen programs, plays, novels—with every conceivable kind of information, instruction, or entertainment, from a statue to a slogan, from a lyric poem to a biological treatise, and from a child's spelling book to a Newspeak dictionary." Since 85% of Oceanic inhabitants belong to the proletariat, special forms of entertainment are devised for them. Their newspapers contain "almost nothing except sport, crime, and astrology." They were also provided with: "sensational five-cent novelettes, films oozing with sex, and sentimental songs." But the ultimate forms of entertainment were "films, football, and beer."[3]

Our contemporary technology—the dazzling montages of images and fragmented segments of visual stimulation—as Richard Harley has observed, might have been incomprehensible to Ellul and Orwell at the time they wrote, but both understood the power of entertainment to distract and to hypnotize.[4]

3. *The Strobe-light Aesthetic.* A third troubling element is the cultivation of what I have termed a 'strobe-light aesthetic' which is based upon our current addiction to novelty and to forgetfulness. This aesthetic is closely related to the other motifs I have mentioned. But I want to draw special attention to it in order to emphasize our celebration of what may be called a Kleenex-culture; a throw away society that wants neither to conserve nor to remember.

---

[2] Jacques Ellul, *Propaganda* (New York: Alfred A. Knopf, Inc., 1973), p. 87.

[3] George Orwell, *1984* (New York: Signet Classics, 1983), pp. 39, 61.

[4] Idem.

Richard Harley spoke of the 'rapid-fire succession' in the presentation of the evening news. I am sure all of us here have experienced the same frustration as I in trying to track down a story which I thought was very important but which passed so quickly I scarcely had time to grasp it. And to make matters worse, the story seemed to vanish and was never brought up again in any detail.

There are, in fact, a number of critics who see TV news in its current form as a communication disposal mechanism which collects the selected information of the day and vacuums it away—out of sight, out of mind, and unavailable for reflection. Indeed Fredric Jameson[5] has suggested that news programs may serve as agents and mechanisms for our historical amnesia as they systematically relegate recent historical experience into the past.

B. Let me turn now from the troubling aspects of television in general to some of the *powerful and positive aspects of the multimedia translation.* While employing the technologies of contemporary mass media, we have sought to depart radically from current goals and processes of commercial television. To add to the comments of Richard Harley and Tom Boomershine, I want to make some brief observations, contrasting the *function, forms and symbols* of this American Bible Society project with current trends in mass media.

First, the basic function of the multimedia project is a translation, accompanied by the presentation of an accessible exegesis through which lay persons can get deeper into the study of the Bible.

This special role of the multimedia project has been uppermost in enlisting, developing, and orchestrating the scholarly and artistic resources for this project. The development of the forms and symbols is guided by its unique function which contrasts sharply with current fads of popular and high art. We are working with multimedia not to

---

[5] Fredric Jameson, "Postmodernism and Consumer Society," *The Anti-Aesthetic: Essays on Postmodern Culture* (Hal Foster, ed., Port Townsend, WA: Bay Press, 1983), p. 125.

entertain or to distract but to re-present, to translate a Bible story in a different language that will speak to the contemporary world, an audio-visual language.

Both the translation and the multimedia techniques discussed by my colleagues are new and revolutionary. But novelty itself is not the aim of this project. Art historian James Ackerman in an essay entitled "The Demise of the Avant Garde"[6] argued that this term no longer had any meaning for a culture totally devoted to what is 'new.' The question for artists and historians today, he concludes, is not "what is new?" but "what is of *value?*" So while there is the challenge to the team to make the most exciting uses of today's amazing technology, we are guided by a commitment, *not* to what is new, *but to what is of value*: a translation in a contemporary audio-visual language and an unprecedented form of study guide for sustained reflection upon the Bible.

The religious dimension of forms and symbols of the multimedia translation challenged the imaginative powers of the team of artists who were responsible for the production.

Let me share with you some of the responses of film makers, stage designers, graphic artists, technicians, and others who worked on this project. There was great excitement and stimulation arising from the fact that they could develop the power of their arts in ways that Hollywood and entertainment-driven productions do not allow. The religious symbols could be creatively explored, for example, without the necessity of dressing the characters up in bath robes and false beards. Instead there was the possibility to re-vision, to bring the human imagination into play, to translate the story in ways that words alone cannot—in short to draw upon the evocative, non-linear power of images to embody a translation. Here was the opportunity to stretch the spiritual imagination and, through dramatic action, color, gestures, staging patterns of light, to translate a story from the Bible in a way that enlivens contemporary consciousness.

---

[6] James Ackerman, "The Demise of the Avant Garde," *L'Arte* 6 (1969): 4-11.

There is another aspect of the project which goes beyond the formal and symbolic challenges of this multimedia translation which I should like to share with you. Among artists there is frequently the sense of isolation, particularly in regard to the life of the spirit. Since the Age of Romanticism, modern artists, unlike those in earlier times, had to choose, indeed to invent as well as to execute the symbols they considered meaningful. This translation and work on the interactive video represented an opportunity to experience a corporate, or communal expression of symbolism. There was a general feeling that the members of the team were not engaged in a solitary or egocentric search, but in a shared venture of religious communication. Among the artists there was a sense that they were collectively involved in rendering visible symbols, not of their own choosing, but ones that stretch back over centuries.

Finally, central to this translation project is the translation. Earlier Richard Harley spoke of the inspiration of translation—of sensing texts as 'strangely alive.' I believe that the interactive video can open up a similar awesome engagement with the Bible to ordinary people. The non-scholar can experience an excitement and can grasp in a tangible way some meaning and beauty of the text that only scholars have known.

I have also learned from Tom Boomershine how important the repeated telling and the hearing of the story is. There is a profound aesthetic and philosophical difference between this audio-visual translation and the stories we have been accustomed to hear and throw away. Traditionally the arts we associate with high culture have been occasions for people to remember. But, as Kenneth Clark noted, the arts have their roots in remembering: ...certain events or objects of contemplation, seen or imagined are so important that they must be recorded.[7] Thus central to this translation project is the story, to be seen and told again, and again, and again.

The multimedia translation project which my colleagues have

---

[7] Kenneth Clark, "Art and Society," in *The Nature of Art* (John Gassner and Sidney Thomas, eds., New York: Crown, 1964), pp. 60, 64.

discussed presents a rare and daring opportunity to show the potential of the electronic media for translations of the Bible appropriate for the 21st century. As a member of the team working on this pilot phase, my hopes and sense of challenge rest on a theological assumption, articulated by H. R. Niebuhr and others, that human creations in all the arts and sciences introduce multiple forms, tools, languages through which faith may be communicated. Clearly also there is a dark side to human creativity, and thus no form—word or picture, print or moving image—is immune to self-aggrandizement. As we survey the destructive dimension of human creativity and corruption, we continually modify our attitudes about the worth of what we create. At the same time, and in tension with this, a revolutionary, redemptive process is at work, continuously opening up the possibility of transformation and renewal.

APPENDICES

BREAKTHROUGHS IN BIBLE TRANSLATING

Eugene A. Nida

For most Americans the activities of translating or interpreting from one language to another seem both mysterious and incredibly difficult. This judgment may simply reflect the fact that so few Americans are bilingual or multilingual, and some even claim that they do not speak English properly, and so translating must be impossible, except for a select few. Translating and interpreting are thought to require years of special training and can only be done by particularly intelligent and well-educated people. Such wrong ideas are often reinforced by the experience of studying a foreign language for a couple of years in high school and never being able to carry on more than a two-sentence conversation.

I. *Translation and Interpreting Are Natural Activities*

In reality, translating and interpreting are very natural things to do. Young children of immigrant parents seem to have no difficulty interpreting for their parents in the check-out lines of supermarkets. And in Africa, where there is probably more multilingualism than in any other part of the world, interlingual communication is simply taken for granted. In China translating is regarded as the fifth skill of language (added to reading, writing, speaking, and listening), and there are now more than 500,000 full-time translators and interpreters in that country.

Even in so-called 'primitive' societies there are some amazingly gifted interpreters. On one occasion I was speaking in Spanish

---

DR. EUGENE NIDA is the former Executive Secretary of the American Bible Society's Translations Department, now serving as special consultant for translations.

through an interpreter to a group consisting primarily of Cakchiquel Indians in Guatemala. The speech was to be about the problems of translating the Bible, and so before the meeting I asked the interpreter just how he wanted me to speak: in short phrases, in brief sentences, or possibly in short paragraphs. But he insisted that I should give the entire speech first, even though it would last almost forty minutes, and then he would interpret it.

My interpreter sat in the front row, but made no notes whatsoever—much to my surprise and consternation. But when he got up to interpret my speech, he reproduced it almost sentence for sentence with remarkable fluency and incredible accuracy.

The best interpreters and translators generally regard their work as so natural and 'obvious' that they do not require special training. In fact, many expert interpreters and translators oppose the offering of courses in the theory and practice of translating since they regard such training as being a waste of time. Some even claim that the only people who become translation theorists are the ones who cannot translate, like the cynical old adage about "those who can't do it, teach it, and those who can't teach, teach in teachers' colleges."

Most first-class translators and interpreters never think about nouns or verbs, clauses or sentences, chiasm or parallelism. For them interlingual communication is as natural as speaking. When people say something, they likewise do not normally worry about grammar, word order, or rhetoric. They know what they want to say, and they say it with automaticity that is as mysterious as it is efficient.

Like effective speakers, interlingual communicators must also have a facility for clear and effective verbalization, in the sense of understanding the designative (or denotative) meanings of what they say and appreciating the associative (or connotative) values of the ways in which they say it. The one diagnostic test given to prospective interpreters for either consecutive or simultaneous interpreting at the Maurice Thorez Institute in Moscow (the leading school of its kind in the Soviet Union) consists of a choice of a topic, one minute to prepare, and one minute to speak, with special attention given to the clarity of utterance and organization.

Translators and interpreters differ exceedingly in natural ability for effective verbalization. Those with only average aptitude can often be greatly helped by thorough courses in various aspects of interlingual communication. But in this same institute in Moscow the head of the interpretation section indicated that during the entire twenty-five years of his experience in teaching translating and interpreting, the institute had not trained one first-rate person. Thousands have learned to do adequate work, but all of Russia's experts in translating and interpreting (and there are many) have been true 'amateurs.'

If this is true of translators in the secular field, then why is it so difficult for the Bible Societies to find translators who can be equally competent in handling the text of the Scriptures? There are two evident reasons: (1) Most biblical scholars are obviously not bilingual and bicultural in the biblical languages and cultures, and (2) as academics they have seldom outgrown the stylistic damage which their Ph.D. dissertation did to their ability to write clear and pleasing English.

There are, however, some sociological and linguistic factors which hamper effective creativity in Bible translators: (1) Centuries of tradition largely inhibit creative rendering of the Scriptures, and any departures from tradition in rendering such terms as *grace, justification, sanctification, expiation,* and *propitiation* are viewed as implying a so-called 'low view' of the inspired word. (2) Ecclesiastical leaders are often suspicious of anything which is not in complete accord with what they learned in seminary twenty-five years earlier. (3) People in the church are dubious of a translation which seems to be prepared for people outside the church, despite the fact that there are more people outside the church than inside. And (4) even the training which is given to potential Bible translators may have been somewhat misdirected. For example, most attention is given to studying the differences between languages, when in reality the focus should be on the similarities of languages at all levels. In addition, most discussions of meaning deal primarily with words rather than contexts, and they concentrate on grammar rather than on discourse. But the most dangerous mistake has been the focus on analysis rather than on creativity, pulling a text apart rather than putting it together, and focussing on the parts rather than on the whole, although the meaning of the whole is normally greater than and/or different from the sum total of the parts.

A creative approach to biblical interpretation seems to many people to be too subjective, and a creative use of language seems antithetical to 'proof-text theology.' Furthermore, it is difficult, if not impossible, to teach creativity or even how to write in a truly fresh way. Also, the study of present-day literary styles has been marginal, if not taboo, in many seminaries and Bible schools.

As already implied in this discussion of interlingual communication, interpreting and translating are in many respects very similar, except for the factor of time: namely, the amount of time which a person has at his or her disposal for producing an equivalent message. And yet it is quite clear that for some persons these two activities seem to be remarkably different. For example, Geronimo Martin, a well-educated blind Navajo, was an unusually skilled interpreter but at the same time a pathetically poor translator when he was reading the English Scriptures in the Braille system. His interpreting was excellent because he was forced to respond in sentences or short paragraphs, which he did with clarity and rhetorical finesse. But when he was reading the Bible text, he became a victim of isolated words and English grammar and seemed incapable of escaping from the grip of the formal elements.

This same phenomenon has been found in other persons who are both interpreters and translators. When forced to interpret simultaneously or sequentially, such persons often exhibit remarkable creativity and intelligibility, even though there may be certain awkward expressions. The dialogic context of having to make sense to an audience and the kind of audience feedback which clearly signals comprehension or mystification force interpreters to be more creative. Some translation teams exploit this fact by having informants or fellow translators respond to hearing the source text read rather than permitting them to read it for themselves.

The dialogic nature of the reading process has been greatly

emphasized in modern literary criticism, but the primary emphasis has been placed on the dialogic encounter of the reader with the author. For the interpreter or translator, however, there is an equally important dialogic encounter with the intended audience.

This concern for the dialogic character of verbal communication has been developed even further by some Jesuits in India, who have set up translation programs in some of the major Dravidian languages in which the basic text of a new Bible translation is drafted by a stylist, rather than by a biblical scholar. In each case the stylist is teamed up with a biblical scholar, and they first discuss in detail the meaning or meanings of the Bible text (a type of dialogic encounter with the source), and then the stylist produces the translation (with the focus on the dialogic encounter with the audience). In this way the maximum expertise of the participants in these 'twin teams' is fully employed. The results of this process are, of course, also reviewed by other persons with competence in biblical studies and in style. But this approach to the problems of interlingual communication is proving to be exceptionally effective, since it guarantees greater creativity through more meaningful dialogue, as well as more effective communication.

II. *Language Universals: the Key to Communicating Equivalence*

Although the naturalness of translating and interpreting provides a number of important insights as to how more satisfactory results can be obtained, a great deal can also be learned from the universals of language. Some people are usually so impressed by the differences between languages that they succumb to the Humboldtian[1] thesis that "We think the way we think, because we speak the way we speak." Some people also back up this view of language determinism by citing

---

[1] Wilhelm von Humboldt, *Über die Verschiedenheit des menschlichen Sprachbaues und ihren Einfluss auf die geistige Entwickelung des Menschengeschlechts,* Berlin: Dummler, 1836.

the Whorf[2] hypothesis about the underlying distinctiveness of languages or Weisgerber's[3] romanticizing about German. In studying any foreign language we are always first impressed by the differences, since contrasts always seem more obvious than similarities. But linguists who have made the broadest analyses of the greatest number of languages are increasingly impressed by the amazing similarities of languages at the most profound and basic levels of both structure and function. In fact, most modern linguists would agree that the basic structures of languages are fully ninety percent alike. In other words, the universals of language far outweigh the differences, and for translators the focus should be on the similarities and not on the differences. The recognition and creative exploitation of these universals is one of the important breakthroughs in interlingual communication.

One of the most evident language universals involves language functions, both psychological and sociological. The primary psychological functions are naming, stating, modeling reality, expression, and cognition. All people sense a need to have verbal means of representing experience. Most children eagerly grasp for new words, because they provide tools for getting things done and for seeming to provide power over objects. 'Word power' is even promoted on television as a way to success.

But names are not enough. People want to say something about objects and events, and so they produce statements, strings of words which identify topics and then make comments about them. These sentences soon become paragraphs, and paragraphs become entire discourses.

Language is, however, more than utterances; it also serves to reflect experience as a 'model of reality,' not the world as it really is, but as it is perceived and talked about. The semantic relations

---

[2] Benjamin Lee Whorf, *Language, Thought and Reality: Selected Writings* (John B. Carroll, ed.), New York: Wiley, 1945.

[3] Leo Weisgerber, *Das Gesetz der Sprache.* Heidelberg: Quelle and Meyer, 1951.

between words form elaborate taxonomies with several layers of classes, e.g. *Fido, dog, canine, animal* and *Minerva, cat, feline, animal.* Classes of words may also model reality: entities (e.g. *boy, dog, hill, tree, star*) participate or are involved in events or activities (e.g. *come, talk, govern, strike, fall*), and both entities and events have characteristics (e.g. *tall, big, good, bad, intelligent, gracious, quickly*). All three classes are complexly related to one another in many ways through relational words such as *in, through, behind, during, because,* and *if.* These universal semantic classes form the core of the language models of experience.

Language is also employed for expression without any intention to influence other people. Exclamations such as *ouch!, damn it!, hurrah!,* and *wow!* do not require an audience. Verbal doodling or playing with words is something young children love to do and something adults do far more than they will usually admit. But language may also be used in aesthetic expression to illustrate balance, proportion, and symmetry or to reflect psychological modes, e.g. serious or playful, content or worried, and happy or sad. Certain features of the function of expression may be purposefully elaborated in rhetorically significant sociological functions, particularly in the emotive function.

The most important psychological function, however, is cognitive, the use of language in thinking (silently talking to oneself). Some thinking is not necessarily verbal in nature (e.g. it may be graphic, formulaic, or temporal), but most complex thought involves verbal symbols. Except for sleeping, people are more occupied with the cognitive function of language than with any other activity.

The primary sociological functions of language form the basis for the ways in which people interact with one another: interpersonal, informative, imperative, performative, and emotive. The interpersonal function involves primarily the ways in which people negotiate and/or maintain social status, that is, their place in the 'pecking order.' The different levels or registers of language, e.g. ritual, formal, informal, casual, and intimate, reflect important differences in roles and relations, relative power and solidarity, and class membership.

The most obvious function is informative, but this function probably accounts for less than twenty percent of what actually takes place in verbal communication. Its purpose is to influence the cognitive content or state of other people, but many speakers talk over the heads of their audiences, and some may simply talk past one another. Too often, lecturers show off knowledge rather than communicate content.

The imperative function of language is designed to effect change in the behavior of people hearing or reading a message, but this is not accomplished merely by means of imperative grammatical constructions. In fact, a pointed joke or an illustrative example may be far more effective. The parables of Jesus have no doubt influenced more behavior than any of his direct admonitions.

The performative function involves primarily a change in the status of others, e.g. solemnizing a marriage, sentencing a criminal, or cursing an enemy. Performative language is often highly ritualized and in some societies is thought to have magical power.

The emotive function is designed to alter the emotive state of an audience, and it depends heavily on the associative or connotative meanings of language. This use of language can inspire deep religious devotion or prompt hilarious laughter. The exploitation of this language function has become the object of extensive study by linguists, a source of enormous wealth for gifted speakers, and the means of great political power for those who can sway the crowds.

Individual discourses, however, seldom if ever involve a single function. Language, the unique implement of the human race, is almost always a multipurpose tool, and the need to appreciate fully its structure and potential is imperative.

The lexical elements of languages also exhibit a number of universal features: (1) figurative meanings (metaphors and metonymies), (2) proper names (representing unique referents) and common names (representing classes of referents), (3) a limited number of word-building possibilities: compounding, affixation, reduplication (complete or partial), change (of parts or wholes, e.g. *sing/sang* and *go/went*), and loss (e.g. French *heureuse/heureux*), (4) the open-endedness of language to addition, loss, and change of both forms and meanings, (5) restriction of reference by means of addition, e.g. compare *men* (potentially millions of referents) with *the three old men I met yesterday* (specific referents), (6) the existence of both designative (denotative) and associative (connotative) meanings, (7) different meanings of the same lexeme (word or idiom) constituting galaxies (central and peripheral meanings), constellations (without a central meaning), and chains, or combinations of these sets of relations, and (8) the related meanings of different lexemes constituting clusters, i.e. semantically contiguous but separate (e.g. *run, walk, jump*), inclusions (e.g. *animal/dog*), overlaps (e.g. *talk/speak*), opposites (e.g. *good/bad*), reversives (e.g. *tie/untie*), complements (e.g. *buy/ sell*), and series: infinite (e.g. *one/two/three...*), repetitive (e.g. *Monday/ Tuesday/ Wednesday...*), and graded (e.g. *hot/warm/tepid/cool/cold*).

The study of syntax in numerous languages has also revealed a number of universals, or at least 'near universals,' in the way in which languages combine words into sentences. The highest ranking structure consists of propositions, a combination of a topic or subject and what is said about it: (1) participation of entities in events (so-called 'case relations'), e.g. agent (*John worked*), experience (*John died, John was hit*), instrument (*the key opened the lock*), and benefactee (*John was given a book*), and (2) class membership, e.g. *John is a dentist* and *John is sick.* But there are also a limited number of other primary semantic relations which occur in languages: (1) restrictive attributives, e.g. *three friends, tall building, very good, come quickly, went home, answer if possible, people who left,* (2) coordination, e.g. *John and Bill, run or jump,* (3) identity, e.g. *Thomas Johnson, the mayor of the town,* (4) relation-axis sets, e.g. *in the house, above the house, through the house* and *when working, while working, if working,* and (5) substitution, e.g. *the man...he* and *he plays tennis better than I do,* in which *do* substitutes for *play tennis.* Languages may differ as to the particular means for signalling these semantic relations, but they all are able to express these sets of syntagmatic and paradigmatic relations.

In view of the enormous variety of possible discourses, it would appear as though there could never be any underlying universals, and yet there are a number of basic features of texts. These elements in the 'framing' of discourse structures are of two main types: (1) primary features of time, space, and class and (2) secondary features of rank, consequence, and dialogic dependencies.

All narratives, personal accounts of happenings, and even instructions for processing involve a so-called 'time line,' and most descriptions depend upon spatial relations, while class is a major factor in lists, classifications, and many descriptions, for example, when a building is described as having so many doors, windows, floors, stairs, etc.

Rank is simply an extension of class, in terms of such categories as importance, size, value, and cruciality, and consequence involves such relations as cause-effect, purpose, result, condition, concession. Dialogic dependencies imply that what follows in a text is somehow formally related to what precedes, e.g. questions and answers, arguments for and against, and 'stream-of-consciousness' sequences.

In addition all languages may enhance the impact and appeal of an utterance by (1) formal devices: shifts in order, repetition, measured lines (e.g. in poetry), embedding, condensation (gnomic utterances), and even nongrammaticality for special effects and (2) semantic devices: figurative language, parallelism/inversion, plays on the meaning of words, paradox, irony, litotes, hyperbole, and specific-for-generic reference.

Not only do such rhetorical features appear to exist in all languages, or are at least readily borrowed as part of the rhetorical inventory of a particular language, but there are also a number of principles which govern the frequency, variety, and distribution of such features in texts. When the focus of rhetorical effectiveness is the audience, then novelty and relevance are primary considerations, but when the focus is on the text itself the major factors are wholeness (completeness and unity) and progression, including cohesion (the relation between the parts) and timing (tempo and rhythm). But when the focus is on the internal context, the coherence of the real or imagined worlds is crucial. When, however, the focus is on the external context of use, then it is the appropriateness of the content and form for the practical circumstances in which a discourse is heard or read.

The amazing number of universals on all levels of language use not only help to explain the translatability of texts, but also point to the need for translators to think more about the similarities than the differences and to exploit more successfully the broad range of universals. This can and should produce an entirely different attitude toward interlingual equivalence and a more meaningful approach to creativity in translating and interpreting. This recognition of language universals constitutes a real breakthrough for translators and interpreters.

III. *Orality in Translation*

The oral form of language is much richer in meaning than any orthographic system designed to reflect it. A snarl in the voice can change a formal compliment into bitter sarcasm, and a slight rise in pitch at the end of a sentence can suggest that the truth of a statement is in serious doubt. Rapid speech can suggest extreme nervousness and tension, and muttered responses can show a rebellious or bitter attitude. But these are only a few of the paralinguistic signs which accompany speech. Note the emphasis in prolonged vowels, the staccato clipping of sounds in terse commands, the gushy tone of voice pleading for favors, and the husky whispers of sexy 'come-ons.'

In addition, oral language normally involves the accompanying extralinguistic features of facial gestures, body movements and stance, eye contact, and muscle tone, which can reinforce or even contradict the meaning of the words which are uttered.

But even more importantly, orality implies dialogic interaction. Dialogic language, however, is not dialectic language, with its cut-and-dried system of thesis, antithesis, and synthesis, in which the answer is decided in advance by Hegelian logic. Dialogic communication is always open, unfinalized, and full of surprises (à la

Bakhtin).[4] This give-and-take of real dialogue offers the best hope of creative insight.

We are so accustomed to the written texts of the New Testament that we often fail to realize how important is the underlying orality: the dictated letters, the conversations, the sermons (even the pastiche of sermon themes in James), and the reports of arguments and disagreements. The Old Testament contains even more material dependent upon oral sources and oral use, e.g. the psalms, the proverbs, and the impassioned pleas of the prophets.

Dialogic language, however, implies more than actual dialogue, since, as Bakhtin has suggested, even listening may be either passive or active. Passive listening means simply hearing what has been said and registering the contents, but active listening means encoding a kind of parallel message, constantly formulating answers, objections, and contradictions, and thinking about other relevant data. Yet some speaking is not dialogic, since it is designed to avoid or to crush response by being meaningless gobbledygook or totalitarian ultimatums. True dialogic communication means the relevant involvement of both speakers and audience.

In order to appreciate the significance of orality buried in written texts, it may be useful to point out some of the major features of such oral language:

1. Bare-bones statements, e.g. the story of the Tower of Babel, with its extreme economy of words. Such texts usually have a bare minimum of description and explanations of motivation, something which is quite characteristic of much of the historical books of the Old Testament.

2. Alternative accounts, e.g. Genesis 1 and 2 and the several resurrection accounts without attempts to explain differences.

---

[4] Gary Saul Morson and Caryl Emerson, *Mikhail Bakhtin: Creation of a Prosaics,* Stanford, CA: Stanford University Press, 1990.

3. Rhythmic features as the result of repeated telling and with the purpose of ease of remembering, e.g. Song of Deborah, Proverbs, Psalms, and liturgical prose (e.g. John 1 and Philippians 2.6-11).

4. Direct quotations, and especially quotes within quotes, as well as shifts between speakers without specifying who says what. Such shifts are frequent in the major prophets. The rather unexpected occurrence of direct quotes, as in Genesis 11.1-9, in which God speaks to himself or to his court, and the conversation between Sisera's mother and her attendants in Judges 5.28-30 (part of the Song of Deborah) seem to be clear evidence of underlying orality.

5. Certain rhetorical features generally associated with oral language, e.g. formal and semantic parallels for emphasis, positive and negative statements which reinforce one another, 'stream-of-consciousness' sequencing (the Epistle of James), and plays on the meanings of words, which depend on sound rather than orthography.

It is also important to recognize that in the ancient world written texts were almost always read aloud, even by a person reading a manuscript in his or her own home. Since reading was almost always an oral process, writing would have been instinctively adjusted to this process, certainly more so than in the case of many modern languages in which reading is almost totally dependent upon sight. Note, however, that stylistic revisions of a written text are largely based on reading a text aloud and hearing the sounds, since our ears are more tuned to the true nature of verbal communication than are our eyes.

By a careful study of the oral literature of receptor languages and the ways in which orality is suggested in written texts, Bible translators can prepare texts which more faithfully reflect the dialogic character of the original texts. But how can the orality of the text be communicated by the orthography, punctuation symbols, and format? First, direct quotations in conversations can be rendered in separate paragraphs, and in those cases in which the participants are evident from the context, it is not necessary to indicate in each case who is saying what. Second, the level of language can reflect different degrees of orality. Certainly, the Gospel of Mark should not be on the same rhetorical level as the Epistle to the Hebrews. Third, contractions can be used in direct quotations of conversations. Fourth, paragraph distinctions can be employed to mark shifts in the internal dialogue, as in Ecclesiastes and Job. Fifth, all transitions must be tested for hearing comprehension; punctuation is not enough to overcome misleading collocations, e.g. a rendering such as "Take us back to the land, Lord" will certainly be heard as "Take us back to the landlord." Sixth, eliminate jingly expressions, final rhymes in prose, and unintended puns, which seem innocent enough in written form but which seriously undermine the dignity of effective prose when heard.

One of the great advantages of multimedia communication of the biblical message is the opportunity to reinstate many of the paralinguistic and extralinguistic features which are so poorly reflected in traditional orthography. Furthermore, since many more people hear the message of the Bible than actually read it for themselves and because there is a growing concern in almost all churches for the liturgical character of worship, far greater attention needs to be given to the oral form of the biblical message.

From psycholinguistics we have become aware of the naturalness of translating, and from linguistics we recognize the potentials of effective communication in view of the universals in language, while from sociolinguistics we see more clearly the significance and power of speech.

Biblical Megatrends: Towards a Paradigm for the Interpretation of the Bible in Electronic Media

Thomas E. Boomershine

I. *Introduction*

The purpose of this paper is to offer some observations about megatrends in Biblical interpretations and, in particular, the interpretation of the Bible in the electronics media culture of the late 20th century. The generative question can be put in several ways: what is the shape of the paradigm of the electronic Bible, of the traditions of Israel's religion on the holy TV and the holy computer as well as in a holy book? What does an electronic hermeneutic look like or sound like? Would you know one if you met one in a vision or walking beside you on the street? And if you met one should you run away, kill it or take it to your heart? We are not at a stage in which a fully documented theory can be formulated. The absence of footnotes is an indication of the seriousness of my intent only to suggest rather than to prove. The value of this type of essay may be in drawing some tentative observations together and submitting them for reaction and further discussion. This is a think piece.

Thomas Kuhn's description of paradigm shifts in the history of science identifies some of the processes involved in paradigm shifts that is appropriate here. Paradigm shifts occur when there is a failure in normal problem solving, when the results yielded by the old methods no longer work. This leads to thought experiments and to a proliferation of various articulations and willingness to try new approaches. Out of this comes a new gestalt, a primary shift in the

---

THOMAS BOOMERSHINE is Professor of New Testament at United Theological Seminary, Dayton, OH.

way in which the material is perceived. Two things happen: 1) the achievements based on a new theory and type of research attract an enduring group of adherents away from competing modes of scientific activity; 2) the theory is sufficiently open-ended to leave all sorts of problems for future practitioners to resolve.

I hear the symptoms of a crisis of paradigmatic proportions in current Biblical research. The primary reason is that the paradigm no longer achieves its purpose. The promise of the historical critical paradigm was that it would render the past alive and would result in illumination and vitality for the religious community. The religious communities that have accepted historical criticism since the 19th century are in decline and the educational enterprise of critical study of the Bible has been massively reduced in theological curriculums since the 1930's because it did not produce spiritual vitality and life. The symptoms of the problem are also reflected in the Society.

The basic paradigm of historical criticism that was generally accepted even fifteen years ago has been fractured. The multiplication of methodologies and research paradigms at an SBL meeting is incredible in comparison to meetings as recent as 1970. But, in spite of all our labor, the impact of historical critical study of the Scriptures on religious communities and the culture in general is minimal in comparison to the beginning of this century. But normal science goes on as if the same formulas and patterns of research will have the same effect. We continue to undertake research projects and to publish books. But increasingly we only write for each other and the results of our research are ignored even by the religious community. We write more and more with less and less effect. To put it simply, the existing paradigm is not producing the results it promised.

Theories have two primary functions: they make it possible to account for the data that can be presently observed and they make possible predictions that can be tested by normal scientific research. I want to suggest a theory that explains why this is happening and generates a radically different paradigm for future research. Arthur Schlesinger made a clear statement of the primary principle of this theory on a recent PBS program on Marshall McLuhan. He said,

"Marx argued that the major movements in history are caused by changes in the modes of production and exchange. McLuhan said that the major movements in history are caused by changes in the modes of communication." Stated in relation to the interpretation of the Bible, the thesis would be that the major movements or paradigm shifts in the history of Biblical interpretation are related to changes in the dominant medium of communication.

The task of Biblical interpretation is to render the primary traditions of the Bible meaningful and alive for persons and communities in later, radically different, cultural and historical contexts. The primary communications system of the community provides the contests within which Biblical interpretation happens. It determines the values, attitudes, and overall hermeneutical options for the interpretation of the Biblical tradition in that cultural context.

II. *The Paradigms of Biblical Interpretation*

If the theory is accurate, the expectation would be that the major changes in communications systems are followed by paradigm shifts in Biblical interpretation. The theory appears to work and a discernible paradigm of Biblical interpretation can be identified in each media age.

A. *The Bible in Oral Culture*

In the oral age, the medium was exclusively sound and the sounds were transmitted by memory. The sounds were generally a kind of chant at least for the narrative, prophetic, and psalm traditions. In the narrative material this chant was improvised on known formulas as in oral poetry now. The way of connecting the present experience of the audience with the holy event of the past was by retelling or representing the material in light of later experience. Thus, the editors of the Pentateuch and the authors of the Gospels all used a common hermeneutical system. Interpreters of this oral tradition were accredited by oral authority generally granted by a master of the tradition. Storytellers and prophet preachers constituted the primary system of distribution.

B. *The Bible in Manuscript Culture*

The historical analysis of the appropriation of writing is more complex. But to make the complex simple, I would propose that writing was appropriated as a servant of oral hermeneutics until the late first century. At that time, a decision had to be made within Israel because of a combination of social, political, and cultural factors of which the prevalence of writing as the dominant communications system in the Hellenistic world was the most important sign of the growing dominance of Hellenistic culture. The new paradigm was based on the distribution of the primary traditions of Israel in writing. Symptoms of this paradigm were: the collection and organization of oral traditions in manuscripts, the production of multiple Biblical manuscripts, the formation of a canon, the cantillation of manuscripts in public worship, the formation of the synagogue/congregation as a place for public readings, and the development of oral forms of commentary on the written manuscripts. Both Pharisaic and Christian Judaism adopted the reading aloud of manuscripts as a primary form for the experience of the written tradition. The words were recited exactly as written and even the chants began to be regulated. This regulation developed until it was written down and fixed by the development of accent systems—in Hebrew the trope marks, and in Greek the accents. The accreditation of an interpreter of the tradition was accomplished by oral disputation. All of these characteristics the movements shared in common.

But Christian Judaism developed a new hermeneutic of Biblical interpretation growing out of this communications system. The primary characteristic of this new hermeneutic was interpretation by ideas. It was essentially an appropriation of the philosophical methods of the Greeks for which Eric Havelock's description of the earlier transition in Athenian culture is instructive. In order to render the Scriptures meaningful in relation to this Neo-Platonic system, allegorical interpretation was developed and became the normative form of Biblical interpretation in Christianity. Theology, the identification and development of doctrine, and the formation of a communications system based on writing in a catholic church—these are symptoms of this paradigm shift.

Pharisaic Judaism also adopted writing as an integral part of Biblical interpretation. But in that new paradigm the oral law remained primary. The oral tradition which produced the Mishnah and the Talmud was organized around memorization of oral law, the interpretation of the written law in relation to the living of individual and communal life, and the maintenance of face to face community. Rabbinic Judaism never developed a full-orbed theological tradition and it appropriated writing in strict subordination to orality. Thus, the paradigm shift associated with writing is evident in the divergent hermeneutics of Christianity and Judaism as each community sought to respond to Hellenistic culture in which writing was the most powerful medium of communication.

C. *The Bible in Print Culture*

The paradigm shift in Biblical interpretation associated with printing is relatively easy to identify. The replacement of the highly allegorical hermeneutics of medieval exegesis by the combination of literal and figural hermeneutics in the Reformation was part of a new paradigm of Biblical interpretation. Vernacular translations, the printing and distribution of the Bible, historical studies of Greek and Hebrew documents in relation to their original meaning, the priority of the sermon, the development of Lutheran hymns and Calvinist psalmody—these were all parts of the new paradigm of Biblical interpretation that emerged in the aftermath of the printing press. The sounds of the Scriptures continued to be read aloud but increasingly in a normal voice without intonation. The availability of texts made it possible for private reading of the texts to be a normal context for study and interpretation. The accreditation of interpreters shifted from an oral disputation to the oral defense of a written thesis. A new distribution system emerged as printed texts of the Scriptures and interpretations of the Bible in printed books and tracts became highly marketable.

D. *The Bible in the Culture of Silent Print/Documents*

Historical criticism developed in the context of the age of silent reading. In the late 17th and 18th centuries in Europe and in the 19th and 20th centuries in America, silent reading became the normal mode for perception of written texts. This is evident in the shift of audience address from "Listen, lordings" in the poems of the 16th century to "Dear reader" in the novels of Henry Fielding and Jane Austen. In this period, for the first time, the Biblical documents were normally studied in silence and the text became increasingly disassociated from sound. Sometimes the sounds continued to be imagined by the readers. But my perception is that this has declined in recent generations as speed reading has become more widely adopted by graduate students as a necessity for survival as secondary literature has multiplied.

Hans Frei's work, *The Eclipse of Biblical Narrative*, is an accurate description of the paradigm of Biblical interpretation in the age of the Enlightenment. As Frei shows, both the radical historical critics and the supernaturalists shared a new common presupposition which he calls "meaning as reference." The meaning of the texts was defined by their value as documentary sources for the establishment of either historical facticity—what Frei calls "ostensive reference"—or theological truths or ideas—what Frei calls "ideal reference." The system of distribution of both Biblical texts and interpretations was and is a massive multiplication of books—thousands and thousands of books—reference sources, the Biblical texts themselves in various arrangements and translations, and books about the Bible in ever increasing numbers up to the present avalanche.

Thus, there appears to be a demonstrable correlation between media change and the emergence of paradigm shifts in the history of Biblical interpretation. And certain characteristics can be identified when one examines each of these paradigms as a separate system. When seen as a whole history, sound, chant, and memorization decline and largely disappear in the dominant paradigm. But the old paradigms do not disappear totally. Instead, the old paradigms are reappropriated and used in new ways within the context of the new paradigm. Thus, the chanting of the original oral medium persisted in the manuscript paradigm and the allegorical hermeneutic of the manuscript paradigm has been continued in new forms in each of the subsequent paradigms.

Furthermore, in each age, other paradigms including virtually all of the paradigms of previous ages have persisted in groups that have resisted earlier paradigm shifts. As a result, paradigm shifts happen at very different stages in the development of different religious and cultural groups. Thus, Raymond Brown in Roman Catholicism and Jacob Neusner in Judaism have been leaders in the quite recent appropriation of the paradigm of historical criticism for the interpretation of the Scriptures in the Catholic tradition, and of the Mishnah and the Talmud in the Jewish tradition. Perhaps not coincidentally, these scholars have generated a prodigious output of books not unlike the output of earlier generations of German Protestant scholars.

III. *A Pattern of Response to Biblical Paradigm Shifts*

There also appears to be a discernible correlation between the major schisms in the communities of the Judeo-Christian tradition and the development of new paradigms of Biblical interpretation. In each period of adjustment to the culture generated by a new communications medium and a new paradigm of Biblical interpretation, there is a patter of response that can be characterized as resistance, appropriation, and capitulation.

The conservative response in each age is to resist the new culture generated by the new medium but to incorporate the medium into the old culture and its hermeneutics. Thus, in the period of the adaptation of the tradition of Israel to the manuscript paradigm, Pharisaic Judaism resisted the Hellenistic culture associated with writing. It incorporated writing and the written law into Jewish culture and even formed a canon of the written law. But the written law was studied and appropriated in the context of orality and the characteristic cultural patterns of the oral age. The ongoing formation of the oral law in first the Mishnah and then the Talmud continued the primary oral hermeneutic of Biblical interpretation. Interpreters of the tradition continued to be authorized by the oral processes of rabbinic education rather than in any sense by publication of written works.

Christian Judaism appropriated the new medium and its culture and formed a new synthesis which integrated the old medium and its culture into a new hermeneutical paradigm. The struggle between the Antiochene and Alexandrian schools of literal and allegorical interpretation were the primary sign of the tensions in this new paradigm. The Antiochene wing maintained close relationships with Rabbinic Judaism while the world of Hellenistic philosophy formed the primary cultural matrix of the Alexandrians. In the end, the new synthesis formed by Christianity adopted the allegorical methods of Hellenistic culture while maintaining essential continuity with the more literal methods of interpretation generated by the oral culture which gave birth to the Scriptures. The tension between Origen and Jerome resulted in a new hermeneutical synthesis.

Gnosticism in both its Jewish and Christian forms can be seen as a capitulation response in which the new medium and its culture became so dominant that the old medium and its culture were rejected. The highly individualistic culture of the world of writing with its consuming interest in speculative and creative ideas became the norm of Biblical interpretation. The new culture and its values generated a hermeneutical system and institutions that actively sought to disassociate the sophisticated present from the primitive past.

In the period of adjustment to the paradigm of print and the culture with which it was associated, the Roman Catholic response was to resist the new culture of which the printing, distribution, and historical interpretation of the Scriptures was a part. In the aftermath of the Council of Trent, Catholics appropriated the essential patterns of the culture associated with printing. But in relation to Biblical interpretation, this adaptation maintained strict subordination to the cultural patterns and "fourfold" hermeneutical paradigms of the manuscript period. In no way was independent interpretation of the Scriptures allowed to compromise the tradition.

Protestantism adopted the new medium and its culture and developed a new synthesis that maintained essential continuity with the tradition. Luther and Calvin were Biblical scholars who generated a massive series of printed texts including vernacular translations, commentaries on the original Greek and Hebrew texts, and doctrinal systems that used the texts as the primary source. The hermeneutical system was primarily theological but made a doctrine based on a literal interpretation of the Biblical texts. This new hermeneutic made possible the widespread distribution of the texts and the formation of communities of independent Biblical interpreters that were held together by a common hermeneutical framework.

Protestant scholasticism capitulated to the culture of the university and rejected both the old culture and the old medium. The university rather than the church became the primary institutional matrix for this form of culture Christianity.

Finally, in the age of silent print, in various stages in Europe and America, the historical critical study of the Bible as a document to be read in silence was resisted by Catholics, Protestant supernaturalists and fundamentalists, and orthodox Jews. In each instance, the new medium and the study of the Bible as a historical document has gradually been incorporated into the old culture. But the synthesis of a scientific interpretation of the Bible and the culture of the Enlightenment took place first within the mainstream of the Protestant churches. The Protestant churches adopted the new medium and its culture and created a new hermeneutical paradigm while maintaining continuity with the tradition. The formation of scientific societies for the study of the Bible, the SBL, SNTS, and CBA are the institutional offspring of this paradigm shift. Kummel's history of interpretation, *The New Testament,* is a chronicle of this paradigm and its development. The critics of the radical liberal tradition capitulated to the culture of the university and eliminated the basic characteristics of the old medium such as, for example, the memorization and recital of the Scripture.

Thus, the theory that changes in the dominant communications medium of the culture are closely correlated with the megatrends of Biblical interpretation also may shed light on the sources of reformation and schism in the history of religious communities. There is a close correlation between the ecclesiastical divisions in the history of Christianity, paradigm shifts in Biblical interpretation, and changes in the systems of communication.

IV. *Biblical Scholarship Today in Light of Media Megatrends*

The implications of this theory for the present context of Biblical interpretation are interesting. In relation to communications technology, the 20th century has witnessed the most extensive changes in the means of communication since the development of writing. The printing press was only a more efficient and uniform way of producing written materials and silent reading was a change in the way in which writing was normally perceived. But the elements of continuity with the written manuscript were primary: marks on paper, bound together in books, read with the eyes, distributed by being moved from place to place, and requiring extensive training in order to be perceived. Electronic communications is a radically different means of communication: no needed paper, widely varied distribution systems, both audio and visual data, instant availability, and no required education to be perceived. The only media change that compares in magnitude with the shift from literacy to electronics is the shift from orality to literacy. In light of the changes in Biblical interpretation that took place in response to earlier media shifts, we live at a critical juncture in the history of Biblical interpretation.

The most powerful interpreters of the Bible in electronic media are conservative evangelicals and pentecostals, most of whom have little or no scholarly training. The Bible is talked about constantly but is rarely presented in electronic media. The Living Bible has been by far the most successful and widely used new version of the Bible. And the religious communities in which this type of interpretation is done are growing at a rapid rate. In my judgment, the interpretation of the Bible in the present world of electronic media is a capitulation to American media culture and is profoundly flawed in ways that do not maintain essential continuity with the tradition. The new culture that has developed with electronic media has become the norm for Biblical interpretation. What will sell on American TV has become the primary norm of exegetical validity. However, while this is in my opinion an accurate generalization, it needs to be tested by more detailed evaluation of the range of Biblical interpretation that is being produced in records, TV, and film.

The community of Biblical scholarship and the churches which it serves have almost exclusively resisted electronic media and its culture. The guild has refused to enter into the interpretation of the Bible in the electronic world. Biblical scholarship has integrated elements of audio-visuals such as slides and some films into its paradigm to a minimal degree. Computers, which make possible the electronic processing of texts, have been enthusiastically integrated into the paradigm of historical critical scholarship. But the world of audio tapes and records, TV, and films has been an alien culture for orthodox Biblical interpretation. At this point in history, the best Biblical interpreters of our culture have abandoned the defense and commendation of responsible interpretation of the Biblical tradition in the most powerful communications medium of our age. That task has been given over to self-appointed religious entrepreneurs.

A projection on the basis of the megatrends of the past would suggest that this response will become increasingly retrogressive and will result in a withdrawal of the scholarly community from the dominant culture into a defensive posture. This response is not necessarily cataclysmic. Those parts of the tradition that have resisted earlier media changes—Rabbinic Judaism, Roman Catholicism, conservative/fundamentalist Protestantism—have made important contributions to the interpretation of the Bible. But the culture that is being formed by electronic media will thereby be ignored. And the consequences of allowing this travesty of authentic Biblical interpretation to go unchallenged in the present religious and political context will be great.

However, while Biblical scholarship has not consciously addressed the issue of media change, the theory does explain the fracturing of the historical critical consensus that has taken place in the last two decades. The collapse of Biblical theology as a strong and viable hermeneutic, the emergence of narrative theology and literary critical methods of exegesis, the impact of semiotics and deconstruction, the development of social science methods of analysis—all are connected by a common epistemological thread which moves away from the distinction between the phenomenal and the noumenal to the phenomena of sense experience itself. In electronic media and its cultures, what is known is what is seen and heard. That is, the theory would suggest that the declining impact of historical critical scholarship is a symptom of a change in the culture. These developments in Biblical scholarship are responses to that new culture and its ways of knowing. This effort is more likely to succeed, however, if the need for a new paradigm of Biblical interpretation is addressed directly.

V. *A Paradigm for Biblical Interpretation in Electronic Media*

The transmission and interpretation of the Bible is a process of communication. The meaning of communication acts is directly influenced by the means or media of communication in any particular cultural setting. This fact is particularly evident when new communications technologies emerge and gradually establish a new communications system. The meaning of the old system of interpretation changes and becomes associated with the past rather than the present. The old system can only be maintained by cutting the connection to the emerging new culture, generally by attacking the new medium and the culture with which it is associated. Inevitably, however, even the maintenance of the old system requires adjustments to the new communications situation and the old hermeneutic is modified.

The transmission and interpretation of the Bible in a new communications system and its various cultural matrices require the development of a new paradigm. Some of the major elements in the paradigms of Biblical interpretation are: the reformation of the Biblical traditions themselves for transmission in the new medium, the development of systems of production and distribution, and the formation of a hermeneutic that will make possible meaningful connections between the traditions in the new medium and the original tradition.

A. *The Bible in Electronic Media*

The first step is to put the Biblical tradition into the new medium, what might be called the transmediazation of the tradition. In each new media age this is the first task: e.g., the writing of the original manuscripts of the oral tradition, the translations into the Vulgate and German, Codex Vaticanus and the Gutenberg Bible, Westcott and Hort and the spate of recent translations for silent reading. In each case, the Bible was put into the new medium of the age in a loving and responsible manner that preserved continuity with the traditions of the past. What is needed, therefore, is an electronic Bible that accomplishes the same purpose for this new media age.

The computer is making this possible in electronic text with relative ease and with much greater breadth than has ever before been possible: e.g., Ibycus and the TLG CD-ROM system. But in the audio and video media the task remains to be done in ways that integrate the previous paradigms into the new paradigm. Audio tapes of the King James Version have been made by Elizabethan actors and videos of dramatized versions of central Biblical narratives are being made in the New Media Bible. But they are anachronistic and poorly conceived. To dramatize Biblical narratives is to change their form from narrative to drama, from a single speaker to a series of actors. However, this is only one of a whole series of problems that need to be solved. Audio is easier than video in which the problem of images must be resolved. But, regardless of the problems, the task is clear. The Biblical tradition itself needs to be made available in the medium of the age, electronic media.

A foundational step will be to reconceive the Bible as sounds rather than as documents. This in turn raises a new set of questions for historical research: how did the Bible sound in its original form? While it may be impossible for us to know precisely how Greek and Hebrew were pronounced in the ancient world and the exact melodies that were used for a particular text, historical research is eminently possible that will at least get us in the ball park. The basic methodology for this study is to compare the extant traditions of Hebrew and Greek cantillation and to reconstruct by comparison the sounds of the original sources from which these extant traditions developed. The scholarship in this area has reached a high degree of agreement that cantillation has been an integral part of Christian and Jewish worship and education throughout the East and until as late as the medieval period in the West. That is, we know that the Scriptures were originally chanted in services of both synagogue and Church. In view of recent research on oral poetry and narrative such as the studies of Lord and Parry, the probability is also high that this practice in the recital of the manuscripts continued and formalized a more spontaneous process of chanting that was characteristic of oral tradition. Thus, we will need to know more about the sounds of the Biblical tradition in order to accomplish an informed translation of the Bible into the sounds of our age.

Thus, a major element in the paradigm shift is the recognition that the Bible is sounds that were recorded in manuscripts so that they could again be resounded rather than texts to be studied in silence. We also need to know the basic units of sound in the history of the tradition. Rather than the units of the documentary tradition as an editing of words or ideas as we have tended to think, the tradition history of the Bible was a recomposition of sounds not unlike the transposition of and development of American hymn tunes in the music of Ives or Copland. The entire paradigm on which the study of the Pentateuch and the Synoptic problem has been based is fundamentally flawed because of an anachronistic reading back of our media world of silent documents into the ancient world. We need, therefore, to reexamine the entire tradition history of the Scriptures historically as a tradition of sound.

Once this is known to a greater degree it will be possible to develop interpretations of the tradition using the melodies and harmonies that are more characteristic of modern civilization in electronic media. Thus, we need to develop a whole new translation of the Bible for recital rather than for study. New ways of printing the texts will indicate the units of sound in the tradition. Various types of recital of the tradition in experimental modes will make the Scriptures directly available in electronic media. Thus, just as a primary task of scholarship has been to produce the best documentary form of the tradition, a new task is to produce the best electronic form of the tradition, the electronic version of Codex Vaticanus, the Masoretic text, the King James Bible, and whatever modern translation you think is best. But a foundational element of that Bible will be the music and melody of the sounds of the tradition.

In relation to video, the question is: what are the appropriate visual components of Biblical texts? Symbols, art (both icons and paintings), photographs and video montage, the sights of liturgy and worship, the faces of living persons, historical documentary footage, and dramatizations—all are possible visual elements of Biblical texts. Answering this question will involve research into the history and theology of images and experimentation with a range of options.

B. *The Production and Distribution of the Electronic Bible*

As is evident from the book display at SBL, the community of Biblical interpreters is presently organized to produce and distribute interpretations of the Bible in the medium of print, primarily print intended to be read in silence. The task before us is the development of systems of production and distribution for the Bible in electronic media. The religious communities will probably be the primary source for these systems but Biblical scholars may need to take their own initiatives. To my knowledge, there are no existing production houses or distribution agencies that have been persuaded of this need. The past sales record of the Bible itself and related materials may eventually provide the commercial motivation once viable projects are generated. But this is unlikely in the early stages. Biblical interpreters will have to fight to maintain integrity because of the complexity and cost of the electronic production and distribution systems needed to accomplish the task.

C. *The Medium of Interpretation of the Electronic Bible*

In the previous paradigms of Biblical interpretation, the earlier media of interpretation were continued and reformed in relation to the new paradigm. The original oral medium of the storytellers, prophets, and psalmists was reformed in the paradigms of writing into oral interpretation of the written texts in preaching and teaching. In an electronic paradigm, oral and written interpretation will be continued and reformed. New forms may emerge. For example, storytelling has experienced a renaissance in the culture and in Biblical interpretation in the last ten years. The development of narrative preaching and Biblical storytelling is a post-literate orality that could only have happened in the context of the culture of the electronic age. The character of books is also changing: e.g., fewer tomes, more short books, multiplication of specialized publications and journals. The medium of interpretation of the electronic Bible will be a media-mix of oral, written, and electronic elements.

D. *The Hermeneutics of the Electronic Bible*

The most complex issue is the way in which meaningful connections will be made between the contemporary world and the world of the Bible in an electronic paradigm of Biblical interpretation. Media change is a major factor that has generally been unrecognized in the hermeneutical literature including that of the "new" hermeneutic. What will be the hermeneutics of the electronic age?

The medium of communication establishes certain constraints that operate in the formation of meaning in that medium. In *Preface to Plato,* Eric Havelock has shown the way in which the transition from orality to literacy necessitated an epistemological revolution of separating the knower from what is known through reflecting on the ideas reflected in sense experience. This primary revolution of the perception of sense experience as pointing beyond itself to transcendent ideas is an essential component of the world of literacy. I would suggest that, in the tradition of Biblical interpretation, this epistemological revolution associated with literacy took place in the development of theology as the primary hermeneutical system for Biblical interpretation within Christianity. In its various forms, theology has been the way in the Christian tradition that connections have been made between the contemporary world and the world of the Bible. Theology as a hermeneutic has been based on the distinction between the phenomena of the Bible itself and the theological truths or noumena to which the Bible points.

The problem of Biblical interpretation in an electronic paradigm is that theological modes of interpretation do not work in this medium of what Ong calls secondary orality. One sign of the problem can be observed when one contemplates the transmediazation of theological works. Imagine the grandeur of Tillich's *Systematic Theology* or Barth's *Church Dogmatics* on TV or audio tape; or the fascination of theologians and Biblical scholars on TV having a theological or exegetical debate. This is death with no resurrection. Electronic media reinforce a thoroughly empirical epistemology. Sense experience is reality, not simply a shadow on a wall. Theology is based on the distinction between sense experience and reality; it relies on abstractions and argumentation. In audio and video, midrash, well done, is far more interesting than theology. The need then is for a non-theological hermeneutic for the interpretation of the Bible in an electronic paradigm.

Narrative hermeneutics, semiotics, phenomenology, and process hermeneutics may all be candidates for this primary role in the transposition of the Bible into this new context. But my inclination is to let the hermeneutic develop from the Bible itself. This has been the mainstream of the Biblical interpretive tradition in which the hermeneutics have never been philosophically pure but have combined elements in unique ways that are finally generated by the Biblical tradition itself. This does not mean that we can go back to proof-texting, pesher, or to simple repetition of the traditions themselves. But it does mean that various interpretive methods will need to be used over a period of time and evaluated in relation to their appropriateness and faithfulness to the spirit that formed the Bible. It is the doing of this evaluative task for which theology will be of indispensable assistance in the future.

The argument can be stated in a less abstract manner. When we have put the authoritative interpreters of the orthodox tradition, namely, scholars who have spent their lives writing books, on TV, they are a disaster. They come off as boring, above it all, irrelevant, wordy, and generally a drag. And because they know that, most of them have never even dreamed of trying. On the other hand, fundamentalist evangelists who have never been to seminary, who practice an utterly irresponsible form of Biblical interpretation and who couldn't write their way out of a paper bag get on the boob tube and they are terrific. They are engaging, sharp, and accessible. Their exegesis sheds light on the Biblical text and helps people connect with it. As interpreters of the tradition, they are far more effective in the medium than scholars.

What are we to conclude? Their content is horrible but it works in the medium; the content of the orthodox is true but it does not work in the medium. Most scholars have concluded that the problem is the medium, that electronic media are demonic and that we should fight it by writing more and more books. This strategy is increasingly becoming like that of the Polish army who sent division after division of calvary against Hitler's tanks.

But another analysis is possible. The tradition of the scholarly community has been definitively shaped by the mastery of writing. We all got our degrees by proving our competence in the medium of silent print. Our tradition has been determined by the hermeneutics of the world of writing. That hermeneutical system and its styles of communication do not work well in electronic media.

The tradition of the evangelicals on TV and radio has been definitively shaped by resistance to historical criticism. Most of the people on TV either never went to seminary and, if they did, learned as little as possible about historical criticism. Most of them cut their eye teeth on the sawdust trail and are masters of oral communication. The oral hermeneutics of the revival and of pesher interpretation work well in electronic media.

We have concluded as scholars that our message is incompatible with electronic media. And theological discourse and scholarly analysis in its traditional forms appears to be. But must we equate our tradition with the Bible itself?

In the paradigm of the world of writing, the Bible has been defined as a set of reference sources for the historical events and theological ideas of the Biblical period. To be faithful has meant, therefore, that one must be faithful to those traditions. In Christianity, authenticity has been defined by theological orthodoxy, by the recognizable presence of certain ideas and styles. But theology is not the Bible nor is it the primary language of the Biblical tradition. It is a hermeneutical language, a secondary, reflective language. If we use the language and literature of theology as our norm for what is authentically Biblical, our approach to electronic media will be as if we would put literary, music, and film critics on TV and never have storytellers, musicians, or athletes. Imagine TV as a series of critical discussions about stories, music, and sports.

I would propose, therefore, that the problem of the Bible in electronic media is a new form of the old problem of the authority of the tradition and the Scriptures. If the tradition of the interpretive paradigm of silent print is the authority of the Bible in electronic media, it is impossible. But if the Scriptures themselves are taken as the authority and the model, the world of electronic media is open to a new world of interpretive possibilities.

We have become radically confused about the character of the Bible. In the traditions of Israel of which the early Christian sect was an integral part, over half of both the Hebrew and Christian canon were stories. The traditions of prophecy and psalm were poetry. The wisdom tradition was proverbs not unlike contemporary advertising. Parables, proverbs, poetry, apocalyptic—those were the primary languages of the Biblical tradition and they will work well in electronic media.

We have equated the Bible and its faithful interpretation with theology. Our entire paradigm is designed to yield information about the ideas of the tradition rather than the experiences. The shape of a new hermeneutic is the shape of experience, of the direct rendering of the revelation of God in story, song, proverb, and vision.

Just as the Church faced a new situation in the second and third century in which the leaders and thinkers of the Church finally had no choice but to develop allegorical and theological methods in order to interpret the traditions of Israel and the early Church in the Hellenistic world, so now we may have no choice but to develop new methods in order to interpret those same traditions in this new cultural context. Thus, we might begin to produce the Bible as a series of audio and video tapes in which connections to the contemporary culture are explored in parabolic, symbolic, and storytelling styles. But the question is: how can we accurately communicate the meaning of the Biblical tradition in its original historical context in the world of electronic media and its various cultures?

VI. *A Personal Paradigm Shift*

I had a paradigm shift once and, while I am not a great scientist who has had a major impact on the field, it might be helpful in clarifying the character of the electronic paradigm. When I was doing research for my dissertation on Mark's passion narrative, I wanted to know what his story meant as a story. So I read all the commentaries and was trying to identify the units of Mark's narrative. And all I could see were the seams between Mark's redaction and the pre-Markan tradition and the implications of those additions for Mark's theology. But I literally could not see anything about the story as a story. And the harder I looked, the more frustrated I became. After weeks of frustration getting nowhere, I decided to start over. The conclusion of most scholars was that Mark's passion narrative had probably been passed on by memory for some years before it was written down. And I knew that narratives in the ancient world were generally chanted, often with a lyre.

I put all my books away, got my guitar, and sat down at my desk and began to memorize Mark's narrative in Greek and to chant it. At first I thought I was crazy, and then later, when I sang it for my friends and my advisor, I knew I was crazy. But I worked on it until I could do the whole thing. In the process, I went through a paradigm shift. I have never been able to experience the documents in the same way since that time. For me, the Bible is no longer a document to be studied in silence. It is sounds that were intended to be heard again.

VII. *Concluding Suggestions*

Changes in the dominant medium of communication create radically new situations for the transmission and interpretation of the Bible. There is a direct correlation between the development of writing, printing, and silent reading and the major revolutions in Biblical interpretation, namely, allegorical interpretation, literal/figural interpretation, and historical critical interpretation. The development of electronic communications in the 20th century is the most radical change in the primary means of communication since at least the printing press and probably since the development of writing.

This communications revolution has had a major effect on Biblical criticism and has been a primary source of the fracturing of the historical critical paradigm in the last 25 years. But the formative cause of this change has largely been unrecognized. Biblical scholarship has continued to operate within the communications world of silent print as if electronic communications has not happened. It may be time now to recognize that the transmission and interpretation of the Bible in the world of electronic communications is the most important shaping influence and constructive challenge for the future of Biblical scholarship. The reason for the declining impact of historical critical work may be that we are not interpreting the Bible in electronic media, specifically radio, audio, and TV. But in order to do that, we will have to change our ways of perceiving and interpreting the tradition. If this theory is accurate, Biblical scholarship is in the early stages of a paradigm shift of major proportions. And if previous media changes are at all indicative of the future, religious communities will experience some significant conflicts over the issues that will be generated by this tradition.

INDEXES

INDEX

Ackerman, James 189
Actium 92
Adam, Apocalypse of 20
Adamo, D. 134, 141
Adan-Bayewitz, David 103
Aelia Capitolina 94, 101
Africa 64, 134, 152, 183, 195
African-American 129, 132, 134, 137, 141, 143, 147, 148, 150, 151, 152, 154-156, 158
'Ain Feshkha 9
Akkadian 87
Al-Udhari, A. Y. 76
Albright, William Foxwell 14, 28
Alexander the Great 100, 101, 111
Allegro, John M. 10
American Bible Society (ABS) 3, 30, 62, 66, 78, 89, 136, 160, 164, 169, 170, 173, 176, 179, 180, 181, 184
American Standard Version (ASV) 39
American Tract Society 180
Antioch 98
Antonia Fortress 92
Arabic 76
Aramaic 7, 11, 12, 17, 18, 27, 48, 61, 85, 90, 97, 111, 182
  Enoch 10, 12
  Gospel 12
  Horoscope 91
  Inscriptions 96
  Proto-Esther 34
  Targum of Job 8
  texts 8, 11, 18
Argarizein 99

Arichea, Daniel C. 50, 54
Aristeas 70, 102
Armenian Convent 92
Asclepius, Apocalypse of 20
Asia 183
Asia Minor 98
Attridge, H. W. 24
Auffret, P. 18
Augustine 50
Avi-Yonah, Michael 92, 109, 110
Avigad, Nahman 110

Babylon 27, 33-35
Bagdikian, Ben H. 186
Bailey, R. 134, 135, 143
Baillet, M. 9, 10
Bar Kochba 90, 94, 113
Barnwell, Katharine 49, 67
Barthélemy, Dominique 28
Baur, F. C. 89
Bechtel, John L. 50
Beekman, John 40, 42
Belloc, Hilaire 41, 43
Bēma (βῆμα) 114, 120, 121
Beroea 106
Beth She'arim 115, 116
Beth tephila (בֵּית תְּפִלָּה) 98
Bethlehem 96
Bickermann, Elias 26, 29
Black 56, 134-136, 143, 155, 156
Black Sea 98
Black, Matthew 45
Boomershine, Thomas E. 5, 167, 169, 176, 179, 188, 190, 209
Boraas, Roger S. 118, 119
Bosphorus 98
Boudinot, Elias 3, 89, 180

Bratcher, Robert G. 41
Breslin, Jimmy 179
Broshi, Magen 102
Bruggen, Jacob Van 51
Budd, P. 128
Buddha 59
Bultmann, Rudolf 17
Burke, David G. 170
Burns, R. 131, 151
Burrows, Millar 15, 90

Caesarea 98, 100, 102
Cakchiquel 196
Callow, John 40, 42
Calvin, John 217
Cantillation 212, 222
Capernaum 103, 104
Carmignac, Jean 18
Carroll, John B. 200
Carson, Donald A. 37, 57, 78,
   84, 85-87
Catacombs 115, 116, 118, 121
Catholic Biblical Association
   (CBA) 217
CD-ROM 161, 163, 221
Charlesworth, James H. 10, 27
Cheek, John L. 37
Chenoboskion 19
China 195
Christ 18, 20, 43, 56, 150, 157
Christianity 33, 55, 60, 88, 89,
   108, 113, 116, 180, 213, 216,
   217, 218, 225, 227
   Early Christianity 4, 19, 109,
   117
   Jewish Christianity 89
   Pauline Christianity 104
Citadel 91, 92

Clark, Kenneth 190
Codex 182
   Jung Codex 19
   Leningradensis 153
   Nag Hammadi codices 20
   Vaticanus 221, 223
Computer 47, 63, 64, 78, 147,
   159-163, 166, 167, 169, 171,
   172-176, 183, 209, 219, 221
Constantine 108, 113, 116
Contemporary English Version
   (CEV) 78-81
Continental Congress 3
Copher, C. 134, 135
Coptic 7, 19, 21, 23, 24
Coptic Museum 19
Corinth 106
Cosgrove, Charles H. 88
Crane, Greg 162, 163, 173
Crim, Keith 47
Critique textuelle de l'Ancien
   Testament (CTAT) 28, 29
Cross 118
Cross, Frank Moore 11, 15, 28,
   35, 129
Culley, R. C. 130, 131, 142, 157
Cush 128, 133, 134, 141
Cushite 126, 128, 132-136, 141,
   143, 152, 153, 156
Cyprus 106

Damascus 33, 34, 101, 106
Damascus Document 31-34
Damascus Gate 92
Dancy, Paul 49
Davies, Philip R. 33
de Mille, Cecil B. 170
de Vaux, Roland 9

de Waard, Jan 38, 170
Dead Sea Scrolls 9-11, 14, 15, 29, 30, 34, 64, 90, 109, 111, 153
Decapolis 100, 101, 104
Deconstruction 52, 129, 155, 220
Deissmann, Adolf 94, 95
Delaney, Paul 167
Delos 98, 99
Dialogue of the Savior 20
Diaspora 27, 97-99, 115
Dimant, Devorah 30
Dionysos 113, 116
Divi filius 18
Dora 98
Doresse, J. 19
Douay Version 39
Dravidian languages 199
Dupont-Sommer, A. 13
Dura Europos 98, 99
Dynamic equivalence 38, 40-43, 45, 46, 68, 74, 85, 170, 175, 176

Ecce Homo Arch 92
Edwards, Douglas R. 103
Egypt 7, 13, 19, 21, 35, 90, 97, 100, 134, 152, 153
Egyptians, Gospel of the 20
Eid, A. 19
Ein Gedi 114
Ein Ghuweir 31
Ekklēsia (ἐκκλησία) 106
Ektrōma (ἔκτρωμα) 157
Ellingworth, Paul 38
Ellul, Jacques 186, 187
Emerson, Caryl 206
Ephesus 106

Epiphanius 98
Episcopal Divinity School 173
Erasmus, Desiderius 49, 50
Essenes 13, 26, 30, 31
Eugnostos the Blessed 20
Eugnostos, Epistle to 20
Evans, Craig 27, 28
Exegesis on the Soul 21

Fehderau, Harold W. 64
Felder, C. 134, 135, 155
Feminist 129, 131, 133, 134, 136, 137, 141, 143, 148, 151, 154, 155, 156
Finegan, Jack 118
First Revolt 96, 97
Fishbane, Michael 27, 29
Fitzmyer, Joseph A. 7, 9, 26-28, 30, 33-35, 90
Formal equivalence 46, 49
Fourdrinier, Henry and Sealy 181
Fox, Everett 68, 69
French 48, 63, 65, 156, 180, 202
Freyne, Sean 101
Functional equivalence 38-42, 46, 68, 69, 170

Galilee 90, 91, 94, 96, 100-104, 113
  Lower Galilee 102-104, 112, 119
  Sea of Galilee 104
  Upper Galilee 101, 103, 112, 118, 120
Gallus 113, 115
Gamala 96, 97
Gassner, John 190

Gaulanitis 112
Gender-bias 41, 53
Gerasene Demoniac 169, 171,
　　172, 179
Geraty, Lawrence T. 119
German 48, 76, 200, 221
Gideons International 62
Giv'at Ha-Mivtar 119
Gnilka, Joachim 54
Gnosticism 22, 216
God's Word to the Nations
　　(GWN) 61
Goethals, Gregor 168, 169, 185
Golan 103, 112, 119
Good News Bible (GNB) 39, 72,
　　77, 79, 82, 83
Goodenough, Erwin R. 109
Goodspeed, Edgar J. 12
GRAMCORD 49
Greek 7, 11, 12, 15, 16, 18, 23,
　　29, 48, 49, 63, 69, 70, 73, 87,
　　90, 97, 102, 106, 111, 113,
　　115, 116, 136, 162, 182, 212,
　　213, 217, 222, 229
　Bible 59
　Biblical Greek 159
　Classical Greek 159
　Inscriptions 96, 105, 106, 115
　Koine Greek 48
　Minor Prophets Scroll 28
　New Testament Greek 49
Greek New Testament
　Nestle-Aland 26th Edition 54
　UBS Fourth Edition 54
　UBS Third Edition 54
Greenspoon, Leonard 68
Greenstein, Edward L. 45, 68-70
Greimas, A. J. 130

Grenfell, B. P. 23
Guatemala 196
Guillaumont, A. 23
Gutenberg, Johann 221
Gutman, Joseph 96, 97, 121
Gutt, Ernst-August 42, 46

Hadas, Moses 26, 29
Hagedorn, Fern Lee 169, 173
Hammat Tiberias 104, 114
Hammond, Gerald 70
Hanna-Barbera 170
Harley, Richard M. 5, 159, 179,
　　185, 187, 188, 190
Harrelson, Walter 131
Harrington, D. J. 12
Harvard University 11, 18, 125,
　　162, 173
Hasidim 13
Hasmoneans 91, 111
Havelock, Eric A. 165, 212, 224
Hebrew 7, 8, 11, 12, 15, 17, 18,
　　27, 48, 49, 69, 70, 76, 78-83,
　　90, 97, 111, 128, 136, 153,
　　182, 212, 213, 222
　Astrological document 91
　Bible 37, 53, 54, 110, 125, 145,
　　146, 147, 150
　Biblical Hebrew 68
　Canon 15, 227
　Hebrew Bible 34
　Inscriptions 96
　paleo-Hebrew script 15
　parallelism 77, 80
　Postbiblical Hebrew 12
　Postexilic Hebrew 12
　Scriptures 11, 15, 61, 85, 111,
　　146, 162

Texts 8, 35, 217
Hebrew Old Testament Text Project (HOTTP) 28
Hebrew University Bible Project 28
Hegel, Georg Wilhelm Friedrich 89
Helios 96, 105
Hellenism 29, 111, 112, 116
Hellenistic culture 212, 213, 215, 216
Hengel, Martin 97, 98
Hermeneutics 51, 52, 112, 133, 168, 213, 215, 220, 221, 224, 225, 226
  Allegorical hermeneutic 213, 215
  Electronic hermeneutic 209
  New hermeneutic 42, 47, 52, 212, 217, 224, 228
  Oral hermeneutic 212, 216, 227
  Process hermeneutics 225
Herod 92-94, 96, 100, 112
Herod Agrippa 93, 101
Herod Antipas 101, 112
Herodium 96, 97
Historical criticism 210, 214, 215, 226, 227
Hodayot 31
Holeczek, Heinz 50
Horn, Siegfried H. 119
Hort, F. J. A. 221
Hubbard, Amos H. 181
Humboldt, Wilhelm von 199
Hunt, A. S. 23
Hypertext 166, 169, 175, 177

Ibycus 221
Iconium 106
Independence Hall 3
Institut für neutestamentliche Textforschung 64
Iwry, S. 13

James, 1 Apocalypse of 20
James, 2 Apocalypse of 20
Jameson, Fredric 188
Japha 103
Jefferson, Thomas 180
Jeremias, Joachim 23
Jericho 114
Jerome 50, 182, 216
Jerusalem 8, 9, 13, 14, 33, 81, 90, 91, 92, 94, 95, 98, 100, 101, 107, 109, 114
  Priesthood 13
  Talmud 115
  Temple 115
Jerusalem Bible (JB) 61, 62
Jesuits 199
Jesus 10, 16, 18, 24, 44, 56, 85, 89, 92, 93, 100, 103, 104, 107, 109, 112, 118, 169-171, 174, 175
  Parables of 46, 86, 103, 202
  Sayings of 23
  The Wicked Priest 16
Jewish Publication Society (JPS) 61, 72
Jobling, D. 130-132, 135, 142, 157
John the Baptist 16, 43, 118
John, Apocryphon of 20, 21
Josephus 13, 18, 30, 31, 33, 92, 98, 102, 104, 105, 113

Judah the Prince 113, 116
Judaism 11, 13, 14, 27, 35, 70,
    91, 110, 113, 115, 116, 144,
    213, 215
  Christian Judaism 212, 216
  Early Judaism 26, 27, 109
  Hellenistic Judaism 26, 89,
    109
  Palestinian Judaism 33, 34, 89,
    113, 116
  Pharisaic Judaism 213, 215
  Rabbinic Judaism 91, 107,
    213, 216, 219
Judea 32, 82, 90, 94, 96, 111
Julian 115

Kaestle, Carl 164
Kanyoro, Rachel Angogo 64
Kapera, Zdzislaw Jan 14
Kee, Howard Clark 3, 89, 118,
    119, 120
Kefer Hananiah 103, 119
Kelber, Werner 165, 168
Kerygma 17
Khabra 11
Khirbet Qumran 7, 9
Khirbet Shema 101
Kidron Valley 92
Kikuyu 45
King James Version (KJV) 39,
    60, 70, 72, 221
Knight, D. 131
Kopesec, Michael F. 40
Koran 114
Kraft, Robert 162
Krause, M. 21
Kuhn, K. G. 97
Kuhn, Thomas 209

Labib, P. 19, 23
Lamentations
    5.11 82
Landow, George P. 166, 167,
    177
Larson, Mildred 42
Latin 18, 49, 182
Layton, B. 24
Lev, Asher 45
Levi-Strauss, C. 130
Levine, Lee I. 94, 95, 97, 117
Liebermann, Saul 26, 29
Lindars, Barnabas 57
Linguistics 47, 48, 208
Literacy 110, 160, 164, 165, 167,
    182, 183, 185, 218, 224, 225
Lithostratos 92
Living Bible (LB) 39, 56, 73
Local texts 15, 35
Lockman Foundation 62
Longenecker, Richard 86
Louw, Johannes 47, 49
Luther, Martin 49, 76, 217

Ma'oz, Z. 97
Maccabees 13, 111
Macedonia 98
Magdala 97
Magne, J. 18
Malta 115
Manuscripts 4, 55, 153, 182, 207
  Manuscript evidence 54, 136
Margolis, Max Leopold 70, 71
Margot, Jean-Claude 44, 48
Mark Antony 92
Marsanes 21
Martin, Geronimo 198
Mary, Gospel of 20

Masada 11, 90, 96, 97
Mason, James 170
Masoretic text 15, 35, 223
Maurice Thorez Institute 196
Mays, J. L. 129
Mazar, Benjamin 110
McKerras, Ross 55
Media 5, 161-164, 167, 168, 172,
    177, 181, 182, 185, 186, 219,
    221
  Electronic media 159, 160,
    164, 165-169, 179, 183-186,
    191, 209, 218-221, 223, 225-
    229
  Hypermedia 167
  Mass media 180, 182, 185,
    186, 188
  Media change 214, 218-220,
    224, 230
  Media pioneers 180
  Media shift 218
  Modern media 160
  Multimedia 162-164, 169, 173,
    174, 188, 189, 208
  Multimedia translation 169,
    170, 172, 175-177, 179, 185,
    188, 189, 191
Melchizedek 21
Ménard, J.-E. 24
Metzger, Bruce M. 41
Meyer, M. W. 21
Meyers, Carol L. 117, 120
Meyers, Eric M. 93, 104, 109,
    117, 118, 120
Michaels, J. Ramsey 154
Midian 134, 152
Midianite 134, 156
Midrash 225

Milik, J. T. 9, 10, 12, 18, 34
Mina, Togo 19
Miqsat Ma'aseh Torah 14, 32
Miriam 126, 128, 131-133, 135,
    136, 141, 142, 146, 152, 155,
    156, 157
Mishnah 12, 107, 108, 113, 116,
    213, 215, 216
Moore, George Foot 26
More, Thomas 50
Morson, Gary Saul 206
Moses 70, 126, 128, 131-135,
    146, 152, 153, 156, 157
Muhammad Edh-Dhîb 8
Mundhenk, Norm 45
Murabba'at 11, 12
Murphy-O'Connor, Jerome 13,
    27, 30, 33
Muslim 33, 65, 146

Naaran 114
Nablus 98
Nabratein 113, 120, 121
Nag Hammadi 7, 19, 21-25, 90
National Council of the
    Churches of Christ (NCCC)
    58
Nature of the Archons 20
Navajo 198
Nazareth 102, 103, 119, 170
Neill, Stephen 44
Nerva 95
Neusner, Jacob 107, 215
New American Bible (NAB) 61,
    85
New American Standard Bible
    (NASB) 39, 56, 61, 62
New English Bible (NEB) 40,

44, 54, 60, 62
New International Version (NIV)
39, 44, 61-63, 73
New Jersey Bible Society 180
New Jerusalem Bible (NJB) 61,
62
New Jewish Version (NJV) 71
New King James Version
(NKJV) 39, 53, 61-63
New Revised Standard Version
(NRSV) 41, 43, 44, 48, 53,
54, 56, 58, 61, 62, 77, 79, 80,
82, 83, 87, 88, 128, 146
Newman, Barclay M. 56, 76,
170
Nichols, A. H. 43
Nida, Eugene A. 5, 28, 38, 45,
49, 50, 52, 59, 60, 74, 170,
195
Niebuhr, H. R. 191
Nirvana 59
Noordtzij, A. 128
Nord, David Paul 180
North Africa 115
Norwich Bible Auxiliary 181
Noth, M. 129

O'Callaghan, José 16
Oikēma (οἴκημα) 98
Olmstead, A. T. 12
Olshewsky, Thomas W. 66
Olson, D. 129-131, 157
Ong, Walter 165, 168, 225
Orality 165, 167, 182, 205-208,
213, 216, 218, 224
Origen 216
Origin of the World, On the 20
Orlinsky, Harry M. 70

Orwell, George 186, 187
Ossuaries 118, 119
Ostia 98
Overman, J. Andrew 103
Oxbridge vernacular 61

Pagels, Elaine H. 22
Paine, Thomas 180
Palestine Archaeological
Museum 9
Paradigm 209-217, 219-221, 224,
227, 228
Electronic paradigm 224, 225,
228
Historical criticism paradigm
215, 219, 229
Manuscript paradigm 215
Paradigm shift 209, 211, 213-
215, 217, 218, 222, 228-230
Print culture paradigm 216
Silent print paradigm 227
Paris, P. 131
Paul 22, 23, 27, 28, 58, 87-89,
106, 147, 157, 168
Letters 46, 87
Literary formulae 86
Paul, Apocalypse of 20
Paul, Prayer of the Apostle 21
Paul, Shalom M. 85
Perkins, Pheme 22, 84
Perseus Project 162
Perushim 107
Pesher 226, 227
Pesher Nahum 32
Peter and the Twelve Apostles,
Acts of 20
Peter to Philip, Letter of 20
Peter, Acts of 20

Peter, Apocalypse of 20
Peters, Melvin K. H. 145
Pharisees 107
Phenomenology 225
Philip, Gospel of 20, 24
Phillips, J. B. 39, 159, 160
Philo 30, 31, 92, 97
Pierpont, William G. 53
Pilate, Pontius 92, 107
Pliny, the Elder 30
Pneuma (πνεῦμα) 44
Pompeii 92
Pope, Anthony J. 49
Porter, Stanley E. 49
Postman, Neil 164, 165, 167, 185
Potok, Chaim 45
Praetorium 92
Priene 98
Propp, V. 130
Proseuchē (προσευχή) 97, 98, 105
Protestantism 217, 219
Proto-Sadducees 32
Psycholinguistics 208
Ptolemais/Acco 101, 102
Ptolemies 91
Puech, Emile 34
Pusey, Nathan 125, 136

Qimron, Elisha 14
Qumran
  Book of Giants 10
  Copper Plaque 8
  Enoch 10
  Genesis Apocryphon 8
  Greek fragments 8
  Habakkuk commentary 8
  Isaiah scroll A 15
  Manual of Discipline 8
  NT writings 8
  Temple Scroll 8
  Thanksgiving Psalms 8
  War Scroll 8

Ranke, Leopold von 52
Raynor, Joyce 120
Reformation 49, 213
Revised English Bible (REB) 40, 41, 53, 54, 61
Revised Standard Version (RSV) 15, 37, 50, 51, 54, 55, 61, 62
Revised Version (RV) 39, 72
Reyburn, William D. 52
Rheginos, Epistle to 20
Rift Valley 112
Robinson, J. M. 21
Robinson, Maurice A. 53
Robinson's Arch 93
Roman Catholicism 215, 219
Rome 98, 112
Rosenbaum, H.-U. 16
Royal Portico 93
Rudi-Weber, Hans 164
Rüger, Hans Peter 54

Safrai, S. 95
Samaritans 99
  Proto-Samaritan group 35
  Samaritan Pentateuch 15, 35
Sanders, James A. 17, 26
Sanhedrin 106
Sardinia 115
Sardis 98, 99
Scanlin, Harold P. 54, 73
Schenker, Adrian 54

Schiffman, Lawrence H. 14, 30, 32
Schmidt, C. 20
Schmithals, W. 23
Scholē (σχολή) 106
Scholer, D. M. 21
Schüssler-Fiorenza, Elisabeth 133
Schwarz, W. 50
Schweitzer, Albert 173
Scott, Bernard C. 86
Scythopolis 102
Second Revolt 90, 94-96
Sekeles, Eliezer 119
Seleucids 91
Semiotics 220, 225
Semitisms 17
Sepphoris 101-103, 107, 112, 113, 116, 117
Septuagint 15, 27, 35, 58, 70, 73, 74, 111
Serekh ha Yahad 31
Sextus, Sentences of 20
Shakespeare, William 159
Shem, Paraphrase of 20
Shuafat 94, 109
Sicily 115
Sidon 104
Silent reading 137, 214, 218, 221, 229
Silvanus, Teachings of 21
Simonides 95
Situational meaning 42, 85
Smalley, William A. 45, 57, 65
Smith, Morton 26, 29
Smith, R. 21
Society of Biblical Literature (SBL) 5, 56, 74, 210, 217, 223

Bible in Ancient and Modern Media Group 167
Sociolinguistics 47, 208
Son of God 18, 19
Son of man 56, 57
Sophia of Jesus Christ 20
South Africa 135
Spanish 195
Speed reading 214
Steely, J. E. 23
Stendahl, Krister 157
Stine, Philip C. 54, 57
Stobi 98, 99
Stone, Michael E. 30
Storyteller 169, 171, 174, 182, 212, 224, 227
Strange, James F. 93, 96, 104, 117, 120
Strugnell, John 10, 11, 14
Studiorum Novi Testamenti Societas (SNTS) 217
Sturdy, J. 129
Sukenik, Eliezer L. 110
Summer Institute of Linguistics (SIL) 49
Sussmann, Y. 14
Swahili 45, 55, 65
Synagōgē (συναγωγή) 97, 105, 106
 Hebraiōn (Ἑβραίων) 106
Synagogue 90, 91, 94-100, 104-106, 108, 109, 113, 114, 116, 117, 118, 120-122, 212, 222
Synedrion (συνέδριον) 102, 106, 107
Syria 98-100, 102

Ta'amireh Bedouin 7
Taber, Charles R. 39, 45, 51
Talmon, S. 15
Talmud 70, 107, 108, 115, 213, 215, 216
Tamil 44
Tanakh 61
Tappert, Theodore G. 49
Targum 8-10, 12, 17, 85
Tarichaeae 98
Teacher of Righteousness 14, 16
Television (TV) 159, 163-165, 167, 168, 170, 183, 185, 186, 188, 209, 219, 225-227, 229
Tell Anafa 101
Tetracomia 112
Textual criticism 15, 30, 34, 46, 53, 54, 64, 153
Thai 59
Thanksgiving, Prayer of 21
Theodotion 72
Theodotus Inscription 94-96
Thesaurus Linguae Graecae (TLG) 162, 221
Thessalonica 106
Thiede, C. P. 16
Thiering, Barbara 16
Thiselton, Anthony C. 52
Thomas, Didymus 24
Thomas, Gospel of 20, 23, 24
Thomas, K. J. 65
Thomas, Sidney 190
Throckmorton, Burton H., Jr. 53
Tiberias 98, 101, 102, 104
Titus 93
Today's English Version (TEV) 39, 44, 50, 51, 53, 59, 61, 72

Tomson, Peter J. 87
Topos (τόπος) 98
Torah 14, 110, 121, 122
Torah shrine 99, 100, 114
Tov, Emanuel 15, 28, 29, 35
Trajan 95
Transmediazation 221, 225
Treadwell, Daniel 181
Trent, Council of 216
Trible, Phyllis 131-133, 135, 136, 142, 151, 156, 157
Trimorphic Protennoia 21
Truth, Gospel of 20
Tübingen School 89
Tuckett, C. M. 24
Turow, Scott 45
Tyndale, William 50
Tyrannus 106
Tyre 101, 104
Tyropoean Valley 91, 93

United Bible Societies (UBS) 28, 164
  Handbooks 49
  Monograph Series 47

Van der Ploeg, J. P. M. 17
Van der Woude, A. S. 17
Van Eck, Arthur 61
Vermes, Geza 31, 33, 91
Vespasian 93
Via Maris 112
Video 169, 173, 174, 176, 177, 179, 184, 190, 221, 223, 225, 228
  Music video 165, 169, 171, 174, 176
  Video images 163

Video translations 183
Vulgate 49, 74, 182, 221

Wacholder, B. Z. 14
Walls, Andrew 66
Weems, Renita J. 136
Weisgerber, Leo 200
Wendland, Ernst R. 55
Wenham, G. 129
Westcott, B. F. 221
White, L. Michael 98, 99
White, Sidnie A. 30
Whorf, Benjamin Lee 200
Wicked Priest 16
Wightman, G. B. H. 76
Williamson, H. G. M. 57
Wilson's Arch 91, 93
Wilss, Wolfram 39
Windows 161, 166, 169, 172, 174

Winter, Werner 66
Wycliffe Bible Translators 49, 58, 60

Yadin, Yigael 14, 110
Yahweh 18, 96, 105, 133, 146
Yiddish 45
Yugoslavia 99

Zadokite 32
Zaire 65
Zealots 94
Zeffirelli, Franco 170
Zenon papyri 111
Zias, Joseph 119
Zion 81-83
Zipporah 134, 156
Zodiac 91, 96, 100, 105

INDEX OF BIBLICAL REFERENCES

Old Testament

Genesis
  1 208
  1.26 50, 51
  2 208
  3 50
  3.5 51
  3.22 51
  4.1-16 130
  11.1-9 209
Exodus
  2 134
  2.19 152
  4 134
  4.6-8 157
  32.35 157
Leviticus
  10.3 157
Numbers
  11-12 130, 131
  11 132, 157
  12 126-128, 130-136, 141, 142,
    154, 155
  12.1-9 134
  12.11 157
  12.12 157
Judges
  5.28-30 209
2 Samuel
  18.19ff 152
2 Kings
  2.23-25 130
  2.27 152
Job
  24.6-7 (Q) 17
  34.12 17

Psalms
  8 56
  18 77, 79, 80
  18.1-2 80
  18.13-15 77
  18.19 77
  18.25 77
  18.28 77
  18.29 78
  18.34-35 77
  22 80
  28.7 (Q) 17
  45.1b 56
  72.2 56
  114.7 18
  151.4 17
Isaiah
  19.19 18
  56.7 98
Jeremiah
  1.18 87
Lamentations
  5.11 81-83
Ezekiel
  4.3 87
  27.17 101
Daniel
  7 56, 57
Amos
  1.3-2.16 85
  7.7 87

Deuterocanon

1 Macc
  2.42 13

New Testament

Matthew
4.23 105
6.2 105
9.18? 105
9.35 105
10.17 105
12.9 105
13.33 86
13.54 105
23.6 105
23.24 105
25.31-46 156
Mark
1.21 105
1.23 105
2.1-4 104
2.4 42
5 171
5.22 105
6.2 105
6.52-53 16
13.1-2 93
Luke
1.32-35 19
7.5 105
8.41 105
10.40 85
12.11 105
13.20-21 86
21.20 94
John
1 209
3 44
6 44
6.59 105
19.13 92

Acts
9.2 106
12.20 101
13.5 106
14.1 106
17.1 106
17.10 106
18 106
18.6-8 106
19 106
19.8-10 106
Romans
3.29-30 88
10.9 18
1 Corinthians
12.3 18
15.8 157
Galatians
3 44
4.10 88
5.4 87
Philippians
1.1 43
2.6-11 209
3.6 88
Hebrews
2 56
3.1-6 157